Avatars of Story

Electronic Mediations

Katherine Hayles, Mark Poster, and Samuel Weber, Series Editors

Avatars of Story

Marie-Laure Ryan

Electronic Mediations, Volume 17

University of Minnesota Press   Minneapolis / London

Sections of chapter 1 were previously published in the introduction to *Narrative across Media: The Languages of Storytelling,* edited by Marie-Laure Ryan (Lincoln: University of Nebraska Press, 2004), 1–40; reprinted with permission of the University of Nebraska Press. Chapter 3 appeared in the online journal *Intensities: The Journal of Cult Media* 2 (Autumn/Winter 2001); copyright 2001; http://www.cult-media.com/issue2/Aryan.htm; reprinted with permission. Chapter 4 is a revision of "Narrative in Real Time: Chronicle, Mimesis, and Plot in the Baseball Broadcast," *Narrative* 1, no. 2 (1993): 138–55; reprinted by permission of Ohio State University Press. Chapters 6 and 7 originally appeared in a shorter version as "Narrative and Digitality: Learning to Think with the Medium," in *The Blackwell Companion to Narrative,* edited by James Phelan and Peter Rabinowitz (Oxford: Blackwell Publishing Ltd., 2005); reprinted with permission of Blackwell Publishing Ltd. Chapter 9 was previously published in *Semiotica* 150, nos. 1–4 (2004): 439–69; reprinted with permission.

Extracts from "Pressing the Reveal Code Key," by John Cayley, and "Perl Port of Jabberwocky," by Eric Andreychek, are reprinted here with permission of the authors.

Published by the University of Minnesota Press
111 Third Avenue South, Suite 290
Minneapolis, MN 55401-2520
http://www.upress.umn.edu

Library of Congress Cataloging-in-Publication Data

Ryan, Marie-Laure, 1946–
    Avatars of story / Marie-Laure Ryan.
        p.   cm. — (Electronic mediations ; v. 17)
    Includes bibliographical references and index.
    ISBN-13: 978-0-8166-4685-2 (hc : alk. paper)
    ISBN-10: 0-8166-4685-6 (hc : alk. paper)
    ISBN-13: 978-0-8166-4686-9 (pb : alk. paper)
    ISBN-10: 0-8166-4686-4 (pb : alk. paper)
    1. Narration (Rhetoric). 2. Interactive multimedia. I. Title. II. Series.
    PN212.R93 2006
    808—dc22

                                                    2006006194

Printed in the United States of America on acid-free paper

The University of Minnesota is an equal-opportunity educator and employer.

12 11 10 09   10 9 8 7 6 5 4 3 2

To those who use the Web for the free dissemination of ideas, rather than putting these ideas under the locks of copyrights: bloggers, participants in online discussions, and masters of scholarly Web sites.

Contents

Acknowledgments

It is a sign of our times that this book is more indebted to e-mail exchanges and online discussions than to live interaction, though the latter, fortunately, has not been fully remediated by digital technology. My thanks go to the following interactors in the scholarship game:

Andrew Hutchison, for the generous gift of his CD *Juvenate*, for going out of his way to answer my questions about it, and for invaluable input about authoring systems. Michael Mateas and Andrew Stern, for sharing and discussing with me their interactive drama *Façade*. Mateas and Stern again, plus Nick Monfort, Noah Wardrip-Fruin, and Scott Rettberg, for maintaining the blog Grand Text Auto, a source of so much inspiration and information that, if I had followed all the leads, I would never have finished this book. Michael Joyce, for explaining to me the more subtle features of Storyspace. Stuart Moulthrop, for thoughts about the functioning of links. Espen Aarseth and Jesper Juul, for being most stimulating opponents in the ludology–narrativism debate. Lisbeth Klastrup and Susanna Pajares Tosca, for risking the life of their avatar, Milagro, in order to take me into persistent virtual worlds. David Herman, for revealing to me the productivity of cognitive approaches to narrative. Emma Kafalenos, for inviting me to participate in her seminars at the Society for the Study of Narrative Literature, which invigorated narratological inquiry in the United States. Sara Gwenllian Jones, adventurous explorer of lands, life, and ideas, for sharing her understanding of media.

Outside the scholarship game, but not outside the realm of intellectual stimulation, the it-goes-without-saying crowd: my family, Phil, Caitlin, and Duncan, as well as Jon Thiem and Jacque Rieux, my fellow members in an exclusive club named Jabberwocky, whose activities consist of jabbering and walking, usually at the same time.

Finally, I thank the following individuals for permission to reprint images from their digital texts: Ingrid Ankerson, Mark Bernstein of Eastgate Systems, Andrew Hutchison, Olia Lialina, Marjorie Luesebrink, Michael Mateas, and Andrew Stern.

Introduction

The recent explosion of "media," "new media," and "comparative media" studies at universities all over the world is premised on the belief that the introduction of a new technology that affects the creation, preservation, and transmission of a certain type of information represents a revolutionary change with potential implications for multiple aspects of life: the economy, social relations, political systems, knowledge and scholarship, art and entertainment, and through all these domains, for that elusive experience that we call "identity," "sense of self," or "subjectivity." The development of some information technologies, such as writing and print, had indeed far-reaching consequences for all areas of social life. By allowing bookkeeping, for instance, writing was a great incentive to commerce and to the creation of wealth, which led to changes in political systems, while by giving permanence to linguistic signs, it transformed improvised storytelling performance into a text-based literature that developed a vast array of new features, as Walter Ong has persuasively shown. Other media have had more restricted effects: cinema and photography, for instance, allowed the preservation of a new type of data, and each created a new form of art, but they can hardly be said to have affected politics and the economy, beyond being vehicles for ideas and introducing new commodities on the market. Our most recent medial revolution, the development of digital technology, has already had a wide-ranging influence on the economy (e-commerce, the loss of jobs to automation), on social life (deterritorialized networks of human relations replacing contacts with neighbors), on how we perform the tasks of everyday life, on politics (dealing with the gap between societies that have widespread electronic access to information and those that do not), and on popular entertainment (the creation of computer games, computer-controlled amusement park rides, and special-effects movies). The computer has also affected the arts, especially the visual arts (digital installations, image manipulation), though its achievements in this domain tend to be rather esoteric, as befits the nature of "high art." But what has the computer done for narrative, a type of meaning that transcends medial boundaries, and the boundary between art and what I will call, for lack of a better term, practical information?

The jury is still out on whether digital technology has bred/will breed major new forms of narrative, and on whether narrative has played/will play a major role in the development of digital textuality, but these issues are currently generating tremendous interest. In the academic year 2003–2004, several books and professional meetings were devoted to digital forms of narrative. The books are Mark Meadows, *Pause and Effect: The Art of Interactive Narrative* (2003); Carolyn Handler Miller, *Digital Storytelling: A Creator's Guide to Interactive Entertainment* (2004); Andrew Glassner, *Interactive Storytelling: Techniques for 21st Century Fiction* (2004); and Chris Crawford, *Chris Crawford on Interactive Storytelling* (2004). All are practical guides offering advice on how to design computer-based narrative entertainment (especially computer games), but none proposes breakthrough solutions to the problem that has plagued the field from its very beginning: how to reconcile interactivity and narrativity. As for the professional meetings, they were the International Conference on Virtual Storytelling (Toulouse, France, November 2003), the conference Narr@tive: Digital Storytelling (UCLA, April 2004), the Digital Storytelling Festival (Sedona, Arizona, June 2004), and the conference Technologies for Interactive Digital Storytelling (Darmstadt, Germany, June 2004).[1] The Toulouse and Darmstadt conferences were heavily technical meetings, with papers on AI story-generating techniques, algorithms for the creation of intelligent agents, robotics (a robot's actions require the same kind of reasoning that we perform in life and that characters perform in a story), computer game design, computer game graphics, narrative in mobile computing, authoring systems, and the use of Global Positioning Systems to connect stories to real-world locations; the UCLA conference focused on poetics, situating digital narrative within the broader phenomenon of electronic art and literature and examining it in the light of contemporary literary, media, and cybernetic theories; and the Digital Storytelling Festival was chiefly a designer's workshop where "enthusiasts and practitioners who use technology to share ideas gather to examine creative work and new concepts being used in the areas of education, community building, business, personal and legacy storytelling, and new media and entertainment."[2] These different emphases reflect four basic approaches to digital narrative: the practical, the metaphorical, the expansionist, and the traditionalist.

The Practical Approach

The practical approach is not concerned with the development of new forms of narrative but, rather, with the importance of stories in people's lives, and with the role of the computer as a disseminator of personal stories. Unlike the other three approaches it does not consider the existence of digital forms of storytelling problematic at all: from the multimedia news stories of CNN, Google, and MSN to the use of stories to advertise products online, and from the global design of certain Web sites to the stories we exchange through e-mail, chat rooms, and blogs, the Internet is an overflowing well of narratives. The special interests of the practical approach include the role of digital narratives in education; the preservation of cultural memories and the archiving of oral history through the Internet, the use of stories in the corporate world; and teaching "ordinary people," that is, people who are neither computer wizards, academics, nor professional writers, how to use digital tools to tell their own stories. The flagship organization for the practical approach is the Berkeley-based Center for Digital Storytelling, and one of its most representative Web sites is Abbe Don's *Bubbe's Back Porch*, a collection of memories by Jewish women. *Bubbe's Back Porch* invites people to submit their own narratives of personal experience and also posts the products of so-called story bees, three-hour workshops during which participants create digital versions of oral storytelling by scanning family pictures and adding their own words.

The Metaphorical Approach

The metaphorical approach seeks inspiration from narrative concepts for the design and promotion of computer applications whose purpose is not in itself the telling of stories. In recent years, the concept of narrative has caught like fire in cultural discourse, and the software industry has duly followed suit by turning the metaphors of narrative interface and of the storytelling computer into advertising buzzwords. Steve Jobs, the founder and CEO of Apple, talks for instance about "the importance of stories, of marrying technology and storytelling skills" (Auletta 1999, 47); Steven Johnson concludes his popular book *Interface Culture* with this pronouncement: "Our interfaces are stories we tell ourselves to ward off senselessness"(1997, 242); Abbe Don titles an influential article "Narrative and the Interface," in which she argues that computers can play in modern societies the role of the storyteller of oral cultures; and Brenda Laurel envisions computers as theater and the use of software as participation in a dramatic plot structured according to Aristotelian principles. The storytelling metaphor provides an antidote to the cold indifference, rigid determinism, and unbending logic of the computer by giving a human face to the machine—the face of compassionate computing. But when it is put to the test of software design, it has so far yielded rather meager results:

1. The creation of a character who guides the user through the program, offers personalized help, and provides comic relief. This character could be the Office Assistant of Microsoft Office (a personage so irritating that most people turn it off), or a guide through a database who provides a customized tour based on certain themes selected by the user.

2. The development of a metaphorical setting or script, such as the supermarket shopping theme of Amazon.com, or the movie-making environment of Macromedia Director.

Those who expect from the term "narrative interface" a spellbinding plot with lively characters and surprising twists will be disappointed by these modest applications, but it is precisely the banality of the narrative scenario that makes it efficient. In the design of software, narrative is not an end in itself but a means toward a goal, and this goal is to facilitate the operation of the program. Interface metaphors, not unlike poetic ones, fulfill their rhetorical and pedagogical function by relating a strange new world to a familiar one.

The Expansionist Approach

Proponents of this approach regard narrative as a mutable concept that differs from culture to culture and evolves through history, crucially affected by technological innovations. This position is epitomized by the title of one of the chapters of George Landow's *Hypertext 2.0*, "Reconfiguring narrative." In this chapter, Landow suggests that in the digital age, narrative could become something entirely different from what it has been in the oral, chirographic, and print ages: "Hypertext, which challenges narrative and all literary form based on linearity, calls into question ideas of plot and story current since Aristotle" (1997, 181). The Aristotelian ideas that hypertext challenges are:

> (1) fixed sequence, (2) definite beginning and ending, (3) a story's "certain definite magnitude," and (4) the conception of unity and wholeness associated with all these other concepts. In hyperfiction, therefore, *one can expect individual forms, such as plot, characterization, and setting, to change,* as will genres or literary kinds produced by congeries of these techniques. (181–82; my italics)

It is not unreasonable to expect that digital environments will produce new variations in plot structure, as well as in the representation of character and setting, but how much transformation can these "forms" themselves tolerate and still retain their basic core of meaning? Judging by the use of the term by some authors of experimental digital texts, it seems that narrative can even do away with characters, plot, and setting. In an essay titled "Narrative Structures for New Media," the visual artist Pamela Jennings argues that the Aristotelian model of plot, because it encourages "linearity and truncation of thought," is "inadequate to the creation of computer-based interactive art" (1996, 349). Jennings is right to point out the existence of a conflict between the inherent linearity of plot and interactivity, but the replacements she suggests—iteration, serialism, open structures, and fuzzy logic—hardly qualify as "narrative structures," at least not to those who expect of narrative a representation of the being-in-time of human existence. In an article titled "Expanding the Concept of Writing: Notes on Net Art, Digital Narrative, and Viral Ethics," Mark Amerika describes the World Wide Web as a "public-domain narrative environment" (2004, 9). By "narrative environment," Amerika does not mean the countless stories posted on the Internet but, rather, the stream of information that flows through cyberspace, waiting to be harnessed into a "nomadic narrative that reinvents what it means to be an artist in a experientially designed cybernetic environment" (10). In Amerika's Web-based *FILMTEXT*, this "nomadic narrative" is a search for "meaningful Life Style Practices" that expand the concept of writing by using "whatever instruments are available to us at our moment in time" (12): "moving and still-life images, typographically experimental text, bits of customized code or raw data, manipulated music/sound/noise, etc." (11). Another digital artist, Talan Memmott, sprinkles his "theoretical fiction" *Lexia to Perplexia* with the term "bi-narrative," which he uses "to represent a degree of reciprocity in the conductivity between agents" (Amerika and Memmott, 5), but these agents seem to be packets of information or cybernetic objects, rather than individuated members of a fictional world that exists in time and space. Nothing really happens in the atemporal webs of symbols, metaphors, and theoretical statements of *Lexia to Perplexia*, and readers would be hard put to summarize the plot, describe the setting, and name the characters. For Jennings, Amerika, and Memmott, narrative has become synonymous with avant-garde writing practice. One may wonder why these authors still see a need to resort to the concept of narrative to describe their works, given the absence in their texts of nearly everything that people normally associate with stories. Narrativity, after all, is not a guarantee of aesthetic merit, nor is it necessary to it, as the case of lyric poetry demonstrates. My guess is that, like software developers, digital authors need to relate the new to the familiar and to give a human face to their textual machines; for there are not enough cyborgs in the world to guarantee a readership. And what could make these textual machines appear more user-friendly than narrative, a term that conjures drama, emotion, adventure, and success, or defeat, in the pursuit of noble or evil goals—everything that matters in human existence?

The Traditionalist Approach

This approach conceives narrative as an invariant core of meaning, a core that distinguishes narrative from other types of discourse and gives it a transcultural, transhistorical, and transmedial identity. With its loose, infinitely malleable conception of narrative, the expansionist approach faced the task of designing new forms of verbal art that took advantages of the affordances of the computer. "Narrative" was the name given to the solutions of this puzzle, whatever form they took. Here the task is more difficult, because the end product must not only take advantage of its medium but also fulfill the relatively rigid demands of narrative form and meaning. Viewing user participation as the most important of the properties of digital media, representatives of this approach conceive their goal as the creation of narratives in which the user controls a character and/or interacts intensively with a fictional world. But most of these scholars and developers are deeply conscious of the difficulty of this project and of the modesty of the results obtained so far, especially if we compare these results with the narrative productivity and diversity of film, drama, and literature. Lev Manovich speaks of interactive narrative as a "holy grail for new media" (blurb for Meadows 2003), Brenda Laurel regards the "interactive story" as "a hypothetical beast in the mythology of computing, an elusive unicorn we can imagine but have yet to capture" (2001, 72), and Chris Crawford laments: "To date, not a single interactive storyworld that commands wide respect has been created" (2003, 259). Yet if the Graal has yet to be conquered, researchers are not giving up the quest, for the pursuit brings its own rewards.

Many representatives of the traditionalist approach (for instance Crawford and Laurel) are game designers who declare themselves tired of the stereotyped plots and violent themes that dominate the video game industry. Their dream is to develop games that people will play for the same reasons they read novels or attend movies: games that will create a genuine interest in the story, rather than treating plot as a mere pretext for the exercise of physical skills, problem-solving ability, and for the adrenaline rush of competitive action. The traditionalist approach is also represented by the OZ projects in Interactive Drama directed by Joe Bates at Carnegie Mellon University in the nineties; by Bates's more recent *Zoesis* project, by the Narrative Intelligence group led by Michel Mateas and Phoebe Sengers (whose work is presented in Mateas and Sengers 2003), and by Mateas's and Andrew Stern's own project in Interactive Drama, *Façade,* which carves an active role for the user in a dramatic action inspired by Aristotelian poetics.[3]

One of the main areas of activity of these researchers is the creation of "believable" characters operated by AI algorithms who respond intelligently and in a dramatically interesting way to the actions of the user. If characters are well programmed, a narrative action will automatically develop out of their interaction with the user, with other characters, and with the world that surrounds them; for what is narrative, if not the representation of the responses of thinking individuals to the behavior of other thinking individuals and to changes in their environment? While the focus on characters exemplifies a bottom-up, emergent approach to narrative, other traditionalist projects apply a top-down, plot-driven approach, in which the various developments are largely predetermined by the designer. As Andrew Stern observes (2003, 225), the top-down approach recommends itself for dramatic projects whose ambition is to implement an Aristotelian pattern of rise and fall of tension because this pattern follows a rigid curve that necessitates a strict control of both the characters' actions and the user's emotions.

For the traditionalist approach to succeed, it must resist the temptation to try to rival the great classics of literature—a temptation that finds its expression in the title of Janet Murray's well-known book *Hamlet on the Holodeck*—and it must learn instead how to customize narrative patterns to the properties of the medium. Fortunately for those who regard narrative as a cultural universal and as a stable foundation of human cognition, adherence to a reasonably strict definition does not exclude diversity, nor does it limit digital narrative to the imitation of literary forms. In this book I endorse two positions that represent a middle ground between a stiflingly traditionalist and a wildly expansionist approach:

1. Narrative is a cognitive construct with an invariant nucleus of meaning, but this construct can take a variety of shapes, which we may call *avatars of story*, and it can be actualized to variable degrees, depending on how many of its core conditions are fulfilled.

2. As a type of meaning, narrative can be called to mind and can manifest itself pragmatically in a variety of ways. I call these multiple manifestations the *modes of narrativity*. The concept of mode, which will be further explained and illustrated in chapter 1, covers traditional literary critical concepts such as fictionality, or diegetic and mimetic presentation, but I propose

to add to this list categories that have been overlooked by narratology, such as utilitarian, illustrative, indeterminate, and
metaphorical. Many of these modes present special affinities
for certain media, and as we will see, digital narrative is indeed
tied to certain modes. I call them simulative, emergent, and
participatory.

Narrative: From Old to New Media

While the main focus of this book is the contribution of digital technology to narrative, it does not approach this issue in isolation but
rather places it in the larger context of the relations between media,
narrative, and modes. The first part is devoted to narrative modes
in "old media," a term I use for its convenience as an umbrella term
and not as a theoretically unified category. I will not, therefore, attempt to define "old media narratives" beyond this negative characterization: narratives that do not depend on the computer to be
performed and experienced. Traditional usage tells us that the term
"old media" is a plural that covers many categories, for instance, literature, painting, film, and drama, but the plurality of "new media"
is much more questionable. Ignoring etymology, according to which
"media" is the Latin plural of "medium," some scholars have developed the habit of using new media in the singular.[4] The theoretical
implications of this usage are not clear to me, but it points to the
ambiguous nature of digital technology: is it an autonomous medium, on par with film and writing, is it a technology that enhances
other non-computer-supported media, such as, precisely, film and
writing, or is it a family comprising many members: the various applications of digital technology, such as computer games, hypertext,
e-mail, blogs, perhaps the Internet as a whole? I will return later to
this question. Throughout this book, I will alternate between "digital medium" and "digital media" (with plural verb, to avoid upset-
ting Latin scholars), depending on whether I focus on the technology
itself or on the variety of its applications.

Since its inception in the heyday of structuralism, narratology
has mainly developed as an investigation of literary narrative fiction. Linguists, folklorists, psychologists, and sociologists have
expanded the inquiry toward oral storytelling, but narratology remains primarily concerned with language-supported stories. The
first chapter of this book, "Narrative, Media, and Modes," outlines the foundations of a transmedial expansion of narratology by

offering a medium-free, cognitive definition of narrative, a catalog of modes, and an investigation of the nature of media. For all its popularity in current academic discourse, medium (or media) remains a surprisingly ill-defined concept whose meaning is too often taken for granted. The trend now is to foreground the technological dimension of media; but as I argue in chapter 1, two other variables enter into the equation: media also differ from each other through their semiotic properties (verbal, visual, or aural; spatial or temporal; single channel or multichannel) and through their cultural usage. No media theory can be complete without taking all of these differentiating factors into consideration.

It would be impossible, within the framework of this book, to give a comprehensive overview of the evolution of narrative in both old and new media. The section on new media attempts to be reasonably wide-ranging, but in the section on old media I have limited myself to three probes. The first one—chapter 2—explores fictionality, the best-known narrative mode, but perhaps also the most difficult to define. My discussion of this mode focuses on two issues: (1) For which media and under what conditions is the concept of fictionality applicable? (2) Has contemporary writing practice, by transgressing the boundary between fiction and its other, rendered their distinction obsolete? Since the crisis of the dichotomy owes to the expansion of fiction at the expense of nonfiction, I attribute this crisis to what I call the Doctrine of Panfictionality. After exposing the disastrous epistemological consequences of Panfictionality, I ask whether the numerous cases of hybridization that have been produced in recent years call for an analog theory that postulates a continuum between fact and fiction, or whether they remain compatible with a digital theory that assumes a well-defined border. The chapter also debates the transcultural validity of the distinction between fact and fiction and its dependency on print technology.

Most digital narratives illustrate the mode that I describe in chapter 1 as emergent, but as chapters 3 and 4 demonstrate, this mode also occurs in old media. In the currently popular genre of reality TV, the quality of emergence is created by placing a number of individuals in a closed environment and letting a story develop out of their interaction. Through a comparison of the fictional reality TV show of the film *The Truman Show* with the real one of *Survivor*, chapter 3 explores the idiosyncrasies and differences in the narrative potential of TV and cinema and investigates the notion of reality that underlies the genre. In my discussion of *Survivor*, I argue that its environment is so visibly and self-referentially staged that questioning its claim to reality becomes pointless if by reality we mean the ordinary, the formless, and the private. If on the other hand we conceive human reality as something that arises from the dynamic interaction between a subject and an environment, something continually produced and presented to others, there is no reason why such a reality could not emerge from a totally artificial environment.

Illustrating the simultaneous mode of narration, chapter 4 takes us into the mental laboratory where stories are dynamically produced out of life data by investigating how radio sports broadcasters emplot a game for the listener without benefiting from the perfect hindsight of the retrospective narrator. Three dimensions of narrative are distinguished: chronicle, which focuses on the what (the linear succession of events); mimesis, which focuses on the how (descriptions); and plot, which gives meaning and form to the events by focusing on the why. Chronicle is the dominant dimension of the sports broadcast, but the success of the performance is heavily dependent on the broadcaster's ability to interweave play-by-play report with mimesis and tentative emplotment schemes. Insofar as emplotment requires a retrospective interpretation of the action, however, it conflicts with the real-time situation. The chapter examines how the game is emplotted through prospective and retrospective interpretations that break up the simultaneous character of the narration, and how the choice of plot patterns and stereotyped narrative themes evolves during the course of the broadcast.

The second part approaches digital narrative from a variety of angles. Chapter 5 asks how classical narratology, whose main concern has been so far texts that represent a certain combination of modes—diegetic, representational, retrospective, scripted, receptive, autonomous, determinate, and literal—can be extended to digital narratives, which are simulative rather than representational, emergent rather than scripted, participatory rather than receptive, and simultaneous rather than retrospective. While digital texts create novel variations in the manifestations of the traditional narrative categories of character, event, time, and space, it is in the domains of textual architecture and user involvement that they open truly new territories for narratological inquiry. Various architectures, among them the network, the tree, the flowchart, the maze, the vector with side-branches, the sea-anemone, and the track-switching system, will be discussed in terms of their ability to provide variations on the level of the two foundational narratological categories of discourse and story. Overlaying these architectures are four basic modes of user participation, obtained from the cross-classifications of two binaries: internal versus external participation; and exploratory versus ontological. Each of these modes of participation will be shown to pair up with certain architectures and certain themes, to produce the various genres of interactive narrative.

If dependency on the hardware of the computer constitutes the distinctive feature of the medium family known as digital, then the various types of text-creating and text-displaying software should be regarded as the submedia of digitality. Chapters 6 and 7 revisit the evolution of digital narrative over the past twenty-five years, presenting it as the story of the relations between software support and textual products and asking of each authoring system: what are its special affordances, and how do these affordances affect the construction of narrative meaning? Looking below the surface, the discussion asks of each text type "how is it made," a question that Christiane Paul (2003, 51) has shown to be central to digital art. Chapter 6 examines early forms of interactive narrative, namely, text-based interactive fiction supported by language parsers and hypertext written with Eastgate's Storyspace, while chapter 7 focuses on Web-based and multimedia texts written with Flash and Director. Concluding chapter 7 is an analysis of Michael Mateas's and Andrew Stern's *Façade,* a multimedia, AI-supported project in interactive drama programmed by the authors by using a variety of tools, rather than created with a standard authoring system.

The rise of computer games as object of scholarly study has created a lively theoretical controversy: is the concept of narrative applicable to computer games, or does the status of an artifact as game preclude its status as narrative? Proponents of the first alternative include the majority of game developers, who customarily describe their projects as storytelling. This association of games with narratives has been attacked by the "ludologist" school of video game studies. Ludologists claim that narrative is based on the retrospective evocation of past events, while the live action of games is based on a real-time simulation. Computer games are therefore like life itself: not the delayed re-presentation but the actual performance of actions. Chapter 8 responds to the antinarrativist position by arguing that games are not unmediated life but an image of life—as are all forms of narrative. Whereas the ludologist school regards the properties of being a game and a narrative as mutually exclusive, I argue that the major contribution of the digital medium to games is to have made strategic play compatible with make-believe and imaginative participation in a fictional world. Through their narrative dimension video games do more than engage our competitive spirit and problem-solving skills; they also speak to the imagination more powerfully than traditional board games or sports games ever did.

Chapter 9 reconnects new to old media by examining the manifestations of metalepsis, a favorite figure of postmodern literature, in written narrative, the cinema, computer science, and digital texts. The narratological concept of metalepsis is explained through the computer-programming concept of the stack, a hierarchical system with distinct levels and a LIFO structure (last in, first out). Metalepsis is an interpenetration of levels that challenges the hierarchical organization and the rigid order of processing of the stack. It represents, on the level of plot, the equivalent of the textual practices described in chapter 2: in one case the worlds and the characters represented in the text jump across fictional levels, in the other it is the text itself that transgresses these boundaries. Two forms of metalepsis are distinguished: rhetorical metalepsis, which opens a temporary window between levels, and ontological metalepsis, which attacks the logical distinction of levels and leads to what Douglas Hofstadter (1980, 21) has called "tangled hierarchies" and "strange loops." After an overview of metaleptic effects in narratology, mathematical logic (Gödel's theorem), and computer science (Turing's proof of the insolvability of the halting problem), I turn to metalepsis in code poetry, computer games, and virtual reality technology. In most of its manifestations metalepsis challenges the boundaries of fictional worlds located on the higher levels of the stack, without affecting reality, but in its concluding section the chapter investigates the theoretical idea of a metaleptic takeover of the ground level of reality by the images that are stacked upon it.

Throughout the second part of this book I will stress the difficulty of reconciling narrativity with interactivity, a feature that I regard as the most distinctive property of digital environments.

One may wonder what is the point of trying to fit the inherent linearity of narrative meaning into an interactive mold that, precisely, challenges this linearity. Wouldn't it be simpler to redirect digital textuality toward other types of meaning, such as those we find in animated visual poetry, code poetry, theoretical fiction, browser art, and self-transforming artworks operated by hidden algorithms, all areas of fecund activity? If it still makes sense to try to overcome the resistance of digital media to narrativity, it is because these media suffer from a malaise that perhaps only the universal, time-tested appeal of storytelling can relieve. With computer games on one hand, and on the other hand experimental forms of writing, electronic textuality has conquered both ends of the cultural spectrum. Games are a wildly popular form of entertainment, but they tend to reduce narrative to stereotyped plots and to subordinate it to gameplay, while the various types of experimental writing, which rejoice in what Alan Liu (2004, 2) would call the "creative destruction" of narrative, remain arcane academic genres read mostly by theorists and prospective authors. While print literature, film, and drama have captured all types of audiences, electronic textuality speaks to the masses (or at least to the masses within a certain age group and gender), as well as to the "cool" intellectual elite, but it has yet to succeed with the broader educated public. I believe that it is only by learning to adapt narrative to the properties of the medium, whether this means giving more attention to the narrative design of games or consolidating the narrative structure of other texts, that digital textuality will be cured from its split condition.

I

Narrative in Old Media

1. Narrative, Media, and Modes

Academic disciplines, unlike people, usually don't have birthdays, but if one could be given to narratology, it would fall on the publication date of issue 8 of the French journal *Communications* in 1966. The issue contained articles by Claude Bremond, Gérard Genette, A. J. Greimas, Tzvetan Todorov, and Roland Barthes. (One of Genette's favorite stories is that Barthes's invitation to contribute to this issue was the incentive that resulted in his lifelong dedication to narrative.) In his contribution, "L'Analyse structurale du récit," Barthes wrote:

> The narratives of the world are numberless. . . . Able to be carried by articulated language, spoken or written, fixed or moving images, gestures, and the ordered mixture of all these substances; narrative is present in myth, legend, fable, tale, novella, epic, history, tragedy, drama, comedy, mime, painting (think of Carpaccio's Saint Ursula), stained glass window, cinema, comics, news item, conversation. Moreover, under this almost infinite diversity of forms, narrative is present in every place, in every age, in every society. . . . Caring nothing for the division between good and bad literature, narrative is international, transcultural: it is simply there, like life itself. (1977, 79)

Two years earlier, in the same journal, Claude Bremond had made a similar point:

> [Story] is independent of the techniques that bear it along. It may be transposed from one to another medium without losing its essential

properties: the subject of a story may serve as argument for a ballet, that of a novel can be transposed to stage or screen, one can
recount in words a film to someone who has not seen it. These are
words we read, images we see, gestures we decipher, but through
them, it is a story that we follow; and it could be the same story.[1]

As these two quotes demonstrate, narratology was conceived by two
of its founding fathers as a field of study that transcends discipline
and media. But the next thirty years would take it in another direction: under the influence of Genette, it developed as a project almost
exclusively concerned with written literary fiction. The purpose of
the present book is to correct this trend and to reposition the study
of narrative on the transmedial and transdisciplinary track. But in
the meantime, hopefully, our understanding of media has grown
more sophisticated. We no longer believe that all media offer the
same narrative resources and that all stories can be represented in
media as different as literature, ballet, painting, and music. Nor do
we believe that the migration of a story from one medium to another does not present cognitive consequences. A core of meaning
may travel across media, but its narrative potential will be filled
out, actualized differently when it reaches a new medium. When it
comes to narrative abilities, media are not equally gifted; some are
born storytellers, others suffer from serious handicaps. The concept
of narrative offers a common denominator that allows a better apprehension of the strengths and limitations in the representational
power of individual media. Conversely, the study of the realization
of narrative meaning in various media provides an opportunity for
a critical reexamination and expansion of the analytical vocabulary
of narratology. The study of narrative across media is consequently
beneficial to both media studies and narratology.

In this chapter I propose to explore the theoretical foundations
of transmedial narratology in both their negative and positive components. The negative component describes the positions that are
incompatible with transmedial narratology, while the positive component explores the concepts of narrative and of medium that are
presupposed by the project.

Positions Hostile to Transmedial Narratology

The main obstacle to the transmedial study of narrative is a position
that comes from within narratology itself, namely, what I call the

language-based, or rather, speech-act approach to narrative. This position (represented by Prince, Genette, and Chatman) defines narrative as an act of storytelling addressed by a narrator to a narratee, or as the recounting by a narrator of a sequence of past events. In these definitions, the condition for being a narrative is the occurrence of the speech act of telling a story by an agent called a narrator. The semantic content of this speech act must be events that already occurred, either actually or in make-believe. This conception of narrative as a language-based phenomenon not only rejects the possibility of visual or musical forms of narrative; it also excludes texts with a language track that do not use an overt narrator, or texts that do not represent events retrospectively. For instance, Gerald Prince writes in the first edition of his *Dictionary of Narratology*: "A dramatic performance representing many fascinating events does not constitute a narrative, since these events, rather than being recounted, occur directly on stage" (1987, 58). According to this view (which Prince abandons in the second edition of the *Dictionary*), the transmedial study of narrative is limited to the distinction between oral storytelling and written literary narrative. Some theorists endorse a milder form of this position that uses the speech-act based definition as a metaphorical model for the analysis of nonverbal texts. In contrast to the radical approach, the mild version accepts the possibility of visual or dramatic narratives, but only if these texts can be fitted into the verbal mold. This approach would analyze drama and movies as the utterance of a narratorial figure, even when the film or the play does not make use of voice-over narration. Its advocates include Christian Metz, Seymour Chatman, François Jost, and André Gaudrault, and its opponents David Bordwell.

Another position incompatible with the study of narrative across media is the doctrine of radical media relativism. A particularly forceful example of this position is Umberto Eco's claim that "there is no relationship at all between his book, *The Name of the Rose*, and Jean-Jacques Annaud's film adaptation of it: they simply share the same name" (Elliott 2004, 221). Radical relativism is latent among theoreticians influenced by doctrines and schools that view the idea of a separation of form and content as heretical, such as Saussurian linguistics, deconstruction, and New Criticism. These theoreticians regard media as self-contained systems of signs, and their resources as incommensurable with the resources of other media. Just as two languages cannot convey the same semantic values under the doctrine of linguistic relativism, two different media cannot convey similar meanings or use similar devices under the doctrine of medial relativism. This view comes in a strong and a weak form. In the strong form, the signified cannot be separated from the signifier. Since a transmedial concept of narrative presupposes a distinction between narrative meaning and the signs that encode it, the strong interpretation kills in the egg the project of transmedial narratology. In its weaker form, medial relativism accepts common meanings but insists on the uniqueness of the expressive resources of each medium, thereby forcing the theorist to rebuild the analytical toolbox of narratology from scratch for every new medium. This position ignores the productivity of transmedial borrowings in narratology: for instance, theme comes from music, perspective from painting, and camera-eye narration from the cinema. In some cases borrowing seems inevitable: for instance when a medium tries to imitate the effects of another medium, or when two media share a common channel. The alternative to medial relativism is to recognize that theoretical concepts can be either medium-specific or applicable to several media. Examples of narratological concepts that apply across media are the distinction story / discourse, as well as the notions of character, event, and fictional world. On the other hand, montage is a technical concept native to film; but literary critics have borrowed it when language-based narrative began to imitate some of the techniques of the cinema.

Defining Narrative

In the past ten years or so, the term "narrative" has enjoyed a popularity that has seriously diluted its meaning. Jerome Bruner speaks of narratives of identity, Jean-François Lyotard of the "Grand Narratives" of a capitalized History, Abbe Don of the narratives of interface in computer software, and everybody speaks of cultural narratives, meaning by this not a heritage of traditional stories but the collective values that define a culture, such as belief in free speech in Western societies, or latent stereotypes and prejudices, such as narratives of race, class, and gender. The dissolution of "narrative" into "belief," "value," "experience," "interpretation," or simply "content" can only be prevented by a definition that stresses precise semantic features, such as action, temporality, causality, and world-construction. A transmedial definition of narrative requires a broadening of the concept beyond the verbal, but this broadening should be compensated by a semantic narrowing down, otherwise all texts of all media will end up as narratives.[2]

As I have already mentioned, the main problem facing the transmedial study of narrative is to find an alternative to the language-based definitions that are common fare in classical narratology. As a point of departure (to be modified later) I will use a definition proposed by H. Porter Abbott. Representing a common view among narratologists, Abbott reserves the term "narrative" for the combination of story and discourse and defines its two components as follows: "story is an event or sequence of events (the *action*), and narrative discourse is those events as represented" (2002, 16). Narrative, in this view, is the textual actualization of story, while story is narrative in a virtual form. If we conceive representation as medium-free, this definition does not limit narrativity to verbal texts nor to narratorial speech acts. But the two components of narrative play asymmetrical roles, since discourse is defined in terms of its ability to represent that which constitutes story. This means that only story can be defined in autonomous terms. As we have seen, Abbott regards stories as sequences of events, but this characterization cursorily equates stories with events, when events are in fact the raw material out of which stories are made. So what is story if it is not a type of thing found in the world,[3] as existents and events are, nor a textual representation of this type of thing (as discourse is)?

Story, like narrative discourse, is a representation, but unlike discourse it is not a representation encoded in material signs. Story is a mental image, a cognitive construct that concerns certain types of entities and relations between these entities. Narrative may be a combination of story and discourse, but it is its ability to evoke stories to the mind that distinguishes narrative discourse from other text types.

Following a proposal by Fotis Jannidis, I suggest regarding the set of all narratives as fuzzy, and narrativity (or "storiness") as a scalar property rather than as a rigidly binary feature that divides mental representations into stories and nonstories. In a scalar conception of narrativity, definition becomes an open series of concentric circles that spell increasingly narrow conditions and that presuppose previously stated items, as we move from the outer to the inner circles, and from the marginal cases to the prototypes. The proposal below organizes the conditions of narrativity into three semantic and one formal and pragmatic dimensions.

Spatial dimension
1. Narrative must be about a world populated by individuated existents.

Temporal dimension
2. This world must be situated in time and undergo significant transformations.
3. The transformations must be caused by nonhabitual physical events.

Mental dimension
4. Some of the participants in the events must be intelligent agents who have a mental life and react emotionally to the states of the world.
5. Some of the events must be purposeful actions by these agents, motivated by identifiable goals and plans.

Formal and pragmatic dimension
6. The sequence of events must form a unified causal chain and lead to closure.
7. The occurrence of at least some of the events must be asserted as fact for the story world.
8. The story must communicate something meaningful to the recipient.

Each of these conditions prevents a certain type of representation from forming the focus of interest, or macrostructure of a story (see list below). This does not mean that these representations cannot appear in a narrative text, but rather that they cannot, all by themselves, support its narrativity.

1. Eliminates representations of abstract entities and entire classes of concrete objects, scenarios involving "the human race," "reason," "the State," "atoms," "the brain," etc.
2. Eliminates static descriptions.
3. Eliminates enumerations of repetitive events and changes caused by natural evolution (such as aging).
4. Eliminates one of a kind scenarios involving only natural forces and nonintelligent participants (weather reports, accounts of cosmic events).

5. (together with 3) Eliminates representations consisting exclusively of mental events (interior monologue fiction).

6. Eliminates lists of causally unconnected events, such as chronicles and diaries, as well as reports of problem-solving actions that stop before an outcome is reached.

7. Eliminates instructions, advice, hypotheses, and counterfactual statements.

8. Eliminates bad stories. This is the most controversial condition in the list, because it straddles the borderline between definition and poetics, and because it needs to be complemented by a full theory of the different ways in which narrative can achieve significance. If we accept 8 as part of the definition, then narrativity is not an intrinsic property of the text, but rather a dimension relative to the context and to the interests of the participants. A sequence of events like "Mary was poor, then Mary won the lottery, then Mary was rich" would not make the grade as the content of fictional story, but it becomes very tellable if it is presented as true fact and concerns an acquaintance of the listener.

The eight conditions listed above offer a toolkit for do-it-yourself definitions. When they are put to the question "Is this text a narrative?" some people will be satisfied with conditions 1 through 3 and will classify a text about evolution or the Big Bang as a story, while others will insist that narrative must be about human experience and will consider (4) and (5) obligatory. Some people will regard a chronicle listing a series of independent events with the same participant as a narrative while others will insist on (6). Those who accept recipes as narratives consider (3) and (7) optional; and there are scholars who draw the line below (8) (for instance, Bruner 1991, who claims that a story must have a point), while others may think that a pointless utterance or a boring account of events can still display a narrative structure (this is my own inclination: I regard the "Mary" story quoted above as narrative regardless of context). But if people differ in opinion as to where to draw the line, they basically agree about what requirements are relevant to narrativity and about their importance relative to each other. If we ask "Is *Finnegans Wake* more narrative than *Little Red Riding Hood*?" we will get much broader agreement than if we ask (mindless of the incompatibility of a yes-no question with a fuzzy set) "Is *Finnegans Wake* a narrative?"

Through its multiple conditions organized into distinct areas, the above definition not only provides criteria for determining a text's degree of narrativity,[4] it also suggests a basis for a semantic typology of narrative texts. While degree of narrativity depends on how many of the conditions are fulfilled, typology depends on the relative prominence of the four dimensions. The Grand Narratives of Lyotard breach the top condition, because they do not concern individuals and do not create a concrete world, while postmodern novels are often low in narrativity because they do not allow readers to reconstruct the network of mental representations that motivates the actions of characters and binds the events into an intelligible and determinate sequence. Through a structure that I call "proliferating narrativity" (Ryan 1992, 373–74), contemporary fiction (especially magical realism and postcolonial novels) may also shift condition (6) from the macro to the micro level, becoming a collection of little stories loosely connected through common participants.

Among narratives that fully satisfy all the conditions, some emphasize the spatial dimension, others the temporal, and still others the mental. With their detailed construction of an imaginary world, science fiction and fantasy locate interest in the spatial dimension, and these genres often treat the plot as a mere discovery path across the fictional world.[5] The demand for action and changes of state that make up the temporal dimension is the dominant feature of thrillers and adventure stories, while the mental dimension, by insisting on the motivations and emotions of characters, rules over tragedy, sentimental romances, detective stories, comedies of errors, and, in the nonfictional domain, narratives of personal experience. In contrast to modernist novels that represent the mind for its own sake, these narrative genres evoke mental processes as a way to explain the behavior of characters.

The definition proposed above presents narrative as a type of text able to evoke a certain type of image in the mind of a cognizing subject. But it does not take a text to inspire the construction of such an image: we may construe stories as a response to life itself, and keep them in memory until we get an opportunity to tell them to an audience. According to cognitive scientists (for instance, Schank and Abelson), most if not all memories are indeed stored in the form of stories. I am not saying that life "is" a narrative, but it can in certain circumstances suggest a quality that we may call "narrativity." The property of "being a narrative" can be predicated of any semiotic object produced with the intent to evoke a story to the mind of the audience. To be more precise, it is the receiver's recognition of this intent that leads to the judgment: this text is a narrative, though we can never be sure that sender and receiver have the same story in mind. "Having narrativity," on the other hand, means being able to evoke such a script, whether or not there is a text, and if there is one, whether or not the author intended to convey a specific story. The concept of "having narrativity," as opposed to "being a narrative," offers a fitting description of the particular narrative quality of music, which remains a theoretical enigma to many scholars (see Nattiez 1990).

My endorsement of a cognitively rather than verbally based definition of narrative should not be taken as an unconditional adherence to a position that has recently taken cognitive science, the social sciences, and the humanities by storm. This position proclaims the fundamentally narrative nature of thought, knowledge and memory, and it equates our never-ending efforts to make sense of the world and of our lives with a process of "emplotting" or "storying."[6] Without denying that storytelling (to oneself or to others) is an efficient way to make life and the world more intelligible, and that the formation of narrative scripts plays an important role in mental life, I believe that there are sense-making operations that do not take narrative form: capturing the laws of physics through an equation such as $E = MC^2$ fails, for instance, the top conditions of my definition, since it produces a timeless law rather than a historical scenario involving particular individuals and one-of-a-kind transformations. Sense making can also result from the drawing of analogies and contrasts between phenomena, rather than from the chronological and causal ordering of individual events.[7] The mental construct that I regard as constitutive of narrative admittedly puts into play cognitive processes that we also use in everyday life, such as focusing thought on certain objects cut out from the flux of perception, a process that also enables us to distinguish discrete states and events; inferring causal relations between these states and events; thinking of events as situated in time; and reconstructing the content of other peoples' minds as an explanation of their behavior. We resort to these mental operations when we drive a nail with a hammer (acting on the basis of inferred causal relations), when we plan our schedules (temporal ordering), when we make grocery lists (focusing on certain items selected from the wide range of available products), and when we participate in social interaction, especially conversation (reading other people's minds). The activation of one or the other of these cognitive processes is not sufficient to produce narratives, because they can operate independently of each other, as my examples suggest. It is only when they all come together and form a reasonably stable mental image that they generate representations that fulfill all the conditions of my definition. Narratives are more than temporary drafts in the theater of the mind, more than transitory firings of neurons in the brain along individual pathways; they are solidified, conscious representations produced by the convergence of many different mental processes that operate both within and outside stories.

Narrative Modes

If narratology is to expand into a medium-free theory, the first step to be taken is to recognize other narrative modes than the standard way of evoking narrative scripts: telling somebody else that something happened. I do not take this term of mode in the traditional narratological sense defined by Genette (1972) (who uses it as a rather vague umbrella term for concepts such as frequency, direct and indirect discourse, perspective, and focalization), but in a personal sense, to mean a distinct way to bring to mind the cognitive construct that defines narrativity. The best way to explain this concept of modality is through a list of concrete examples. This list, which I regard as open-ended, is organized for convenience's sake into ten binary pairs and one triple. In each group the left-hand term can be regarded as the unmarked case, because the texts that present this feature will be much more widely accepted as narrative than the texts that implement the right-hand category. The conjunction of all the left-side categories yields the prototypical narrative situation, while the actualization of one (or more) of the right-hand categories leads to marginal forms. If the set of all narratives were the bird family, the left-hand elements would correspond to robins and nightingales, its most exemplary members, and the right-hand terms to penguins, kiwis, and ostriches.[8] The terms of the oppositions described below are not freely combinable and I do not claim that my "system" can generate $2^{10}*3$ types of narrative. Some modes presuppose or exclude others, and the list could be organized differently.

External/Internal. In the external mode, narrative meaning is encoded in material signs; it is textualized. In the internal mode, it does not involve a textualization: we can tell ourselves stories in the privacy of our minds (see Jahn 2003).

Fictional/Nonfictional. Of all the pairs of modes listed here, this is the most widely recognized and the most extensively theorized, but also the hardest to define. I will not discuss it here, since it forms the subject matter of chapter 2. I do not personally regard fiction as a more prototypical form of narrative than nonfiction, but some scholars do (Wolf, Fludernik, Jannidis), presumably because of the greater variety of its discourse. Moreover, as we will see in chapter 2, some scholars deny the possibility of a nonfictional form of narration.

Representational/Simulative. This distinction is based on the idea that a given process may be actualized in many different ways, or that a given action may have many different consequences depending on the global state of the world. A representation is an image of one of these possibilities, while a simulation is a productive engine that generates many different courses of events through a combination of fixed and variable parameters. A narrative mode specific to digital media, simulation is found in story-generating programs and in computer games. (Simulation will be further discussed in chapter 8.)[9]

Diegetic/Mimetic. An expansion of the representational category of the preceding pair, this distinction goes back to Plato. A diegetic narration is the verbal storytelling act of a narrator. As the definition indicates, diegetic narration presupposes language, either oral or written; it is therefore the mode typical of the novel and of oral storytelling. A mimetic narration is an act of showing, a visual or acoustic display. In forming a narrative interpretation the recipient works under the guidance of an authorial consciousness, but there is no narratorial figure. Mimetic narration is exemplified by all the dramatic arts: movies, theater, dance, and the opera. But each of these two modes can intrude into a narration dominated by the other. The dialogues of a novel are islands of mimetic narration, since in direct quote the voice of the narrator disappears behind the voice of the characters; and conversely, the phenomenon of voiced-over narration in cinema reintroduces a diegetic element in a basically mimetic medium.

Autotelic/Utilitarian. In the autotelic mode, the story is displayed for its own sake; in the utilitarian mode, it is subordinated to another goal, such as making a point in a speech or sermon, explaining a situation through an example, or motivating people to adopt certain behaviors.

Autonomous/Illustrative. In the autonomous mode, the text transmits a story that is new to the receiver; this means that the logical armature of the story must be retrievable from the text. In the illustrative mode, the text retells and completes a story, relying on the receiver's previous knowledge of the plot. The illustrative mode is typical of pictorial narratives, for instance, medieval paintings of biblical scenes. Halfway between these two poles are texts that offer a new, significantly altered version of a familiar plot, such as a modern retelling of a classical myth.

Scripted/Emergent. In the scripted mode story and discourse are entirely determined by a permanently inscribed text. Examples include both print narratives and dramatic performance relying on memorized text. In the emergent mode, discourse, and at least some aspects of story, are created live through improvisation by the narrator (oral storytelling), by the actors (commedia dell'arte), by the recipient (see participatory), or through computer programming (see simulation).

Receptive/Participatory. In the receptive mode the recipient plays no active role in the events presented by the narrative nor in their presentation: she merely receives the account of a narrative action, imagining herself as an external witness. In the participatory mode (a subcategory of emergent), the performance of the recipient actualizes the narrative and completes it on the level of either discourse or story. In discourse-level participation (hypertext fiction), the recipient-participant determines the order of presentation of the text, while in story-level participation (pencil and paper role-playing games *[Dungeons and Dragons]*, interactive drama, and computer games) she impersonates an active character who influences the evolution of the storyworld.

Determinate/Indeterminate. As the image of a world that undergoes metamorphoses, a story traces an arc, or a trajectory, that traverses many points in time. In the determinate mode the text specifies a sufficient number of points on the narrative arc to project a reasonably definite script. In the indeterminate mode, only one or two points are specified, and it is up to the interpreter to imagine one (or more) of the virtual curves that traverse these coordinates. The indeterminate mode is typical of narrative paintings that tell original stories through the representation of what Lessing calls a pregnant moment. The pregnant moment opens a small temporal window that lets the spectator imagine what immediately preceded and what will immediately follow the represented scene. But a full-blown story normally covers an extended stretch of time, and every spectator will probably imagine the remote past and the remote future in a different way.

Retrospective/Simultaneous/Prospective. In the retrospective mode, narrative recounts past events; in the simultaneous mode (TV and radio commentaries of live broadcasts), it recounts events almost as they happen; in the prospective (prophecies and political speeches), it focuses on future events. Setting events in what is from our historical point of view the future does not necessarily result in a prospective narrative: science fiction stories are usually told in the retrospective mode.

Literal/Metaphorical. What constitutes a literal or metaphorical narration depends on the particular definition given to narrative. While literal narration fully satisfies the definition, the metaphorical brand uses only some of its features. The degree of metaphoricity of a narrative thus depends on how many features are retained, and on how important they are to the definition. The great advantage of recognizing a metaphorical mode is that it enables narratology to acknowledge many of the contemporary extensions of the term "narrative" without sacrificing the precision of its core definition.

Here are some examples of what I consider metaphorical types of narrative. If we define narrative as the representation of a world populated by individuated characters, and if characters are intelligent agents, the following relaxations of the definitions should be regarded as metaphorical: scenarios about collective entities rather than individuals (for example, the "Grand Narratives" of Lyotard, as well as their heirs, the "narratives of class, gender and race" of contemporary cultural studies); narratives about entities deprived of consciousness (for example, Richard Dawkins's exposition of biology as the story of "selfish genes"), and dramatizations that attribute agency to abstract concepts (Hegel's "ruses of Reason").

If we want to stretch the metaphor to its limits, we can apply it to art forms deprived of semantic content, such as music and architecture. In the case of music, the metaphor can be invoked to analyze the structure of the work in terms of narrative effects or narrative functions. Narrative terminology is indeed common in music theory: relations between chords are described as exposition, complication, and resolution. Given a specific exposition and complication, only certain chords will provide a satisfactory resolution. In this metaphorical interpretation, all music becomes narrative, while if we use an illustrative interpretation, narrativity is a feature that occurs in only some compositions—those that allude to a narrative through their title, such as the *Don Quixote Suite,* by Telemann, or the *Sorcerer's Apprentice,* by Paul Dukas. In the case of architecture, a metaphorical interpretation would draw an analogy between the temporality of plot and the experience of walking through a building. In a narratively conceived architecture, the visitor's discovery tour is plotted as a meaningful succession of events. This occurs in Baroque churches, where the visitor's tour is supposed to reenact the life of Christ.

Some of the modes listed above have strong affinities for certain media, while others can appear in several physical supports, but no mode is totally medium-independent. For instance, the distinction fictional-nonfictional appears in written and oral language, film, and television, but it is questionable in other media, as we will see in chapter 2. The diegetic mode presupposes language, illustrative occurs mainly in visual media, and the participatory mode is most common in digital environments, though not entirely limited to them. It is precisely this dependency of certain modes on certain media that makes the concept useful for transmedial narratology.

What Are Media?

The concept of medium is no less problematic than the concept of narrative. As Joshua Meyerowitz observes, "it is a glaring problem for media studies" that "we have no common understanding of what the subject matter of the field is" (1993, 55). This may seem a strange problem for the layman: don't we all instinctively know what media are? And yet, if we ask specialists of different disciplines to propose a list of media, we will receive a bewildering variety of answers. A sociologist or cultural critic will answer TV, radio, cinema, the Internet. An art critic may list music, painting, sculpture, literature, drama, the opera, photography, architecture. An artist's list would begin with clay, bronze, oil, watercolor, fabrics, and it may end with exotic items used in so-called mixed-media works, such as grasses, feathers, and beer can tabs. An information theorist or historian of writing will think of sound waves, papyrus scrolls, codex books, embossed surfaces (for Braille texts), and silicon chips. A philosopher of the phenomenologist school would divide media into visual, aural, verbal, and perhaps tactile, gustatory, and olfactory. In media theory, as in other fields, what constitutes an object of investigation depends on the purpose of the investigator.

These various answers reflect the ambiguity of the term. The entry for "medium" in *Merriam Webster's Collegiate Dictionary* (11th ed., 2003) includes, among other meanings, these two definitions: (1) a channel or system of communication, information, or entertainment; (2) material or technical means of artistic expression. Type 1 regards media as *conduits,* or methods of transmitting information; and type 2 regards them as *languages.* (I am borrowing these terms of comparison from Joshua Meyerowitz.)[10] Media of type 1 include TV, radio, the Internet, the gramophone, the telephone—all distinct types of technologies—as well as cultural channels, such as books and newspapers. Media of type 2 would be language, sound, image, or more narrowly, paper, bronze, or the human body.

In the conduit, or transmissive conception of medium represented by type 1, ready-made messages are encoded in a particular way, sent over the channel, and decoded on the other end. Before they are encoded in the mode specific to the medium in sense 1, some of these messages are realized through a medium in sense 2. A painting must be done in oil before it can be digitized and sent over the Internet. A musical composition must be performed on instruments in order to be recorded and played on a gramophone. Medium in sense 1 thus involves the translation of objects supported by media in sense 2 into a secondary code.

Some media theorists (Ong 1982, 176) have objected to the transmissive conception of medium, arguing that it reduces them to hollow pipelines, through which information passes without being affected by the shape of the pipe. It is almost an axiom of contemporary media theory that the materiality of the medium—what we may call its affordances, or possibilities—matters for the type of meanings that can be encoded. On the other hand, if we regard meaning as inextricable from its medial support, medium-free definitions of narrative become untenable and we fall back into the doctrine of radical medial relativism. This doctrine, as we have seen, makes it illegitimate to compare messages embodied in different media and to view them as manifestations of a common narrative structure. To maintain the possibility of studying narrative across media we must find a compromise between the hollow pipe interpretation and the unconditional rejection of the conduit metaphor. This means recognizing that the shape and size of the pipeline imposes conditions on what kind of stories can be transmitted, but also admitting that narrative messages possess a conceptual core which can be isolated from their material support.

Insofar as they present their own configuring properties, channel-type media can be simultaneously conduits and languages. Take, for instance, the case of television. As a transmissive medium it can play any kind of movie, but as a means of expression it possesses its own idiosyncrasies, which have led to the development of new forms of narrative, such as the soap opera or the reality show. Moreover, the experience of watching a movie is significantly different when it is shown on a small screen in the home and on a large screen in a dark theater that holds spectators prisoner for a couple of hours.

Media may or may not be conduits, but they must be languages to present interest for transmedial narratology. This leads to another question: what do these medium-specific languages consist of, and what kind of features distinguish them from each other? The answers of the imaginary informants quoted above suggest three possible approaches to media: semiotic, material/technological, and cultural.

Media as Semiotic Phenomena

The semiotic approach looks at the codes and sensory channels that support various media. It tends to distinguish three broad media families: verbal, visual, and aural. It is only our habit of not ranking cuisine and perfume among media—probably because they do not transmit the proper kind of information—that prevents this list from including olfactory and gustatory categories. The groupings yielded by the semiotic approach correspond broadly to art types, namely, literature, painting, and music, but the three classes extend beyond the aesthetic use of signs; language, for instance, has both literary and nonliterary uses; pictures can be artistic or utilitarian. In its narratological application, the semiotic approach investigates the narrative affordances and limitations of a given type of signs or stimuli. The following list of narrative *can do* and *can't do* for language, static images, and instrumental music illustrates the scope and concerns of the semiotic approach. (Moving pictures without sound track can be considered a fourth semiotic type, but I leave it to the reader to figure out their narrative properties.)

Language

Can easily do: Represent temporality, change, causality, thought, and dialogue. Make determinate propositions by referring to specific objects and properties. Represent the difference between actuality and virtuality or counterfactuality. Evaluate what it narrates and pass judgments on characters.

Can do only with difficulty: Represent spatial relations and induce the reader to create a precise cognitive map of the storyworld.

Cannot do: Show what characters or setting look like; display beauty (language can only tell the reader that a character is beautiful; the reader cannot judge for herself and must believe the narrator). Represent continuous processes. (Language can tell us: Little Red Riding Hood took two hours to reach her grandmother's house, but it cannot show her progression. It usually segments time into discrete moments.)

Images

Can easily do: Immerse spectator in space. Map storyworld. Represent visual appearance of characters and setting. Suggest immediate past and future through "pregnant moment" technique. Represent emotions of characters through facial expression. Represent beauty.

Cannot do: Make explicit propositions (as Sol Worth observed, "Picture cannot say 'aint'"). Represent flow of time, thought, interiority, dialogue. Make causal relations explicit. Represent possibility, conditionality, or counterfactuality. Represent absent objects. Make evaluations and judgments.

Makes up for its limitations through these strategies: Use intertextual or intermedial reference through title to suggest narrative connection. Represent objects within the storyworld that bear verbal inscriptions. Use multiple frames or divide picture into distinct scenes to suggest passing of time, change, and causal relations between scenes. Use graphic conventions (thought bubbles) to suggest thoughts and other modes of nonfactuality.

Music

Can easily do: Capture flow of time in pure form. Suggest narrative pattern of exposition-complication-resolution through relations between chords. Create suspense and desire for what comes next. Arouse emotions.

Cannot do: Represent thought, dialogue, causality, virtuality. Single out distinct objects, characters, or events in a storyworld. Tell a specific story, since its stimuli have no fixed meaning.

Makes up for its limitations through these strategies: Use titles and subtitles to suggest a "narrative program." Individuate characters though musical motifs or distinct instruments (Peter as the strings in Prokofiev's *Peter and the Wolf*).

The relative narrative importance of the items on the "can do" and "can't do" lists for the three semiotic types confirms Werner Wolf's (2002) ranking of the three major media families, or art types, in this decreasing order of storytelling ability: verbal, visual, and musical. Whereas verbal signs can implement the strongest narrative modes—autonomous and determinate—pictures are either illustrative or indeterminate, and music is either illustrative or metaphorical. Because only language can explicitate the relations that turn individual events into a story, such as "x caused y" or "a did p because she wanted q," it is the medium of choice of narrative. In pictures and music, motivations and causal relations can only be suggested indirectly, and as Wolf observes, these media require a far more extensive gap-filling activity than verbal texts to be interpreted narratively, though they can usually be appreciated aesthetically without paying attention to their narrative message. It seems safe to assume that narrative competence developed concurrently, and in intimate relationship with language,[11] a semiotic code that enables users to extend topics of communication to entities not situated in the immediate context, such as third parties and past events. If language is indeed the native tongue of narrative, the narrativity of pictures and music is not a feature original to these media but a relatively late attempt on their part to emulate the cognitive template that language activates so efficiently. The limited storytelling ability of pictures and music doesn't mean, however, that they cannot make original contributions to the formation of narrative meaning. The affordances of language, pictures, and music complement each other, and when they are used together in multichannel media, each of them builds a different facet of the total imaginative experience: language through its logic and its ability to model the human mind, pictures through their immersive spatiality, and music through its atmosphere-creating and emotional power.

Media as Technologies

Left by itself, the semiotic approach yields only broad families. To bring further refinement to media theory, we must ask about the *raw materials* (such as clay for pottery, stone for sculpture, the human body for dance, or the human vocal apparatus for music) and the *technologies* that support the various semiotic types. It is further necessary to distinguish technologies of pure reproduction, such as sound recording or xerox copying,[12] from technologies that create new media objects and open new expressive possibilities. Only the latter present interest for transmedial narratology. Moreover, not all technologies that bring expressive diversity in a media family do so in a narratively significant way. In the sound category, for instance, diversity is created by the various musical instruments developed through the ages, but none of them has significantly increased the limited narrative potential of music. Much more consequential for narrative are the technologies that affect language-based and visual media. In the language category, these technologies correspond to the various ways to inscribe verbal signs (manuscript writing, print, and digital encoding),[13] as well as to the various methods of encoding and transmitting spoken language (radio and telephone). In the visual domain, the most narratively significant technologies correspond to methods of capture, such as photography, film, and television. The digital encoding of images has also brought new expressive possibilities, but their narrative impact is questionable.

The technological approach not only refines semiotic categories; it also cuts across them and reorganizes media into different families: media of long-distance communication, media of the moving image, and above all, "old media" versus "new media." This label of "new media" may be used in a narrow sense to cover media or submedia that only perform through the computer (VR installations, video games, e-mail, Internet chat, hypertext), and in a wide sense, to describe media that use digital technology as mode of production but end up being taken out of the computer (digital photography, digital recordings, and films with computer-generated scenes). Technology also regroups semiotic families into multiple-channel media (or "multimedia media") that affect several senses.

The classic example of an approach to transmedial narratology based on technological categories is the work of Walter Ong on the influence of writing on narrative form. The enormous impact of writing technology on thought, and, by extension, on narrative, can be captured in one brief formula: a permanent inscription serves as a prosthetic memory. In oral cultures, narrative was used as a mnemonic device for the transmission of knowledge; its memorization was facilitated by prosodic features, fixed formulae, and standardized images; and the limitations of memory were compensated by a relatively free episodic structure which allowed, within reasonable limits, permutation of its units. The development of manuscript writing transformed this open epic structure into the tightly knotted dramatic plot described in Aristotle's *Poetics*. Though drama was meant for oral performance, Ong regards it as the first narrative form controlled by writing. With its organization of events into an exposition, complication, crisis, and resolution, its symmetrical, carefully controlled rise and fall of tension (known as the Freytag triangle), and its climactic reversal of situation at the apex of the triangle, the dramatic plot exploits the significance of the sequential ordering of events to an extent that would not be possible in oral improvisation.[14] But as Ong observes, the chirographic age remained a basically oral culture, and its written texts were mainly used for reading aloud or memorization. Its longer narratives retained consequently the episodic structure and the prosodic features of ancient oral epics.

The invention of print, by encouraging silent reading, made mnemonic features obsolete and led to the birth of the novel,[15] a relatively unconstrained narrative form that took plot to unprecedented levels of complexity: framing, embedding, branching, digressions, disruptions of temporal sequence, and multiple plot lines. But it wasn't until the nineteenth century that the novel developed an alternative to the episodic structure of its epic forbearers. This alternative, according to Ong, is the "perfect pyramid" of the detective story, a plot type heavily indebted to the dramatic structure: "In the ideal detective story, ascending action builds relentlessly to all but unbearable tension, the climactic recognition and reversal releases the tension with explosive suddenness, and the dénouement disentangles everything totally—every single detail in the story turns out to have been crucial—and, until the climax and dénouement, effectively misleading" (1982, 149). By making reading a solitary activity, print also encouraged an inward turn that favored the creation of psychologically complex characters—what E. M. Forster called "round characters," as opposed to the flat character of oral narratives who delight the reader by "fulfilling expectations copiously" (Ong, 151). In high modernism, the representation of mental processes becomes indeed so invasive that it threatens to expel narrative action from literary fiction. The last major feature that Ong attributes to print is self-reflexivity, a feature most dominant in the early and late stages of the novel: "The very reflectiveness of writing—enforced by the slowness of the writing process as compared to oral delivery as well as by the isolation of the writer as compared to the oral performer—encourages growth of consciousness out of the unconscious" (150).

Writing technology has recently taken a new leap forward with the development of digital media, and a whole new chapter in the technological history of narrative remains to be written. Theorists such as Jay David Bolter, George Landow, and N. Katherine Hayles have prepared the ground by investigating the differences between print and digital writing, but we are still waiting for a comprehensive study of the more narrowly *narrative* applications of digital encoding, such as hypertext, blogs, or computer games. The second part of this book initiates such a study; but as Terry Harpold observes (2005, 108), we are still in the *incunabula* phase of digital narrative, and we lack the temporal distance needed for the assessment of the long-term viability of the current attempts to put computer technology in the service of narrative. The understanding and exploitation of the properties of a new medium are often slow to develop. Ong observes, for instance, that chirographic and early typographic cultures retained a "residual orality" that delayed the development of the narrative features typical of writing technology. Similarly, we have just entered the digital age, and our first attempts with digital narrative may be more indebted to the print tradition than we would like to think.[16]

Media as Cultural Practices

The third important dimension of media is their cultural use. This dimension is not entirely predictable from semiotic type and technological support. In fact, some ways of disseminating information are regarded as distinct media from a cultural point of view, despite their lack of a distinct semiotic or technological identity.

Newspapers, for instance, rely on the same semiotic channels and printing technology as books, but "the press" is widely regarded by sociologists as a medium in its own right, on par with the other so-called mass media of TV, film, radio, and the Internet. Drama, similarly, is a well-recognized cultural institution, but as a live performance using multiple sensory channels, it cannot be distinguished from ballet or the opera on strictly semiotic or technological grounds. Yet we traditionally call drama, ballet, and the opera media rather than genres.

By far the majority of media studies have been devoted to cultural use. These studies will ask, for instance, about the social impact of film violence, Internet pornography, television news reporting, or multiusers computer games. In a study of cultural use, consideration must also be given to the network of relations among media, a network commonly described through the metaphor of media ecology (Heise 2002). For instance, the cultural role of the cinema shifted after the invention of television, though the technology itself did not undergo significant changes. In the pretelevision days, movie theaters showed a variety of features: newsreels, documentaries, cartoons, and a feature film. They combined reality-based and fiction films in a continuously running show. This diversity and continuous running has been taken over by television, and nowadays movies deal mainly with the fictional, with a distinct preference for the fantastic, while TV favors reality (or reality effects), in the form of news, documentaries, and fictional representations of everyday life. It has even turned the real into a spectacle in the increasingly popular genre of reality TV.

The evolution of narrative forms depends as much on cultural pressures as on the semiotic or technological properties of the medium. What Ong writes of the oral-written distinction is valid for all contrasts between media: "Obviously, other developments in society besides the orality-literacy shift help determine the development of narrative over the ages—changing political organization, religious development, intercultural exchanges, and much else, including the development of other verbal genres" (1982, 139). Ong observes, for instance, that in recent decades the tightly knotted dramatic plot, a product of writing, has "fallen out of favor as too 'easy' (that is, too easily controlled by consciousness) for author and reader" (151). This development was a cultural reaction against the well-constructed plots of realism, though it cannot be entirely disconnected from writing technology: it would be hard to imagine an audience being held entranced by the oral presentation of a plotless text, unless it is a multichannel dramatic preformance. Culturally conditioned developments sometimes involve a return to a previous medium, or an attempt to imitate another medium. An example of this situation is the recent emergence of what I call the "novel of proliferating narrativity," a narrative type that replaces the overarching climactic plot with multiple "little stories." Particularly prominent in fantastic realism and postcolonialism, this narrative type developed both as a reaction to the deplotting of the New Novel and as an attempt to reconnect narrative with its oral origins.

Defining Media from the Perspective of Transmedial Narratology

For students of narrative, what counts as a medium is a category that truly makes a difference as to what stories can be evoked or told, how they are presented, why they are communicated, and how they are experienced. Narrative differences may concern three different semiotic domains: semantics, syntax, and pragmatics. In narrative theory, semantics becomes the study of plot, or story; syntax becomes the study of discourse, or narrative techniques; and pragmatics becomes the study of the uses of narrative. On the semantic level, different media favor different variations of the basic cognitive template: for instance, film prefers dramatic narratives shaped according to the Freytag triangle, TV prefers episodic narratives with multiple plot lines, and computer games prefer quest narratives with one plot line but several autonomous episodes corresponding to the levels to be passed. On the discourse level, media may produce different ways to present stories, which will necessitate different interpretive strategies on the part of the user. For instance, narrative is broken up into distinct frames in comic strips, while it is represented by an image that seems to evolve continuously in film, at least until the next camera take. On the pragmatic level, finally, different media may offer different modes of user involvement and different "things to do" with narrative. An example of these new things to do is the posting of private diaries on the Internet, a phenomenon known as "blogging." With digital media, it is now possible to share narrative of personal experience with millions of strangers.

In summary, a medium will be considered narratively relevant if it makes an impact on either story, discourse, or social and personal use of narrative. This approach implies a standard of comparison: to say, for instance, that "radio is a distinct narrative medium" means that radio as a medium offers different narrative possibilities from those of television, film, or oral conversation. "Mediality" (or mediumhood) is thus a relational rather than an absolute property.

For a type of information support to qualify as a distinct narrative medium, it must also offer a unique combination of features. An overview of the kind of media features that affect the experience of narrative follows.

Spatiotemporal extension. Media fall into three broad categories: purely temporal ones, supported by language or music exclusively;[17] purely spatial media, such as painting and photography; and spatiotemporal media, such as the cinema, dance, image-language combinations, and digital texts. A temporal medium is not merely one that requires time to be processed—don't they all?—but one that imposes an order and a directionality on the act of processing. A painting, for instance, may be scanned by the eye, one region after another, rather than being perceived instantly in its totality, but it is not a temporal medium, because the eye remains free to wander on its own paths, even when the work tries to direct it along certain lines.

Kinetic properties. By this I mean whether a medium is static or dynamic, that is, whether the texts of this medium stand still or change over time. With a static medium, appreciators can process the text at their own pace, but with a dynamic medium, the text imposes a tempo, and consequently time limits, on the act of perception. Spatial media should in principle be static, and media with a temporal dimension should be dynamic, but the distinctions static/dynamic and spatial/temporal do not always correspond, because language, a temporal medium which is scanned one word at a time, can be immobilized by writing, so that all its signs will coexist in space. We can have media that are spatial and static—painting, sculpture—media that are temporal and static—printed texts and combinations of image and texts, such as comics and illustrated books—and media that are temporal and dynamic, for instance, dance, movies, TV, oral storytelling, and digital media. The only combination not represented is media that are purely spatial and dynamic, because dynamism presupposes evolution in a time frame.

Number of semiotic channels. In the spatial category there is only one channel, unless one considers that sculpture and architecture have a tactile and kinesthetic dimension. In the temporal category we have either one-channel media (language or music), or combinations of the two temporal media, language and music, in songs and sung forms of poetry. Most spatiotemporal media have multiple channels, but mime and silent films use only visual data. The channel combinations of the spatiotemporal group include still pictures-language (in illustrated books); moving pictures-music (in silent films accompanied by a pianist); moving pictures-music-language (in film, drama, and the opera); and touch,[18] moving pictures, language, and music in certain digital installations and VR technology.

Priority of sensory channels. The opera should be considered distinct from a theater production that makes use of music, even though the two media include the same sensory dimensions and semiotic codes, because the opera gives the sound channel higher priority than the theater. In the opera the plot serves as a support for music, while in drama it forms the focus of interest.

Another important issue for transmedial narratology is the delimitation of medium with respect to genre. Both medium and genre exercise constraints on what kinds of stories can be told, but while genre is defined by more or less freely adopted conventions chosen for both personal and cultural reasons, medium *imposes* its possibilities and limitations on the user. It is true that we choose both the genre and the medium we work in. But we select media for their affordances, and we work around their limitations, trying to overcome them or to make them irrelevant. For instance, painters introduced perspective to add a third dimension to the flat canvas. Genre by contrast deliberately uses limitations to optimize expression, to channel expectations, and to facilitate communication: for instance, tragedy *must* be about the downfall of a hero and use the mimetic mode of narrativity; and sonnets *must* consist of fourteen lines, organized in two quatrains and two tercets with a certain rhyming pattern. These conventions are imposed as what Jurij Lotman has called a second-order semiotic system on the primary mode of signification. Genre conventions are genuine rules specified by humans, whereas the constraints and possibilities offered by media are dictated by their material substance and mode of encoding.

It is not always easy to distinguish genre from medium; but I would like to suggest a criterion based on the old question: what comes first: the chicken or the egg. Let the text be the chicken and genres and media be the egg. With genres, the chicken comes first. Genres originate in innovative texts that create a desire to duplicate their generative formula. With media, on the other hand, the egg comes first, since a text can only come into existence when the material support for its signs and the technology for their transmission are already in place. But if media and genre are distinct categories, this does not mean that the development of new media has no impact on the development of genres. Insofar as media are sets of affordances, or possibilities, new media give birth to new forms of text and to new forms of narrative, which in turn may be codified into genres.

Let's test this idea on the case of computer (video) games: are they a genre within the medium of digital technology, or are they a medium in their own right? Many people call computer games a medium, but the two-part label "computer games" tells us that they lie at the intersection of two categories: they are a certain type of activity that uses a certain technological platform, namely, the computer. As games they belong to a family that includes chess, Monopoly, football, roulette, and playing house, while as uses of computer technology, they are on par with e-mail, hypertext, and Internet chat. Computer games thus owe some of their features to being games, and some others to their being supported by the digital medium. But genre also intervenes within this hybrid notion of computer games in the form of categories such as adventure games, shooters, horror, and god games (or simulations). So what are computer games? A subset of a broader type of activity characterized by its reliance on a specific technological medium, and itself divided into genres.

The difficulty of categorizing computer games points to the ambiguous status of digital technology: is it a medium with its own language, a medium family divided into submedia, or a metamedium that synthesizes and transmits all other media? It is now fashionable to regard digital technology as the end of distinct media. The art critic Rosalind Krauss speaks of a "post-medium condition,"[19] and the media theorist Friedrich Kittler of a blending of all media into a universal coding system:

> When films, music, phone calls, and texts are able to reach the individual household via optical fiber cables, the previously separate media of television, radio, telephone, and mail will become a single medium, standardized according to transmission frequency and bit format . . . The general digitalization of information and chan-

nels erases the differences between individual media. Sound and image, voice and text have become mere effects on the surface, or, to put it better, the interface for the consumer . . . In computers everything becomes numbers: imageless, soundless, and wordless quantity. And if the optical fiber network reduces all formerly separate data flows to one standardized digital series of numbers, any medium can be translated into another. With numbers, nothing is impossible. Modulations, transformations, synchronization; delay, memory, transposition; scrambling, scanning, mapping—a total connection of all media on a digital base erases the notion of the medium itself. (1997, 31–32)

But if inside the computer all data are represented as zeros and ones, the execution of the code, which outputs a sensory manifestation of the data, restores the differences between media. Though critics have argued that an analog text and its digital version are no longer the same text (Hayles 2003), the digitized version preserves the major semiotic and cultural features of the original. For the human user, an online version of a daily newspaper or a DVD version of a TV show played on a computer retain their identity as "daily newspaper" or "TV serial," despite their new encoding. It is only from the nonhuman point of view of the machine, which of course is not a genuine point of view at all, that the differences between media disappear.[20] But the transmission of other media is not the only function of the computer; it has also developed original uses that turn digital technology into a medium in the language sense of the word. These original uses stand halfway between medium and genre. What are we going to call e-mail, hypertext, and Internet chat within media theory? My suggestion is to regard them as submedia—just as oil or watercolor are the submedia of the visual arts—and to view the supporting software as the differentiating factor within the technological family of digital media, just as raw material supports such as pastel, ink, marble, or bronze is the differentiating factor within the semiotic family of visual media.

Playing with the Medium

As the study of the configuring effect of media on narrative, transmedial narratology cannot avoid some degree of medial determinism. But it should also recognize the limits of this determinism. Far from being narrowly conditioned by the properties of its supporting medium, narrative has developed various relations to these properties. First, narrative may go with its medium and take, if not full, at least significant advantage of its affordances. But, as I observe above, it may take a while to understand what can be done with a medium: the history of the novel, of film, television, and digital narrative could be written as the gradual emancipation of these media from their respective predecessors: the novel from oral narrative, film from the theater, television from film, and digital narrative from all of the above, especially from print novels. Second, narrative can ignore the idiosyncrasies of the medium and use it purely as a transmission channel. This is what happened when Stephen King posted one of his novels on the Internet. The text was meant to be printed, and it took no advantage whatsoever of the artistic resources of a digital support. Third, narrative can actively fight some of the properties of the medium for expressive purposes. For instance, a print narrative with multiple branches subverts the linear reading protocols typical of novels distributed in book form, and it anticipates the possibilities of electronic textuality. Here we can say that the text yearns for another medium—one that will "remediate" (in Bolter's and Grusin's term) the limitations of its own medium. And fourth, a text may expose latent properties in its medium, properties that expand its expressive potential beyond current practice. This happened when postmodern print novels began playing with graphic layout and made us aware of the spatiality of the print medium,[21] a spatiality that is forgotten when print is considered to be nothing more than the translation of spoken language.[22] The diversity of games that narrative can play with the resources of its medium is one of the many reasons that make the study of the relations between media and narrative, an area still largely unexplored, one of the most promising new fields of narratological investigation.

2. Drawing and Transgressing Fictional Boundaries

Fiction lies at the intersection of two fundamental modes of thinking. One is narrative, the set of cognitive operations that organizes and explains human agency and experience. Fiction does not necessarily fulfill all the conditions of narrativity that I have spelled out in chapter 1, but it must create a world by means of singular existential propositions, and it must offer, to the very least, an embryonic story.[1] The other mode of thinking is what we may variously call "off-line thinking," "virtual thinking," or "nonfactual thinking": the ability to detach thought from what exists and to conduct mental experiments about what could be or what could have been. Most instances of virtual thinking are practical, in the sense that they subordinate the virtual to the actual; for instance, an engineer will imagine all sorts of possible catastrophes—floods, earthquakes, terrorist attacks—in designing a bridge that will resist these situations, while a historian will examine all the possibilities that faced a certain individual in order to evaluate his actual decisions. Because action involves planning, and planning is about what could be, all narratives, whether fictional or not, presuppose some amount of thinking about virtual situations. But fiction differs from other modes of virtual thinking in that it contemplates the virtual for its own sake, rather than using it as an instrument to shape the real.[2]

Fiction as Philosophical Issue

The earliest attempts to capture the phenomenon that came to be known in the twentieth century as fiction are formulae coined by poets. Sir Philip Sidney famously claimed, "Now for the poet, he nothing affirms and therefore never lieth," and Samuel Taylor Coleridge described the attitude of the reader of poetry as a "willing suspension of disbelief." A long hiatus separates these isolated observations from the discovery of fiction as a theoretical issue in the 1970s.[3] This discovery is attributable not to literary critics—who until recently have tended to take fiction for granted—but to members of the analytic school of philosophy, also known as the Oxford school. Generally associated with philosophy of language, analytic philosophy is mainly concerned with logic, formal semantics, and the relations between language and the world. One of its lasting legacies is speech act theory, as developed by J. L. Austin and John Searle. It is therefore not surprising that fiction was first approached by philosophers as something that one does with language.

Central to the analytic approach are the questions of truth and reference. In the first part of the twentieth century, under the influence of Russell and Frege, logicians assumed that sentences concerning nonexisting objects, such as unicorns or cyborgs, did not have reference and could not have a truth value: these sentences were either false (in a binary system) or indeterminate. This approach was consequently unable to distinguish statements such as "Emma Bovary committed suicide" and "Emma Bovary married a rich aristocrat and lived happily ever after" in terms of their validity with respect to Flaubert's novel. Moreover, if all the statements in and about fiction are indeterminate or false, it becomes impossible to explain on the basis of what information readers construct mental images of fictional worlds. Starting with John Searle's pathbreaking 1975 essay "The Logical Status of Fictional Discourse," the analytic approach broadened the notion of reference to include fictional entities and investigated under what conditions statements of and about fiction can yield truth. Here is a quick review of the major accounts of fiction inspired by analytic philosophy and speech act theory.

John Searle. For Searle, fictionality is an operator that affects the speech act of assertion. Though the bulk of novels consists of assertive (or constative) sentences that seem to make truth claims, the novelist, in writing these sentences, is only pretending to make assertions, or imitating the making of assertions. Searle distinguishes a deceptive from a nondeceptive form of pretense, the first corresponding to lies, and the second to fiction. Though the language of fiction is often indistinguishable from the language of nonfiction, the reader's recognition of the author's act of pretense protects him from taking the assertions within the text as information about the real world. Insofar as fictionality is determined by the author's intent, a text cannot pass from nonfiction to fiction or vice-versa. Through the intent constitutive of fiction, the author delegates responsibility for making true statements to a narratorial figure when the story is told in the first person, or suspends responsibility altogether, in the case of nonindividuated, third-person narration. In this type of fiction, according to Searle, the author is not pretending to be somebody performing speech acts but just pretending to perform speech acts. This subjectless act of pretense goes against the habit of literary critics to postulate a narratorial figure even when the text does not create an individuated narrator. Another controversial point of Searle's account is his division of fictional texts between serious and pretended speech acts. According to Searle, "most fictional stories contain nonfictional elements" (1975, 330): for instance, Conan Doyle pretends to make assertions when he refers to Sherlock Holmes, but he makes serious assertions when he refers to London. It is hard to reconcile this patchwork of fiction and nonfiction with the homogenous impression that the world of the Sherlock Holmes stories makes on the reader.

David Lewis. For David Lewis, theorist of the plurality of worlds, fiction is a story told as true about another world than the one we regard as actual by a narrator situated within this world. A nonfictional story by contrast is told as true about our world by one of its members. (This does not mean that the story has to be true: nonfiction encompasses lies and errors as well as accurate representations.) The difference between fiction and nonfiction is thus a matter of reference world. In Lewis's model, members of the actual world have counterparts in alternative possible worlds, so that when a novel refers to Napoleon, it does not describe the historical individual but imports an alter ego of the emperor, possessing somewhat different properties, into its fictional world. This idea of counterpart relation solves the problem encountered by Searle with texts that refer to actual entities. For Lewis, the world of the Sherlock Holmes stories is not created by a mélange of fictional and nonfictional statements but by a fully fictional discourse that describes a possible world linked to the actual world through many common features (or counterpart relations). Lewis also proposes a criterion for assessing the truth value of statements about fiction: "A sentence of the form 'in the fiction f, p' is non vacuously true iff [if and only if] some world where f is told as known fact and p is true differs less from our actual world, on balance, than does any world where f is told as known fact and p is not true" (1978, 42). Thus, it is false to claim that Emma Bovary was a devoted mother, because a society where her attitude toward her daughter is regarded as devotion would be further removed in its values from our cultural pocket of the actual world than a society in which she is considered a neglecting mother. One of the most important implications of Lewis's account of fiction is the self-denying quality attributed to this narrative mode: fiction is not just a product of the imagination but an invention that passes as a report of fact. An overt prescription to the imagination ("think up a one-eyed, one-horned flying purple people eater") or a counterfactual statement ("if p had happened, so would have q") are not fiction, because they construct a world overtly flagged as "other."

Gérard Genette. The great narratologist came relatively late in his career to the question of fictionality. In *Fiction and Diction,* he proposes an account that answers a question left open by Lewis: what are the truth conditions for the text-internal statements that constitute a fiction, as opposed to the external statements that describe it? In other words, what makes the reader accept without questioning the fact that there was a woman named Emma in the world of Flaubert's novel, and that she committed suicide after two unsuccessful extramarital affairs? For Genette, fiction belongs to the type of speech act that Austin calls performative. Rather than describing a world existing independently of language, the fictional speech act creates its world through the very act of describing it, and its statements are automatically true within its reference world. This account runs into difficulties in the case of unreliable narration; but even unreliable narrators must be unconditionally believed most of the time if the reader is to construct a fictional world on the basis of their discourse.[4] It is indeed from the clash between believable and nonbelievable statements that the reader diagnoses narratorial unreliability. Genette also endorses a layered account of fiction, by which a real-world communicative act between an author and a reader frames an imaginary exchange between a narrator and narratee that takes place in the fictional world. It is therefore the dissociation of the author from the narrator that distinguishes fiction from nonfiction.

Gregory Currie. While Searle describes fiction as a particular modality of the speech act of assertion—this is to say, as a metaspeech act—Currie regards it as a speech act in its own right on par with assertion, or rather, as an alternative to assertion. He also opens up the definition from a purely logical to cognitive and phenomenological account by introducing the important notion of make-believe. Though Currie recognizes the possibility of nonverbal fiction—drama, film, and the visual arts—his definition of fictionality is formulated through the same model that Searle uses for the speech acts of assertion, command, and promise. According to Currie, a speaker S performs the illocutionary act of uttering fiction if S utters a proposition P to an audience A with the intent that

1. A would make-believe P,
2. A would recognize S's intention of 1, and
3. A would have 2 as a reason for doing 1.[5]

To put this more directly: nonfiction is offered for belief, fiction for make-believe. Still, as the case of the unreliable narrator reminds us, not every statement in a fiction is supposed to be imagined as true of the fictional world. Rather than directly "make-believing P," the reader make-believes a world on the basis of P.

Kendall Walton. While definitions of fiction in terms of pretended speech act, autonomous speech act, telling as true of another world, performative utterance, and contrast between author and narrator all imply the medium of language, Kendall Walton puts the theory of fiction on the transmedial track by relying on the notion of make-believe without trying to define make-believe through a model borrowed from speech act theory, as does Currie. For Walton, "Not all fiction is linguistic. Any adequate theory of fiction must accommodate pictorial fictions, for instance, as well as literary ones" (1990, 75). Drawing an analogy between a certain type of children's games and the representational arts in general, Walton defines fiction as a "prop in a game of make-believe," this is to say, as an object that inspires imagining rather than belief. Just as children playing cops and robbers adopt imaginary personae and pretend that a certain tree is the jail, spectators of a painting of a ship pretend that they are facing a ship, and readers of literary fiction pretend that the text is the description by a narrator of a world that exists independently of the text, when they know that this world is in reality the product of the author's discourse. In all three examples, fictionality derives from a decision by the "player" to take something as something else.

Fiction as Transmedial Concept

If the concept of fiction encompasses verbal texts and pictures, it should be easily extendable to combinations of these two channels—to movies, drama, and photography. But the parallelism of Walton's account of games, pictures, and texts hides a profound asymmetry that calls into question its transmedial validity. For Walton, the set of all texts is divided between nonfictional ones that invite belief, and fictional ones that invite make-believe. But in the pictorial domain, no such distinction obtain: all representational pictures—all pictures that depict—are inherently fictional, because they pass as something that they are not. As Walton categorically claims: "Pictures are fictions by definition" (1990, 351). The global fictionality of pictures thus implies the global fictionality of all media using a visual channel: photography, film, drama, and comics. But if all representational pictures are intrinsically fictional, this amounts to saying that fictionality is not a valid concept within visual representation. The reader of a text will interpret it differently if it is fictional or nonfictional, but in the case of pictures, the diagnosis of fictionality is vacuous, since it does not carry cognitive consequences. It will not help to make fictionality a label for whole media rather than for individual texts, because in the case of language it splits the medium in two.

Why do all pictures, for Walton, participate in a game of make-believe? Apparent counterexamples are not difficult to find; for instance, the illustrations of a textbook contribute to our knowledge of the world and therefore induce beliefs rather than make-believe. Walton answers this objection by saying that in order to recognize a picture as representing something—let's say, a cow—we must imagine ourselves facing and seeing a cow. Since what we are actually seeing is not a cow but an image, this constitutes an act of make-believe. The question is whether or not "imagining ourselves as facing an x" is necessary to the recognition of what the picture depicts. I believe that this type of imagining occurs only with illusionist pictures that draw the spectator into their space through their use of perspective and overall realistic rendering of the depicted scene. Walton regards a sketchy line-drawing with faulty perspective as no less fictional than a Vermeer painting done with the help of a camera obscura, but I personally process the sketchy image as "a picture (or sign) of an x," rather than as "an x." We could, against Walton, restrict fictionality to the case of the Vermeer painting, but this is not a satisfactory solution, because fictionality would then depend on style in visual media but not in language, and different criteria would be used in each case: the binary criterion of pretended truth and existence in verbal texts (we pretend that fictional characters actually exist), the analog criterion of impression of presence in pictures. As Jean-Marie Schaeffer observes (1999, 286), the experience of presence is a matter of "immersive mimeticism," not a matter of fictionality.

If the concept of fiction is to extend beyond language, it should be based on comparable criteria in all the semiotic domains for which it is valid, and it should cut across them rather than applying wholesale to some domains. My claim is that fictionality is not a property inherent to certain media but a specific use of the media for which the concept is valid. I believe furthermore that the importance of Walton's distinction between belief and make-believe does not hinge on his analysis of visual media, and that we can use it as a basis for a transmedial theory of fiction without regarding all visual depictions as fictional.

Film, Television, and Photography

A consequence of conceiving the opposition fiction/nonfiction in terms of make-believe *versus* belief is the restriction of the opposition to those media that are capable of asserting truths; for to believe is to hold a statement as true. These truths, moreover, should be about individuals rather than universals or abstract concepts, because they should be able to evoke concrete representations in the mind of the appreciator. Visual media as a semiotic family may not share the ability of language to articulate definite propositions, but within the visual family there are technologies that do make particular claims to truth, and consequently, that invite us to believe because their images are produced by mechanical means. These technologies are photography, film, and TV recording. It is not by accident that film and TV are the two media, other than literature, in which the distinction fiction/nonfiction is the most solidly established.

An image obtained by mechanical means is not only an icon bearing a visual resemblance to an object but also an index related to its referent through a causal relation: the mark on a sensitive surface of the patterns of light reflected by the object. Let's focus on the case of photography, though the following observations are equally valid for film. Though the photographer plays an active role in determining both what the picture will show and how it will show it, and though the photograph reflects her interests, aesthetics, and goals, the human agent does not inscribe her vision on film, glass plate, or digital memory: it is the scene that inscribes itself on these devices. Roland Barthes, who cannot be accused of naïve realism, writes: "The photograph is literally an emanation of the referent" (1981a, 80). Or again: "Discourse combines signs which have referents, of course, but these referents can be and are most often 'chimeras.' Contrary to these imitations, in Photography I can never deny that *the thing has been there*. There is a super-imposition here: of reality and of the past" (76). Even though a photograph can "never preserve all the information available to the observer" (of the original scene), even though it can only present "*selected* and *degraded* information" (Plantinga 1996, 315), it makes a determinate and *almost* irrefutable truth claim: "What I am showing, really existed." The only way to refute this claim would be to prove that the photograph has been manipulated, or that the recorded scene has been faked. In both of these types of failure, the objectivity inherent to the technology has been interfered with by a human agent. Unlike language, which is uttered by humans, photography does not permit honest mistakes; the only options are truth, if humans did not tamper with the image, or lie, if they did. This is why the photos from the Abu Ghraib prison that surfaced in May 2004 were so shocking. The admission by the U.S. government that they weren't forgeries gave to the public incontrovertible proof of the mistreatment of Iraqi prisoners by American troops—a proof that the most thorough journalistic report or the most realistic artist sketch would be unable to provide.

Photography has been overwhelmingly used as a window on the world, especially in our days of easily transportable pocket-size cameras; but in the early days of the technology, when heavy equipment and long times of exposure made it very difficult for the photographer to work in the field, the fictional use of the medium was much more widespread than it is today. The work of the Victorian photographer Julia Margaret Cameron includes, for instance, not only studio portraits of family, friends, and prominent members of

British society—all works that make a believable truth claim—but also illustrations of literary works ("King Lear allotting his kingdom to his three daughters") and biblical stories ("Jephthah and his daughters"), allegories ("Love in idleness"); compositions inspired by individual verses ("Call and I follow," a title borrowed from a line by Tennyson); and imitations of Renaissance paintings ("A Study of the Holy Family"). All these fictional photos record real people posing in various roles in a scene that has been artfully designed by the photographer. In all the cases mentioned above, fictionality resides not primarily in the subject matter (though some subject matters can only be represented fictionally) but in the act of make-believe required of both the model and the spectator. Just as the subjects who posed for the camera pretend to be Cupid, the Madonna, or one of King Lear's daughters, the viewers pretend that the photographic subject is one of these characters, and that the picture represents spontaneously occurring events, rather than a staged spectacle.

The argument for the fictionality of some photographs can be easily extended to film. The fiction film induces make-believe rather than belief because the spectator knows that the represented action is *both* staged for the camera and simulated by actors, rather than lived by characters. I insist on these two conditions occurring simultaneously, because neither one is sufficient to define the fiction film. The documentary status of Leni Riefenstahl's movie *Triumph of the Will* has been questioned on the ground that the events of the 1934 Nuremberg Nazi Party Congress were choreographed for the camera, but these events really constituted a party congress, and while the participants may have been executing a script, they were not playing roles. The film should therefore be regarded as nonfiction. Even dramatic roleplaying is not incompatible with nonfiction if it is properly framed. Trevor Ponech (1997, 205) mentions a documentary film by Margaret Mead and Gregory Bateson, *Trance and Dance in Bali,* that depicts the traditional *Tjalonarang* (Witch) play of Balinese culture. Even though the people shown in the film impersonate mythical beings, the film is not fiction, because it captures a tradition that exists independently of the movie.

The two criteria I list above for the fiction film also hold for drama: in the theater, the action is both staged and simulated, and there is no such thing as nonfictional drama. This seems to contradict my earlier claim that the distinction fiction/nonfiction, to be valid for a given medium, should cut across it, rather than applying wholesale. Here I should perhaps refine my claim, by saying that the distinction should cut across semiotically and technologically based media, but not necessarily across cultural ones (cf. the distinction made in chapter 1).

Man-Made Pictures

Belief and make-believe are attitudes that we take toward propositions; if these notions are to provide the foundation of a theory of fictionality in the classic visual arts, we must coax paintings, drawings, and sculptures into expressing statements capable of being true or false, in spite of Sol Worth's claim that picture cannot make propositions. Here I outline some proposals, though none of them satisfies me entirely.

1. Man-made pictures make an existential statement. A painting titled "ship" implicitly says "there are ships," a painting of a unicorn says "there are unicorns," a painting of Napoleon says "Napoleon existed," and a painting of Ophelia says "Ophelia existed." We will then believe the ship and the Napoleon paintings, but only "make-believe" the claim made by the unicorn and the Ophelia paintings. This proposal seems much less satisfying in the case of "ship" and "unicorn" than in the case of Napoleon and Ophelia. Paintings of ships and unicorns do not refer to a specific representative of the category, and I am not convinced that they make existential statements: instead of implicitly stating "here before you is a unicorn," a painting could be simply saying "this is how the imaginary object called unicorn looks like," without committing itself to the existence of the fabulous animal. How, furthermore, would this proposal classify paintings of blue horses (Franz Marc) or of women with distorted features (Picasso's cubist paintings)? Are these fantastic creatures, or the product of visual symbolism? Any deviance from reality could lead to a judgment of fictionality.

2. Man-made pictures are not inherently fictional or nonfictional, but they can inherit these properties from other objects. Rather than applying to all pictures, the features of fictionality and nonfictionality would only concern those artworks that either refer to texts or are included in books. An illustration in an anatomy textbook would be nonfictional because the text, as a whole, is offered for belief; while an illustration in a fairy tale book would

participate in the act of make-believe mandated by the story. This proposal leaves a large number of paintings outside the dichotomy, while most if not all films, photos, and texts can be classified as either fiction or nonfiction.

3. Representational paintings imply an assertion by the painter: "This is what I saw." If the painter did not really see what is shown in the picture, the spectator make-believes that he did, and the picture is fictional. For instance, Leonardo da Vinci did not attend the Last Supper; the painting is therefore fictional, even though the event was historical. But Leonardo really saw Mona Lisa and painted his perception of her; therefore his portrait of Mona Lisa is nonfictional. But the perception of the painter is always transformed by the imagination. Painting uses external reality as a more or less free source of inspiration, but in contrast to photography, there is no strict causal relation between this reality and what ends up on the canvas. It is a safe bet that what Monet saw when he painted fields of poppies did not look exactly like his painting, but it would be absurd to postulate an imaginary observer and to regard the painting as fictional.

4. Pictorial fictionality is restricted not only to pictures that represent but to those that represent narratively. By the definition I gave in chapter 1, a story represents a world populated by individuals and presupposes existential statements. To interpret a narrative painting such as *Breakfast Scene* from the series *Marriage à la Mode* by William Hogarth (a painting that creates its own story rather than illustrating a preexisting tale), spectators will form in their mind propositions such as: "There's a drunk man slumped in a chair next to a tipsy woman. All the furniture is overturned. A man with a notebook is talking to a servant. Judging by his appearance and demeanor he must be a debt collector. The drunk couple is in for a rude awakening." The picture's fictionality depends in this case on the attitude of make-believe taken toward these statements. But what would this proposal do with a painting based on a true story, such as *The Raft of the Medusa*, by Théodore Géricault, which shows the dying survivors of a shipwreck on an overcrowded raft? Because the models were not the actual participants, and because the scene was either recreated in the studio or painted from imagination, we could regard the painting as a fictional adaptation of a true story—the pictorial equivalent of the journalistic genre known as "true fiction" or "the nonfiction novel" (to be discussed

in the next section). Since we can invoke similar arguments for all pictorial illustrations of true stories, this proposal ends up classifying all narrative paintings as fictional. The same verdict holds for two other types of narrative that relies on man-made images: cartoon movies and comics. In visual media, nonfictional narrativity would then be the exclusive domain of film and photography—a conclusion justified by the semiotic difference between mechanical and human-made representation.

To justify my personal judgments of pictorial fictionality I had to draw on a heterogeneous collection of criteria rather than on a unified definition. Some of these criteria are quite fuzzy: for instance, how much imaginative transformation can a portrait or a landscape tolerate without ceasing to pass as a document of visual appearance? The fact that my principles leave a vast number of artworks outside the dichotomy fiction/nonfiction departs from the situation offered by the media previously discussed, but through their loopholes, these principles reflect our cognitive attitude toward the fine arts more accurately than a theory that forces spectators to decide for every painting "is it fiction or nonfiction." When I look at a Monet painting of a field of poppies, the question simply does not come to my mind. Because they cannot make overt and unambiguous claims to truth, as do language, film, and photography, man-made visual representations do not fit cleanly in a theory of fictionality. Nor do, for the same reason, media deprived of semantic content, such as music and architecture.[6]

Hybridizing Fiction and Nonfiction

In the past few decades, the border between fiction and nonfiction has been the site of numerous violations which have caused, if not the spilling of blood, at least the spilling of ink. As authors developed ever new ways to crossbreed the two narrative modes, literary theorists began to wonder whether their distinction still serves a useful function in the new geography of postmodern textuality, or whether the controversial border will eventually share the fate of the Berlin wall.

It all started with the movement known as New Journalism, which gave birth to a genre variously labeled "Nonfiction Novel," "True Fiction," and "Faction" (Truman Capote, *In Cold Blood*; Norman Mailer, *The Executioner's Song*). This movement represents an attempt to introduce narrative techniques typical of fic-

tion, especially those of the nineteenth-century novel, into journalistic reports of real-world events. Tom Wolfe, one of the most
vocal advocates of New Journalism, argues that the realistic novel
enjoyed a "unique power, variously known as its 'immediacy,' its
'concrete reality,' its 'emotional involvement,' its 'gripping' or 'ab-
sorbing quality'" (1973, 31). This power is the result of such techniques as the predominance of scene over summary, detailed record
of dialogue, the depiction of everyday gestures, and variable focalization allowing direct access to the minds of characters. While the
realistic novel immerses the reader in its textual world, traditional
journalism is bound by an allegiance to objectivity and verifiability
that restricts the representation, dulls the narration, and hampers
the reader's emotional involvement in the narrated events. Through
its controversial use of fictional techniques in the description of the
real world, New Journalism mounts a charge against the lack of
imaginative appeal of the traditional brand. Its reference world is
simply a more knowable, and consequently more completely rep-
resentable, counterpart of the real world. In contrast to the historian, who either says "things happened this way" (when there is
solid evidence) or "it is possible that things happened this way"
(when speculating), the author of True Fiction suggests possibility
through a narrator who claims factuality.

The borderline between verifiable facts and fabulation is particularly fuzzy in autobiographical writing, despite what Philippe
Lejeune calls "the autobiographical contract": the promise by the
author, and expectation from the reader, that the text presents authentic memories of personal experiences. Far from constituting
fixed snapshots of past events, memories are representations that
change over time, enhanced by the imagination, revised in the light
of more recent experiences, and redrawn every time they are replayed in the theater of the mind (Schank and Abelson 1995). It
is consequently very difficult to draw the line between authentic
recollections and made-up memories. Yet autobiographies are the
most interesting in their most unverifiable assertions, when they
report what only the author could know.[7] Some authors of self-
representations, for instance J. M. Coetzee in *Boyhood* (1997),
acknowledge the fundamental uncertainty of memories by with-
drawing the generic labels that would categorize the text as either a
memoir or a novel, thereby avoiding the autobiographical contract
(the subtitle of *Boyhood* reads: "Scenes from Provincial Life"). For

those who conceive identity as the product of a narrative process of self-representation, furthermore, autobiography does not capture a preexisting subjectivity but creates the subject dynamically through the act of writing, in much the same way the discourse of a novel creates characters by telling the story of their lives.

Biography differs in principle from fiction through its avoidance of fabulation. But this taboo has been recently violated. In *Dutch: A Memoir of Ronald Reagan* (1999) by Edmund Morris, the author delegates the narration to a fictional character, a counterpart of himself born some thirty years earlier, whose life frequently crosses paths with the life of the future president. Not content to create a fictional point of view, Morris develops his authorial persona into a fully fleshed character, surrounds him with a circle of imaginary relatives and friends, and interleaves his life story with the main narrative. The fabrication is not directly acknowledged in the text, though critics have found subtle hints of the artifice, and the author further blurs the boundary between the fictional and the historical by documenting the lives of the made-up characters with fictional footnotes. This daring narrative move enables Morris to weave a much more immersive and fluid narration than allowed by the standards of historical scholarship. The relatively unknown figure of the young Reagan can be described with the same vividness of purely physical observation as the better-documented old one, without resorting to the clumsy hypothetical statements of traditional biography.

Much less controversial than biography imitating fiction is fiction imitating biography, because fiction is a land of liberties, while nonfiction is a land of constraints. Wolfgang Hildesheimer's *Marbot: A Biography* presents itself as the lifestory of a historical individual, the nineteenth-century British aesthetician and philosopher Sir Andrew Marbot, who committed suicide in 1830 at the age of thirty. His life is reported with the fastidiousness of a biographer more interested in maintaining historical credibility than in bringing his subject to life. The narration of Marbot's life adheres to what John Updike has sarcastically called the "must have" school of biography[8]: the text is overflowing with claims of limited knowledge. The reality effect is strengthened by an index of names, by meticulous reference to sources in the body of the text, and above all by visual documents. Who could still doubt the historical accuracy of the text, after seeing reproductions of paintings of Marbot and his parents by Sir Joshua Reynolds and Eugène Delacroix, as well as photographs of his estate in the English countryside? When the book first appeared, it was read by some critics as a genuine biography; and yet Sir Andrew Marbot is a fully imaginary character. More recently, the fictional status of the work of W. G. Sebald has raised heated controversy. *The Emigrants* and *Austerlitz* recount the lives of European Jews whose lives were directly or indirectly affected by the Holocaust. These lives are presented as the personal recollections of a narrator who personally knew, heard about, or briefly encountered the characters. The text, which bears no generic label,[9] limits itself to the knowable, and the impression of authenticity is strengthened by the inclusion of old photographs, newspaper clippings, maps, and sketches. Trusting the testimonial power of photography, I initially read *The Emigrants* and *Austerlitz* as fact-based stories, but critics have suggested that Sebald worked from found images, inventing stories about the characters shown in the pictures.[10] I must confess to a slight disappointment when I learned about this method of fabrication. While I gained admiration for the writer's performance (and slight deception), my emotional attachment to the characters decreased, because I could no longer relate "this face" and "this body" to "this destiny."

Whereas Sebald's texts cultivate ambiguity with respect to the reality status of their reference world, Richard Powers's *Galatea 2.2* constructs an obvious blend of lifestory and invention. The novel is a work of autofiction whose narrator/protagonist, named Powers, is a counterpart of the author. The past of the narrator could be that of the novelist, but the plot involves a science-fictional element (a much more advanced state of Artificial Intelligence than currently available) that retrospectively brands the whole text as fiction. Thanks to the smooth morphing of the autobiographical into the imaginary, *Galatea 2.2.* presents itself as a homogeneous montage.

Another way to play with the fictional boundary is to borrow elements from both sides of the divide and to link them together in a deliberately heterogeneous collage of individually identifiable fragments. This strategy is illustrated by *The Many Lives of Josephine B.*, by Sandra Gulland, a novelized life of the French empress that combines the fictive diary of the heroine with letters from her actual correspondence. This operation can cross the border in either direction. While *Josephine B.* remains solidly anchored in fiction, some texts of literary theory interweave a fictive voice with theoretical statements for which the author remains personally responsible. *Writing Machines,* by Katherine Hayles, creates, for instance, a fictional alter ego of the author named Kaye, and *Avatar Bodies,* by Ann Weinstone, offers a collage of "philosophy, literary criticism, fiction, autobiography, and real and imagined correspondence," as the book cover tells us. Digital hypertext has given a boost to the principle of the collage, or patchwork, by making it possible to interlink documents of any type.

It is tempting to regard these practices as "assault[s] on the ever-weakening line between fact and fiction," as Thomas and Meacham wrote about *Dutch* (1999, 24). The postmodernist way to deal with phenomena of hybridization is to claim that there is no fundamental difference between fiction and nonfiction. I have called this approach the Doctrine of Panfictionality (Ryan 1997), because the crisis of the dichotomy owes to the expansion of fictional territory at the expense of nonfiction.

Panfictionality

The main proponents of the Doctrine of Panfictionality were Roland Barthes and Hayden White, but the roots of the idea reach further back, into the structuralist interpretation of Saussurian linguistics. One of the firmest beliefs of postmodern theory is that Saussure's doctrine of the arbitrary nature of language has dealt a fatal blow to the idea that language can speak objective truth about the world. Saussure, of course, was not the first to insist that the relation between meaning and sound is based on convention rather than naturally dictated, but his formulation of the principle of arbitrariness is much more radical than the view of his predecessors because it affects not only the relation between signifier and signified but also the delimitations created by language in the very substance of sound and meaning. For Saussure, signs acquire their meaning and their identity not from vertical relations to objects in the world but from horizontal relations with other signs: "In language there are only differences *without positive terms*" (1966, 120). In a purely differential framework (and with its *only* and *without,* Saussure's formula left no room for compromise), language is a self-enclosed, self-regulating system whose terms receive their value from their relation to all the other terms, and its evolution results entirely from internal forces. This hypothesis has been fruitfully applied to phonology. What makes *p* and *b* into distinct phonemes in English is their ability to produce differences in meaning, such as the difference between *pin* and *bin*. But once the differential principle has been used to determine phonemes, it cannot be reused to determine meaning. We must therefore refer to the world to establish that *bin* and *pin* have distinct meanings. Or to borrow an argument from Benveniste (1971, 44): when Saussure spoke of the different values of English *sheep* (which contrasts with *mutton*) and French *mouton,* which includes both meat and animal, he could not have found these terms comparable in the first place if they did not refer to the same general area in the domain of *reality.*

How does the differential theory of language support the Doctrine of Panfictionality? As Robert Scholes points out, the structuralist and poststructuralist disciples of Saussure believe that if language is arbitrary, it cannot represent reality:

> Many believing deconstructivists . . . accept as an article of faith that it is impossible to utter the truth because there is an unbridgeable gap between human language and the world. According to this view, everything we speak or write is fictional because there is no such thing as the literal meaning of words. . . . Because perception is always coded by language, and because language is never "literal" but always figurative, perception is never accurate, is always distorted. (1993, 179–81)

This argument rests on the assumption that we can only make true statements about the world if the structure of language, prior to its use, truly reflects the order of the world. It would take a one-to-one correspondence between words and things for language to be "literal" rather than "figurative." But according to logicians, the predicate "true" applies to individual utterances and expressions, not to language as a code. Sentences make truth claims but individual words do not. Confusing language and language use, *langue* and *parole,* this line of reasoning tells us that in a rather circular way, language in itself must be a true statement about reality if it is to provide the tools for making true statements about reality. Yet as J. L. Austin observes, "there is no need whatsoever for the words used in making a true statement to 'mirror' in any way, however indirect, any feature of the situation or event" (1970, 125).

The constructivist idea that language creates reality, rather than reflecting it, is a recurring theme in the work of Roland Barthes.

In *Camera Lucida,* alluding to the testimonial value of photography, he writes: "No writing can give me this certainty. It is the misfortune (but perhaps also the voluptuous pleasure) of language not to be able to authenticate itself. The *noeme* of language is perhaps this impotence, or, to put it positively: language is, by nature, fictional" (1981a, 85–86).[11] But it is through an earlier essay, "The Discourse of History," that Barthes gave momentum to the Doctrine of Panfictionality:

> The facts [of history] can only have a linguistic existence (as a term of discourse), and yet everything proceeds as if this existence were nothing but a pure and simple "copy" of another existence situated in the extrastructural domain, in the "real." This discourse [historiography] is doubtless the only type in which the referent is aimed for as something external to the discourse, without it ever being possible to attain it outside this discourse. (1981b, 16–17)

History masks its inability to reach the real by creating, through narrative, a "reality effect." "Narrative structure, which was originally developed within the cauldron of fiction (in myths and the first epics) becomes at once the sign and the proof of reality" (18). Barthes is suggesting here that every discourse that uses narrative form inherits the fictionality of its origin. But the fact that the oldest surviving stories were epics and myths does not constitute evidence that "narrative developed within the cauldron of fiction." What if all the nonfictional ones, such as narratives of personal experience, had simply been forgotten, because they were not considered worthy of preserving? What if myth were truth and not fiction? What if ancient cultures classified discourse along different lines than fiction and its other? I will return to these questions later. The point I want to stress here is that with Barthes's essay on history, the rampant skepticism of structuralism and poststructuralism concerning the possibility of accurate representation of the world takes on a narrower form. Fictionality may be inherent to language, but it is above all an effect of the artificiality of narrative representation.

Barthes's implicit equation of narrativity and fictionality is the kernel of Hayden White's theory of historiography, or "metahistory." In *Tropics of Discourse,* White claims that the meaningfulness of historical narrative is achieved by configuring events into literary models of coherence, such as the archetypal plot patterns described by Northrop Frye: tragedy, comedy, romance, or satire:

Historical narrative succeeds in endowing sets of past events with meaning by exploiting the metaphorical similarities between sets of real events and the conventional structures of our fictions. By the very constitution of a set of events in such a way as to make a comprehensible story out of them, the historian charges those events with the symbolic significance of a comprehensive plot structure. Historians may not like to think of their work as translations of facts into fictions; but this is one of the effects of their works. (1978, 91–92)

Why should narrativization turn historical facts into fiction? In a later text, White answers this question through a rhetorical question: "Does the world really present itself to perception in the form of well-made stories, with central subjects, proper beginnings, middles and ends, and a coherence that permits us to see 'the end' in every beginning? Or does it present itself more in the form that the annals and chronicles suggest?" (1981, 23). By annals, White means a chronological listing of uninterpreted, causally unrelated events. Chronicles are slightly more connected than annals, because they concern the deeds of one individual or group, and they contain more details, but unlike proper narratives, "they do not so much *conclude* as simply *terminate*" (17). Here is an example of annals:

709. Hard Winter. Duke Gottfied died.
710. Hard year and deficient in crops.
711.
712. Flood everywhere. (*Annals of St. Gall,* quoted in White 1981, 7)

White's critique of narrative as a potentially truthful representation of historical reality presupposes a secure sense of how reality presents itself to perception: *not in narrative form*. As evidence of the superimposed and consequently fictional character of narrative form, White invokes the arbitrariness of the Aristotelian pattern of "beginning, middle and end": since history is always in the making, there is no such thing as natural boundaries, climaxes, denouements, and narrative closure. To this argument one can reply that if life is made at least in part of actions, agents experience it as a succession of structured episodes delimited by the formation, pursuit, fulfillment, or abandonment of goals. Another aspect of the supposedly alien form imposed by narrative on the events of the past is their organization into causal chains and their interpretation as actions performed by agents; for causal relations and the intents that turn gestures into actions can only be inferred by historians. By denouncing narrative form as extraneous to "life" or "reality," White opts for a vision of the real that excludes anything that cannot be directly observed by the senses. The alternative to the assimilation of narrativity to a fictional mold borrowed from literature is to regard narrative as a cognitive template wired into the human mind through which we filter and interpret certain aspects of human experience—ours as well as that of others. This approach explains the similarities between the plot structures of fiction and history by assuming that we activate the same cognitive processes to give coherence and intelligibility to imagined and real events: those inferential processes, precisely, that bind together and explain events through causal relations and human motivations. For the cognitivist approach, "narrative" is not an artifice, it is the only way, should we say the *natural* way for the mind to represent (or configure, as Paul Ricoeur would say) action, desire, change, being in the world, and the temporality of human existence.

None of the objections I have raised so far against Panfictionality is nearly as damaging as the argument that Lubomír Doležel calls "taking the Holocaust test." How could a theory that regards historiography as fiction justify the rejection of texts that deny the existence of the Holocaust? The question was presented to a number of historians by Saul Friedlander. "It is to Hayden White's credit," writes Doležel, "that he agreed to take the Holocaust test" (1999, 251). He did so by splitting historical discourse into two levels. The first level is the "account[s] of events already established as facts"; the second is constituted by "poetic and rhetorical elements by which what would otherwise be a list of facts is transformed into a story" (White 1992, 38). Here White clearly retreats from the Barthian formula that he uses as epigraph to *The Content of the Form*: "the fact can only have a linguistic existence." What is fictional is not the facts that the historian deals with but their narrativization. White's distinction between facts and emplotment may provide grounds for rejecting texts that deny the existence of the Holocaust, but it offers no criterion for assessing the validity of a particular emplotment of facts, though White claims that an emplotment that presented the Final Solution as comedy, satire, or the Nazis' tragedy would be unacceptable. This problem can be easily circumvented by regarding the various narrativizations of the

Holocaust not as *fictions* but as *interpretations* of a common reference world. Whereas truly fictional texts create their own world and constitute the only mode of access to it, nonfictional texts refer to a world that forms the potential target of many texts, because this world possesses an extratextual existence. Fictional texts are automatically true of their reference world, but nonfictional texts must establish their truth in competition with other texts that describe the same world.

In the last analysis, the claim that all representations are by necessity fiction is itself based on a fiction—in the nontechnical but widespread sense of the term as illusion or falsity. Postmodern theory postulates a dichotomy in representations: some are artifices, made up, culturally determined, convention-laden. These representations are fictions. Others are true, natural, not made up, not influenced by cultural conventions, free of prejudice, totally objective—the language spoken by reality itself, what Foucault calls "prose of the world."[12] These texts are nonfiction. Not surprisingly, postmodern theory discovers that the latter do not exist: they were just a straw man, constructed and then destroyed to serve the ideological agenda of the writer. But even if one concedes the unavoidable artificiality of representation, the thesis of universal fictionality rests on a faulty syllogism: All fictions are artifices. All representations are artifices. Hence, all representations are fictions.

Let's assume, however, that the Doctrine of Panfictionality is true—in a blatant contradiction of its own claim. This would not really affect the question of the distinction between fiction and nonfiction, because Panfictionality is an epistemological issue, while the distinction I am investigating is a pragmatic one. While the epistemological issue is concerned with whether the world is knowable, or whether it is a construct of the human mind, the pragmatic issue asks: how are we supposed to *use* a text? Until philosophers can prove that reality is constructed by texts, we will continue to take some texts as representations of the real world, and others as representations of imaginary worlds, and we will bring different attitudes and expectations toward these different types of texts. The concern of the theory of fiction is not with the objective relations of texual worlds to reality, nor with the decidability of this relation, but with how readers, spectators, or players apprehend textual worlds.

I will not put Panfictionality to rest, however, without saying a good word about it, as is customary in a eulogy. The Doctrine of Panfictionality took narratology out of the complacency with which it has long approached nonfiction. If narrative form, tropes, conventions, rhetorical devices, and the idiosyncrasies of the medium produce meaning in fiction, so do they in nonfiction. Until the Doctrine of Panfictionality came along, nonfictional genres of discourse enjoyed an illicit immunity from textual or semiotic forms of investigation. Thanks to the postmodern critique, we are now better aware that texts of nonfiction display an image distinct from their reference world (I call it the textual world), and that the construction of this image deserves consideration.

The Analog versus the Digital Approach to Fiction

If we want to preserve the distinction fiction/nonfiction in the face of hybrid phenomena, we have a choice of two options. (1) Fiction and nonfiction are the two poles of an analog continuum, and there is no definite, stable boundary between the two; or (2) the distinction is closer to digital than to analog, in the sense that fiction and nonfiction are separated by a clearly marked boundary. If we imagine fiction as white and nonfiction as black, the analog interpretation describes hybrid texts as homogeneous shades of gray, while the digital interpretation views them as more or less finely grained combinations of black and white elements. Which view is the more appropriate?

The obvious advantage of the analog model lies in its flexibility. It welcomes every new combination of fact and invention and seems therefore particularly appropriate in a time of literary experimentation such as the present period. Between the white of fiction and the black of nonfiction, the analog model accepts a whole spectrum of gray shades. But if it dispenses the theorist with the difficult task of drawing a border, the model still needs to define the two poles of the continuum. The most obvious solution is to use a semantic criterion: the black pole is the factual, the white pole the imaginary, and the position of a text along the continuum is determined by the distance between its textual world and the real world. One could, in this framework, create a scale leading from straight history, to slightly fictionalized history *(Dutch),* true fiction, historical novels, novels with a historical setting *(Madame Bovary),* and stories taking place in fully imaginary worlds *(Lord of the Rings).* The analog model explains the differing attitudes of readers toward these texts as different shades of belief: there are texts that we believe literally, and others from which we are willing to learn, but without expecting too much accuracy. But the analog model is not without problems. If a text's location on the continuum is determined by its similarity to the real world, *Madame Bovary* is less fictional than *Lord of the Rings*, but this conclusion ignores a major difference between Flaubert's and Tolkien's texts on one hand, and works of history on the other: the former refer to their own world, the latter to the real world. Moreover, not all texts can be neatly arranged on a linear axis. Where, for instance, does the model place works of history that are riddled with factual errors? Novels that contain lengthy essays with potential real-world validity? The analog approach reduces the cognitive process through which we apprehend fiction to the weakest form of belief—that is, nonbelief; but isn't there a qualitative, rather than quantitative, difference between the way we read, on one hand, a historical novel, and on the other a work of history? In an analog model, fiction cannot be associated with make-believe, because make-believe does not admit degrees.

The alternative to the analog model is to view fiction and nonfiction as the two terms of a binary opposition and the border between the two as clearly marked and stable.[13] The digital model deals with hybrid phenomena by allowing texts to borrow elements from the other side of the border without being infected by these elements, because the reader makes separate judgments of fictionality on the local and the global level. For instance, the fictional narrator of *Dutch* can be bracketed out, and the text as a whole should be evaluated as a biography. Conversely, the many believable facts of a novel of true fiction should not place the text in the territory of nonfiction, because the author declines responsibility for the historical accuracy of the text as a whole. This checkerboard approach presents the advantage of explaining how readers can learn precise facts about the real world from a work globally categorized as fiction: the reader will assume that some statements are true in both the real and the fictional world, while others describe the fictional world only.

It could be that fiction is like light according to the Copenhagen interpretation of its behavior: sometimes it is best described as particles (the digital approach), sometimes it is more efficiently modeled as a wave (the analog approach). The digital model has a clear advantage in the domain of formal definition. All the theories discussed above support a clear distinction: either you believe or make-believe, assert or pretend to assert, refer to the real world or to an alternative possible world. With its idea of an open, shifting, or nonexisting border, the analog model is consistent with the rejection of binaries of contemporary thought, but it also takes the easy way out, for it is always easier to deny the existence of boundaries than to try to define them. On the other hand, a model allowing a fuzzy middle ground is more efficient than a strictly digital model at supporting what psychologists may call a "folk theory" of fictionality. If the formal definitions discussed above reflect the textual competence of the members of Western cultures, the reader of a standard biography or a science fiction novel should be able to tell unambiguously, when confronted with the question, whether she should believe or make-believe the text; whether it describes the actual world or an alternative possible world; and whether the author speaks in his own name or hides behind a narratorial figure. But these questions become pointless (or unanswerable) in the case of a piece of New Journalism or a creative autobiography. The ordinary reader simply accepts the text as "part fiction, part truth" or as "freely based on facts." For this reader, the continuum is reduced to three classes: fiction, nonfiction, and "inbetween"—a hybrid, if this can be, of the analog and the digital model.

The three-part version of the analog model is also preferable for oral storytelling. While some oral narrative genres are clearly fictional (jokes and tall tales) and others factual (courtroom testimonies), the narratives of personal experience that we tell during conversation are only loosely subjected to criteria of truth. When a participant in a conversation volunteers to tell a supposedly true story, the audience expects both information and entertainment. This means that truth should not get in the way of a good story. For the sake of entertainment, listeners will be quite tolerant toward embellishments, exaggerations, dramatizations, transpositions, invented dialogue, and concrete details that memory could hardly retain. The audience does not sort out the story for statements to believe and statements to make-believe but evaluates it globally as "mostly true" or "partly true," as well as "well told" or "poorly told." Conversational narratives of personal experience thus fall into the no-man's-land between fiction and its other.

Fiction and Writing

The difficulties created by oral narrative for the digital theory of fiction suggest that the strict distinction between fictional and nonfictional texts, as we know it in Western cultures, is the product of writing.[14] Today we regard the myths and epic poetry of oral cultures as fictions, but in their culture of origin, these forms did not enter into a contrast with history, science, or any other truth-functional discourse. On the contrary, myths were both science and history. They told about the origins of culture, and they offered explanations of natural phenomena: what happens to the sun between the time it sets in the west and rises in the east, or how the rainbow came to be. But above all they were sacred stories given to the people by supernatural creatures. In contrast to modern science and history, they were not falsifiable, and they did not enter into a competitive relation with other texts. Myth is the voice of Truth itself, the foundation of a culture, a definitive representation that refuses to acknowledge the existence of any other version.[15] Its truth is so secure that the narrators of myth never need to justify the source of their information (Booth 1996, 244), and its authority so complete that "belief in the myths of a community is compulsory" (Pavel 1986, 61). Since the truth of myth is guaranteed by its origin—ancestors, tradition, or the gods—myth shares the declarative status and world-creating power of fictional discourse. But the analogy stops at the world of reference: while our modern fictions establish truth for a world that is ontologically not ours (we must transport ourselves in imagination to regard it as actual), myth concerns the most real of all worlds, the very center of the believer's ontological system. Mircea Eliade has observed that the heroes of myth live *in illo tempore,* in a sacred time and place rigidly delimited from the realm of the profane, but this separate domain is an integral part of the real, rather than one possible world among many others. From this derives what is perhaps the main difference between myth and fiction: there is only one corpus of myth per culture, because there is only one actual world, but there are many fictions, living in peace with each other, because each one creates a different possible world.

Did preliterate societies distinguish myth from fiction and both of them from "fact" (as I will call, for lack of a better term, discourse about regular individuals and everyday life that can be true or false), or do these categories represent what Dan Ben-Amos calls "analytical genres," classes forged by scholars in order to compare text types across cultures, as opposed to the "ethnic genres" recognized by native taxonomies? Even if we find narratives in oral societies that we would categorize today as fact, fiction, or myth (gossip for fact, jokes, fables, and tall tales for fiction, epic poems for myth), this does not necessarily mean that these categories had cultural significance. Since the only way of preserving knowledge in preliterate cultures was the limited resources of human memory, oral cultures may have distinguished narrative types according to whether or not they are worth preserving. The forgettable stories deal with the individual and the ephemeral, while the stories preserved in the cultural heritage provide atemporal truths and useful knowledge. To facilitate preservation, stories of the second type were encoded "in mnemonic patterns, shaped for ready oral recurrence," such as meter, alliterations, assonances, repetitions, antitheses, and formulaistic expressions (Ong 1982, 34). Narrative itself was a potent mnemonic device—try to memorize a list, as opposed to memorizing a plot—and practical knowledge was often transmitted in the form of stories. *Pace* Roland Barthes, the myths and epics that survived from oral societies were not born in the "cauldron of fiction," and to assimilate them to the modern narrative entertainment of novels, short stories, and movies would be to ignore the particularities of their cultural function.

I will leave it to others to draw detailed connections between the invention of writing and the erosion of myth, but both played an important role in the emergence of fiction as a culturally recognized narrative mode. According to Thomas Pavel, when myth dies it turns into fiction. "When a mythological system gradually loses its grip on a society, the ancient gods and heroes start to be perceived as fictional characters" (Pavel 1986, 41). As the countless plays and novels inspired by Greek mythology in Christian societies testify, the loss of belief in myth makes its material available for fictional treatment. Meanwhile, factual types of discourse received an enormous boost from the invention of writing. As Ong writes, "Literacy . . . is absolutely necessary for the development not only of science but also of history, philosophy, explicative understanding of literature and of any art, and indeed for the explanation of language (including oral speech) itself" (1982, 15). Writing allows the complex logical reasoning of philosophy, the preservations of eyewitness testimonies of chronicles, the use of documents of historiography, the cumulative development of science, and the system of quotations of textual exegesis. When writing became print, and texts became more widely accessible, discourse developed strict criteria of verifiability that widened the gap between imaginative and factual discourse. Nonfiction, in both its narrative and non-narrative varieties, was born when it became possible to consult documents, check out facts, repeat experiments, and compare written results. As facts became verifiable, a polarization of fact and invention took place, and through a backlash effect, the emergence of factual discourse as a culturally recognized category led to the cultural recognition of fiction. It is no coincidence that modern science and the modern novel were both born in the century that followed the invention of print.

It is common knowledge that the rise of scientific discourse accelerated the demise of myth. The analytical categories of fact, fiction, and myth had been able to live peacefully with one another during the age of manuscript writing. In the Middle Ages, what we regard as fact was represented by history, annals, chronicles, and commentaries; what we label fiction by romances and fabliaux; and myth survived in religious texts, but the borders were fuzzy. With its fantastic elements, for instance, hagiography was a blend of all three types. But when science developed in the age of print, its incompatibility with myth led to the collapse of a loose three-partite textual system into the strict dichotomy of fiction and non-fiction. Fiction is no rival for science, despite its frequent dismissal of scientific laws, because it creates its own world. But myth and science target the same reference world. Insofar as they attempt to provide explanations for natural phenomena, the two modes of knowledge also overlap in their subject matter: science tells us that certain atmospheric conditions cause the optical phenomenon of rainbows, myth tells us that rainbows were created as a sign of an alliance between man and God; science explains menstrual periods in terms of hormonal cycles, myth may do so in terms of a mystical bond between women and a moon goddess. As the raging debate between creationists and partisans of evolutionary theory in contemporary American society reminds us, the common reference world and the overlapping concerns of myth and science place the two modes of discourse in a fierce competition: if one is true, the other cannot be. Having to contend with other representations is a normal situation for science, but in the case of myth, it is a sign of degeneration. The rivalry of science and myth that divides modern cultures internally and pits them against each other was never supposed to happen: the narratives that are still active as myths in contemporary societies are mostly the legacy of an age when science was still in its prehistory. The three types of discourse I have discussed above adopt strikingly different stances toward competition: science thrives under it, fiction protects itself from it by isolating itself in its own private world, and myth cannot accept it, because it is threatened in its very essence by any challenge to its authority. As myth disappeared from the discourse system of vast segments of Western societies,[16] the features of the dying narrative mode were divided between the two survivors. Nonfiction, like myth, describes the real, but it lacks the authority of myth and must consequently defend the truth of its claims by enrolling the support of experiments or other texts. Fiction preserved the authority of myth, its declarative power to create a world, its irrefutable truth, but it diverts all of these properties toward imaginary worlds.

If postmodern skepticism could speak for the public at large, fiction would now be doing to factual discourse what factual discourse did to myth, and we would be heading toward the undifferentiated system of panfictionality. But the reactions of outrage that greeted Edmund Morris's Reagan biography[17] demonstrate the enduring cultural vitality of the distinction between fact and fiction. The play with boundaries of postmodern hybrids does not bring down a repressive dichotomy but, on the contrary, heightens our awareness of an epistemologically responsible distinction. For without this distinction, what would motivate us to examine critically the claims of nonfiction, rather than accepting them as automatically true performative statements?

3. Narrative in Fake and
Real Reality TV

If the producers of the so-called reality TV shows have any say in defining reality, Jean Baudrillard and Michel Foucault are not merely towering figures of postmodern thought; they are the true prophets of this young millennium. By placing human subjects under the never-ending surveillance of cameras, and by labeling the resulting spectacle reality, these shows seem to have been conceived for the specific purpose of implementing Foucault's dystopic vision of a panoptic society, and Baudrillard's doctrine of the (hyper)reality of the image in contemporary culture. Postmodern theory tells us that "reality" is what comes *out* of the media, but if we want to understand the specific working of a medium, we must also take into consideration the input to its machine and the operations performed on this input. Moreover, if media fabricate hyperreality, it would be simplistic to assume that their products automatically become the spectator's own reality. In this chapter I propose to compare the fictional TV show of *The Truman Show* to the real one of *Survivor* with two questions in mind: (1) how dependent on other genres and media is the TV reality show, and through what cultural patterns, especially narrative ones, does it filter live data; and (2) in what sense does its output deserve to be called reality? In asking this second question I am not claiming that reality TV has anything to say about reality in any ontological sense of the term, but by eliciting reactions in the spectator about the nature of its offering, it is instrumental to the building of a "folk theory" of what is real and what is not. Through this folk theory, it makes a significant contribution to the phenomenological study of reality.

The Truman Show

In a classic example of what Bolter and Grusin call "remediation"—media striving to refashion, improve on, or simulate other media—*The Truman Show* represents in movie form the run of a TV show, which itself exploits the fascination of the public for webcams, a phenomenon based in yet another medium. Through this cross-medial narrative embedding, *Truman* invites us to reflect on the idiosyncrasies and differences in the narrative potential of TV and cinema. Even though cinema and TV sometimes transmit the same material, the experience of a movie shown on a TV screen is significantly different from its experience in a theater. A movie theater envelops us like a dark cave and creates the optimal conditions for an immersive experience. We are a captive audience in a magic spectacle that requests and receives our undivided attention. The film plays without interruption for about ninety minutes, and when it finally releases us from its world we have a hard time adapting again to the brightness of natural light. A movie shown on a TV screen is a far less immersive experience, visually speaking, because it competes with countless potential sources of distraction. We can surf to other channels, the showing is interrupted by commercials, the screen occupies only a small part of our field of vision, and the quality of sound and image is much lower than in a movie theater. This is why McLuhan has called TV a cold medium, in contrast to the hot medium of cinema. The different viewing conditions of TV and movies have significant consequences for the type of narrative that best fits each of these media. Since movies last on average ninety minutes, about the time of a theatrical performance, their narrative plots favor strict Aristotelian patterns of exposition, complication, climax and resolution. In fact, Aristotelian dramaturgy has become something of a bible for Hollywood scriptwriters. Meanwhile, since TV runs twenty-four hours a day, seven days a week, fifty-two weeks a year, its narratives may stretch over a considerable period of time, even though they occupy a limited slot in the weekly schedule. The type of narrative that takes full advantage of the idiosyncrasies of the TV medium is not the self-contained Aristotelian plot but the never-ending serial with multiple characters, parallel plot lines, and largely episodic structure.

As Sarah Kozloff has observed, this endless stretching of narrative time deemphasizes action and redirects attention toward the characters. Viewers develop emotional attachment (or passionate distaste) for the main characters of a show and for the often eponymous actors who play these characters. Because TV narrative stretches out indefinitely in time, its plot is continually in the process of being written, which means that the audience can offer feedback to the scriptwriters, either indirectly through polls or directly through such institutions as fan clubs, fan magazines, and online chat groups. This feature makes the TV serial narrative far more interactive than movie drama.

Another narrative dimension that distinguishes TV from movies is the possibility to narrate "in real time" through the live broadcasting of real-world events. This real-time potential of TV narrative does not successfully combine with the indefinite temporal extension of serials; the favorite topics of live coverage are not ongoing wars or time-consuming rescue efforts but well-scripted and dramatically engrossing rituals of strictly delimited temporal extension, such as sports events, royal weddings, and Oscar ceremonies. In addition, TV serials make up their own narratives, since they specialize in fiction, while the events shown on live broadcasts are supposed to happen independently of the camera. TV narrative thus opens two possibilities that are not available to the cinematic brand, but these two distinctive properties of the medium are mutually exclusive in commercial programming. About the only actual shows that run *all the time* and *in real time* are the abovementioned webcams, as well as the closed-circuit *surveillance* cameras that we find in stores, banks, and prisons.

The reason why we don't have TV narratives that never go off the air and run in real time are commercial rather than practical. As the webcam phenomenon has shown, it is easy to place a camera in a location where something interesting might happen and to make this camera record and broadcast continually until some dramatic event "walks," so to speak, in its field of vision. But a show of this kind would have such a low degree of narrativity and so many dead moments that nobody would want to watch it for an extended period of time. Internet webcams are indeed meant for quick "grabs," not for the lengthy couch-potato camping in front of the tube that enables TV viewers to ingest enough commercials to keep their favorite show on the air. It is only in the realm of the imagination that a continuous live broadcast could generate sufficient interest to justify sustained watching. This of course is what happens in the Truman show,[1] a fictional TV show embedded in the real film by the same name. Narrative embedding has always been a convenient way to present virtual artworks that stand no chance of being actualized—think of the painting in *The Picture of Dorian Gray,* a portrait that ages instead of its subject, or of the Chinese novel in Borges's "The Garden of Forking Paths," a narrative that follows all the branches of the possible, and that we find paraphrased, but significantly not directly quoted, in the very real story by the same name. Similarly, in *The Truman Show,* the embedding technique is used to present a show that could never be implemented in the real world for reasons that involve not only the technological and the narratological but perhaps also the ethical, though not many people are willing to concede a sense of human decency to a medium as maligned as TV. Insofar as they use volunteers and lure them with the promise of a rich money prize, real shows such as *Survivor* and *Big Brother* are a far cry from the carceral situation of *Truman.*

The subject matter of the show is nothing less than the entire life of its hero, a very ordinary insurance salesman named Truman Burbank. Truman was adopted by a television company—the first individual legally adopted by a corporation, we are told—and from the moment of his birth, unbeknown to him, every instant of his life has been recorded by a camera and shown live on TV to an adoring audience. The people who surround Truman are not his genuine wife, mother, buddies, colleagues, or neighbors but actors whose every action and utterance is scripted and piped in by the producers of the show. To prevent Truman from escaping from the eye of the camera, the TV company built a giant bubble dome that covers an entire town, a perfectly clean and well-planned island community that looks like a hybrid of California real estate development (Truman *Burbank!*), seaside tourist resort, and suburban paradise from a TV show of the fifties. Whenever Truman attempts to take a trip to the world at large, a carefully planned "accident" brings him back within the range of the recording equipment. But after thirty years on the show, Truman begins to suspect that there is something fishy about the world he lives in, and one day he manages to sneak away from the camera and to escape in a sailboat. He eventually hits the wall of the bubble and confronts Christof, the creator of the show, who tries to persuade him to resume his TV life for the sake of the audience: "You are the hero of a TV show that brings joy to millions." Ignoring the plea, Truman walks off the show, to the thunderous cheers of the fans. If these cheers salute the liberation of the audience from the tyranny of the media, the euphoria of a TV-free existence turns out to be short-lived. The movie ends with the all too familiar question "What else is on?" as two dejected spectators frantically search with the remote control for an active channel.

When a medium embeds a representation of another, the logic, discourse, and aesthetics that prevail are inevitably those of the embedding medium. In the movie, by necessity, the thirty years of the show are condensed into about an hour of footage. Whereas in the TV show Truman's life is broadcast "live and unedited," the actual movie filters it down to its dramatic highlights. The episodic and character-centered TV narrative has been reshaped by the movie into a plot-centered Aristotelian structure, with a clear exposition, complication, climax, and denouement. The discrepancy between the two logics and the prevalence of the resources of the embedding medium is particularly evident in the use flashbacks. As a real-time and continually produced narrative, the fictional Truman show would not allow a dissociation of the orders of story and discourse, since organizing the presentation of a story into narrative discourse is an editing process that requires a temporal distance from the events and a comprehensive knowledge of what can be used as narrative material. In a genuine real-time situation, producers have no choice but telling events in the exact order of their occurrence, and they cannot delete meaningless or nonfunctional events since narrative functionality is a dimension which is assessed after the facts. The only choice allowed is among the many cameras that simultaneously record the events from various points of view. But in the movie, the life story of Truman is presented in a classical nonchronological style, with a beginning in medias res and flashbacks to earlier episodes in the show. This rearrangement is obviously meant to arouse the interest of the actual spectator, but it is naturalized within the fictional world of the movie as the familiar broadcasting practice of rerunning earlier episodes of TV serials. There is, for instance, a flashback that shows Truman's encounter during his college years with a beautiful woman who tried to warn him of the whole scheme. When the scene is over, we see a shot of two female viewers who comment, "I can't believe he married Meryl on the rebound."

From a narratological perspective, the impossible character of the embedded Truman show lies in its hybrid status between fiction and nonfiction. As we saw in chapter 2, postmodern literature has accustomed us to works that challenge the strict dichotomy of fiction and nonfiction by alternating between the two modes, by exploring their fuzzy boundary, or by making the question of fictionality undecidable. But the virtual narrative of *The Truman Show* manages to be at the same time, and quite unambiguously, fiction and nonfiction, a feat that to my knowledge no real narrative has been able to accomplish. Here we have a text whose fictionality depends on the perspective of different characters. From Truman's point of view, the show is as clearly "life" as it is "fiction" from the point of view of the actors who play roles. The reason for this discrepancy lies in the fact that fictionality requires a duplicity of actor/character in dramatic media, and of author/narrator in strictly narrative works. The actors are duplicitous, since they are playing roles, but Truman has only one identity. The obvious staging of Truman's life is not sufficient to make it fiction, because in real life also, we find many scripted events that count as genuine performance. One need only think of the carefully planned protocol that regulated the life of Louis XIV. Every gesture of the king's daily life was turned into a ceremony, and the noblemen of the court could even buy the right to attend the spectacle, but the king was really performing the actions specified by the script and not simply acting them up. In *The Truman Show,* this compatibility of staging and authenticity is expressed by the actor who plays Truman's best buddy when he tells the audience in a documentary program: "Nothing is fake. Everything is true. It is merely controlled."

The Truman show is not only a paradoxical hybrid of fiction and nonfiction, it also manages to be at the same time reality show and soap opera. Through its combination of raw life and staged action, the show cleverly taps into the two fundamental sources of narrative appeal. We are fascinated by true stories because we are citizens of the same world as their participants, because we experience a sense of community with all human beings, and because real events may impact our personal life; on the other hand, we are attracted to the made-up stories of narrative fiction because they fulfill formal and thematic patterns that engage the imagination.

If we combine these two sources of pleasure or interest, nothing should be more satisfactory than life imitating popular literature, a formula that tabloid journalism understands only too well. In *The Truman Show*, the continuous surveillance of Truman by the cameras that are hidden everywhere on the island offers a guarantee of truth. Truman has no off-camera life, and except for his inner thoughts, he cannot hide anything from the audience. This sense of authenticity is strengthened by the already mentioned impossibility to edit live broadcasting and to tamper with its narrative sequence. Christof, the producer of the show, woos the audience with the promise "Live and unedited, twenty-four hours a day, seven days a week." If the show is unedited, this means that it must go on even in the narratively barren moments of Truman's life, for instance, when he is asleep. The scriptwriters of the show make up for these barren moments by filling the daytime with the kind of events that one might expect from a soap. These events introduce a tellability into Truman's life that rescues it from the tediousness of normal life. In his broadcast about the show, Christof titillates the audience with a preview of the excitement to come: "Meryl will soon leave Truman. A new romantic interest will develop. And watch for the first live conception on TV." (The show seems to become sexually bolder as the years go by, as does indeed the culture that produces it.) The dual allegiance of the show to the randomness of life and to the control of narrative art is reflected in the ambiguous stance of the audience with respect to the hero. The insignium of belonging to the club of Truman fans is the wearing of a button that says "How will it end?" The cheers that salute Truman's definitive departure from the show can be read as an expression of aesthetic satisfaction with the resolution of the plot, even though this resolution deprives the fans of the show that gives meaning to their daily life.

Through its eschatological overtones, the message "How will it end?" is also the first intimation of a religious theme that becomes more and more explicit as the movie nears, precisely, its climax and its end. Truman, the ordinary man whose life is scripted from above, becomes the sacrificial lamb of a media religion that redeems the tedium of everyday life by making its banality into the object of a TV show. Through the mediation of Truman, everybody is vicariously raised to the highest glory that humanity can hope to attain in a media-dominated culture, namely, to the status of TV celebrity. In the religion masterminded by Christof, Hamlet's dilemma, "to be or not to be," is reinterpreted as "to be on TV or not to be." According to a standard mythical pattern, the fulfillment of the redemptive scheme requires the sacrifice of the redeemer's life. In keeping with the preoccupations of contemporary culture, this sacrifice does not mean the loss of life, but simply the loss of privacy. Truman's life is indeed offered to mankind by being put on public display. According to Mircea Eliade, the great historian of religions, the performance of religious ceremonies transports cult members into mythical time and makes them contemporaries of the hero whose life is being reenacted. In the case of Truman this interpenetration of profane time and mythical time is automatic, since the cultural hero fulfills his destiny in the eternal present of the live broadcast.

As is the case with most organized religions, the worship of Truman involves responsibilities as well as benefits. To earn the privilege of having the show brought to them, the audience must support the church financially through the purchase of paraphernalia that bear the likeness of their hero. Every object that appears on the show is for sale through a catalog, and even though the show is technically free of commercial interruptions, the hawking of various products is an integral part of the script. In the middle of a conversation with Truman, his wife will, for instance, turn toward the audience and say, "Truman, let me prepare for you a cup of cocoa 'Mococoa.' It's the best cocoa I have ever tasted, and believe me, I have tasted them all." Consuming these goods strengthens the unity of the community of worshipers and functions as mediation between the cult figure and ordinary mortals. Drinking the same cocoa as Truman is not merely an imitation of the hero but a ritual that enables the worshiper to become one with him, just as in Christianity practicing the "Imitation of Jesus Christ" is a way to reach a state of spiritual communion with the Savior, and in the religion of sports, just as wearing Michael Jordan sneakers is a way to "be like Mike."

The obvious target of this somewhat heavy-handed satire is the tendency of TV to usurp the place of myth and to define cultural values in modern society. Recent treatments of the importance of TV shows in the popular press suggest that far from being regarded as fictional worlds created for the sake of pure entertainment, these shows are credited with the power to determine what is allowed and forbidden. The currently much-maligned show *Father Knows Best* was the expression of the patriarchal values of the fifties, and the more recent *Ellen* serial was hailed as the official acceptance of homosexuality in American culture. In archaic societies the absolute truth of myth is guaranteed by the authority of the source—gods, prophets, shamans, or ancestors—but the erosion of faith in the sacred in contemporary society, as well as the general rejection of institutional forms of authority, has voided the traditional sources of authentication and turned over responsibility to celebrities. Many of these "mythical shows," such as *Roseanne, Ellen, Seinfeld,* or *The Cosby Show,* bear indeed the name of the actor who plays the leading role. The homonymy between the name of the character and the name of his or her real-life impersonator creates the expectation that the private life of the actor respects the cultural values expressed in the myth. By declaring her homosexuality, for instance, Ellen DeGeneres established the legitimacy of her lesbian character as a role model in contemporary society. (At least, this is what the press said at the time—the subsequent demise of the show may have shown those pronouncements to be premature.) When the myth falls out of cultural favor, discrepancies between the private lives of the actors and their fictional personae are invoked to kill it off. After the death of Robert Young, the actor who plays the infallible Jim Anderson in *Father Knows Best,* the media's insistence on his private mental problems and suicide attempts was an implicit rejection of the truth of the myth. In *The Truman Show* there is no chance of a discrepancy between actor and character ever taking place, since Truman has no private life other than what is shown on the screen. As long as it maintains its panoptic surveillance of the hero, the camera functions as the guarantee of the absolute truth of the myth.

Survivor

Truman walked off the show before the heir promised by Christof could be conceived live on TV, but as the several real-world imitations of the concept demonstrate, he did indeed manage to reproduce himself. In a further case of remediation, Truman's nonfictional epigones range from webcam simulations of the "live and unedited twenty-four hours a day" TV broadcast that we only glimpse at in the movie to TV simulations of the highly edited cinematic mediation of this show.

The numerous TV adaptations of the Truman formula—the so-called reality shows or "voyeur TV" (VTV)—all resort to various degrees of compromise between scripted movie drama and the raw spectacle of the surveillance camera. *Survivor,* the most popular U.S. TV show in the summer of 2000 (still going strong at the time of this book's publication), takes the formula as close as it can go toward the scripted pole without becoming a fully acted TV movie. (*Big Brother,* the other, less popular show of the 2000 summer season, stayed closer to the raw pole.) For those who equate reality with the banal, the quotidian, the spontaneous, the unstaged, the intimate—in short with how "ordinary people" behave in certain spaces culturally designated as sanctuaries of privacy—dismissing the reality claim of *Survivor* is like complaining that Las Vegas is fake. Making no attempt at hiding the camera from the participants nor at pretending to record the daily grind of a random sample of the population, *Survivor* openly exploits its own power to create behaviors. At the risk of rehashing what every reader who doesn't live on a desert island already knows, let me summarize the formula. The producers of the show selected sixteen people out of a huge number of applicants (over six thousand, according to *Time* magazine) and placed them in a blatantly artificial situation that severed all ties with their personal environment. Marooned, or rather implanted, on an uninhabited island in Southeast Asia, the participants fought to survive the doubly hostile environment of nature and their fellow cast-offs (the latter far more dangerous, since nature's parsimony was somewhat compensated by supplies dropped from the sky). Every three days a participant was voted off the island by the others, and the last one to survive received a prize of one million dollars.

If the opposition of life and art is one of formlessness versus design (a popular conception admittedly belied by the presence of pattern in nature), *Survivor* aggressively pursues the artifice of art. The weekly script of *Survivor* transposes onto the temporal level the spatial concept of windowed display. The hour-long show was so predictably divided into thematic (or strategic) units that I was able to skip the parts that did not interest me—namely, the organized activities. The Aristotelian pattern favored by movies thus prevailed on the level of the weekly episode, though over the course of its twelve-week run *Survivor* did generate the emotional reaction to characters that Kozloff considers typical of TV narrative. The broadcast began with a panning of the landscape, followed by a few shots of the cast-offs engaging in life-sustaining activities (fishing, cooking, eating), accompanied by bits and pieces of spontaneous dialogue. After an interlude of comments directly spoken into the camera on such topics as the harshness of life, interpersonal relations, or the participants' assessment of their own chances to survive the day's vote came a contest whose winner (tribe or individual) was rewarded with a luxury item from the outside world: fresh fruit, beer, a useful piece of equipment, or a video phone call to the loved ones at home, for the show was big on family values. A second contest, after another interlude of talk or nature shots (not to mention the commercials), was fought for the much more substantial reward of immunity. A session of comments on interpersonal relations directly spoken into the camera, which, to many viewers, constituted the crux of the show, prepared the climax of the "tribal council" (as the voting event was called) and the denouement of the loser's expulsion.

In a show of this type, the discrepancy between what Genette (1972) calls narrated time and time of narration makes selective editing inevitable. This further precludes any claim that reality is just "showing itself." The boredom of island life, a feeling born out of the temporal *durée* of repetitive experience, is, for instance, condensed into thirty-second shots of idle people commenting into the camera about the emptiness of their days. Thanks to the weekly compression of time, as well as to the fact that *Survivor* as a whole aired some three months after the filming, the editing process often takes the allure of retrospective narration. (The *Big Brother* experiment, by contrast, ran in the same time span as the show; each installment was a selection of the day's materials, and some shows even contained live footage.) The retrospective tampering with the data was most obvious in the tribal councils. As the contestants took their seats in the designated area, the camera typically dwelled on the face of one of them, raising the suspicion that this contestant was going to be "it." When this foreshadowing became too predictable the editors resorted to another tactic: the camera framed an individual who would narrowly survive the vote. This trick too became predictable, but by that time the producers seemed to have run out of ideas; deceptive foreshadowing ruled the show for most of the second half.

Narrative shaping is not only a matter of structure and techniques but also a matter of symbols and themes. *Survivor* plays against each other, in oxymoronic fashion, two themes that stand for the opposite ends of a cultural spectrum: capitalist materialism and native spirituality. As was the case in *Truman*, the show invests in the facile readability of cultural stereotype and mythical archetype. The Southern California planned community has given way to Polynesian clichés (exotic tribe names, tiki-room decor), but in both shows the setting provides the stage for a secularized version of religious drama. In *Survivor*, this drama rewards virtue in this life with financial heaven in the afterlife of postshow existence. The ceremonial pump that surrounds the tribal councils tells the spectator that there is more to the moment than getting rid of obnoxious comrades and potential rivals: the vote expresses the communal wisdom of a sacred entity named Pagong, Tagi, or Rattana. As they write down a name on the ballot, many participants movingly speak of their love and respect for the person they are about to cast off, for sending people back to the world beyond the ocean is the hard rule of life, not an expression of personal resentment. The voting takes place in a circular area separated from the profane space of the island by a suspended bridge and illuminated by torchlight: one burning torch for each surviving member of the tribe. As the participants prepare themselves to scribble a name on their ballot (this usually done with spelling mistakes), the show host intones the ritual formula: "The voting is irrevocable, and the person voted out will have to leave the island immediately." When the vote has been tallied, the torch of the loser's life is extinguished, and another formula, "the tribe has spoken," punctuates the walk of the newest victim of tribal wisdom across the symbolic bridge that leads from life to death. Eliminated contestants may have been unable to get along with the other members of the tribe during the day, but in the moment of expulsion, they are revered as dead ancestors, and their memory is kept alive through the extinguished torches that decorate the ceremonial area. In the final weeks of the show, these dead ancestors (or at least, those who survived long enough to become truly venerable) are invited back to the voting ceremony to observe the living, for they will be the ones who cast the final vote. During the last installment, the remaining three participants are made to perform a rite of passage by walking on (symbolic) hot coals through a double row of palm fronds held by their "fallen comrades." Their faithfulness to the tribal spirits is tested by a contest that grants immunity to the player who can answer the most questions about the Dead Ancestors. In another contest, they must hold as long as they can onto a wooden pole that stands for an idol. (The winner, Kelly, held on for more than three hours.) The contestant who was best able to please the Dead Ancestors during the Last Judgment is rewarded with mythical gold, but in the end everybody gains access to Heaven. The show concludes with a happy reunion of all participants, during which all feuds and grudges are erased by Love Triumphant. Thanks to the miracles of cosmetics, the bodies we saw battered by nature and deprivation are gloriously resurrected for their affluent after-island life; for, thanks to media appearances, book contracts, and endorsements, everybody walks out a financial winner.

The kitschy New Age spirituality of the native theme is thus undermined by the cynicism of the capitalist theme. Many of the immunity contests are so silly that they seem to have been designed for the express purpose of demonstrating how much public humiliation people will tolerate for a chance to win a million dollars: eat worms, stay on a plank in the ocean and under the sun for many hours, or, as already mentioned, "hold on for dear life" onto a wooden pole. Relishing in their power to give and take away, the omnipotent gods of the networks tantalize the materially deprived contestants by dangling before their hungry eyes the luxuries of conspicuous consumerism. After winning a contest, for instance, a player is flown to a yacht off the island, where he or she is served Champagne by a tuxedoed waiter. When the two tribes merge into one, a representative of each group is taken to a sand spit to negotiate a symbolic marriage. While the tribe members left on the island gripe about having nothing to eat but rice, the two ambassadors, not coincidentally male and female, and both young and handsome, are treated to a gourmet candlelight dinner in a glorious sunset, before retreating into a night that we are made to imagine rich in other pleasures.

The capitalist theme is so openly flaunted that its ideology almost negates itself. Exposing the theses of the French philosopher Guy Debord on the relations between capitalism and fascination for the spectacle in contemporary society, Scott Bukatman writes:

> The spectacle is the ultimate commodity in that it makes all others possible: in its role as advertisement, the spectacle generates the condition for consumption, and therefore for production as well.

> The spectacle is infinitely self-generating: it stimulates the desire to consume (the only permissible participation in the social process), a desire continually displaced onto the next product and the next. (1993, 37)

Survivor does more than verify these observations—it does so with typically late-capitalist, postmodern self-consciousness. The blatant consumerism of the show is acknowledged through the playful interplay between the commercials and the game itself. While the contestants ecstatically feast on the product of one of the sponsors (Budweiser), the commercials display the same setting as the show, reenact some of its most memorable moments, such as the infamous worm-eating contest, and even feature some of the participants voted out in the early stages. The contestants themselves practice self-consciousness through frequent allusions to the made-for-TV nature of their situation: "Its like being in a game show," says Colleen. "Which of course it is." Or Susan, before an archery contest, which she lost: "I am going to beat a guy. And on national TV."

Where is reality in all of this? The two dominant themes create a overflow of meaning that seriously compromises the credibility of the show as "reality TV"; for, as Roland Barthes observes, it is the meaningless, the random, the found object that create "l'effet de réel" (reality effect). Through its forceful pursuit of thematic and dramatic legibility, *Survivor* offers a classic example of what Baudrillard calls the hyperreal, namely, a copy that kills the desire for the original, because it is better shaped, more coherent, more predictable, and therefore more intelligible. Baudrillard explains our fascination for the hyperreal as a self-seduction, a phenomenon that involves a more or less willing abdication of defenses ("to seduce is to weaken"; 1988, 162). This idea of seduction can be understood in two ways. In one interpretation, which I would like to dismiss right away, critical faculties are so debilitated by the rhetoric of the show that the audience becomes blind to its artifices; the show is consequently taken as the authentic, unmanipulated image of life. But today's TV audiences are far too sophisticated to miss the work of the camera, the dramatic scripting of the data, and the intertextual borrowings from other TV shows. If this sophistication weren't sufficient to kill off illusion, the self-referentiality of the show should dissipate any remaining chance of taking *Survivor* as a candid window that "catches in the act" the fully spontaneous behavior of true representatives of ordinary humanity. To the idea of a gullible audience thrown into mental arrest by the mystifying power of the media, I prefer the thesis advanced by Cynthia Freeland with regard to other types of reality TV, such as *Rescue 911* or *When Animals Attack*: these programs are so badly acted and so amateurishly produced that they have "gotten to the point of parodying themselves" (2004, 259). *Survivor* achieves the same effect through the opposite route of overproduced, technically perfect images. According to Freeland, audiences watch these caricatures "in a subversive, ironic spirit," deriving their pleasure from the thought that this is not reality but rather its made-for-TV version. This attitude falls along the same lines as the fascination of many supermarket shoppers for the headlines of tabloids such as *National Enquirer* or the *Weekly World News*: these readers (here I speak for myself) do not view the stories as something to believe but rather enjoy them in a spirit of schadenfreude, as examples of "what other people are dumb enough to believe." (These other people, of course, are a construct of the reader's imagination, so my schadenfreude may ultimately rest on delusion.) If indeed the spectator is not fooled by the reality-claim of the image, we must opt for an interpretation of seduction as the deliberate choice of the fabricated over the authentic. As the current popularity of personal history, "true fiction," "true crime," or memoirs of traumatic events indicates, neither raw life nor well-made fiction can rival the appeal of "true" facts cast in a properly dramatic mold. The need to compromise between narrative form and authenticity may pose a dilemma to historians and biographers, but in the entertainment sector, allegiance to "the real" weighs little against the seduction of plot, because it is not a value in itself but a means toward an end. As the victory in the ratings of *Survivor* over its less scripted relative *Big Brother* indicates, American audiences want a flavor of reality, but they want their reality properly cooked and dressed.[2]

The claim to reality of reality TV has been so widely deconstructed by critics, however, that rather than joining the chorus line, I would like to play the devil's advocate. If the various episodes of *Survivor* achieved viable ratings for at least eight seasons, it is because something genuine, something worth calling reality took place in their artificial environments. The claim that what happened in the fishbowl does not capture reality because participants were selected by the producers, were aware of the presence of the camera, and were placed in an artificial situation presupposes an essentialist interpretation of human reality. In this view, the real equals the normal, the everyday, the private, and the intimate. We are only truly ourselves in the familiar circumstances of our daily life, and preferably behind closed doors, when we no longer play the game of social behavior. The "false," controlled self of public life is thus opposed to the "true," impulsive self of privacy, which the reality show can only hope to capture when the participants forget the camera and let raw feelings speak out. This hope of seeing "what happens when people stop being polite and start being real" (slogan of the MTV show *The Real World*) is admittedly a strong motivation for watching *Survivor* and *Big Brother*. According to this conception, "reality" happens in flashes on the show, for instance, when Susan places a curse on Kelly, when Jenna wipes away a tear, thinking of the loved ones at home, or when Greg and Colleen disappear into the night for an alleged dalliance. "We don't see real life in these series," claims Paul Romer, a producer of *Big Brother*. "But sometimes, we touch on real personalities. There is a momentary reflection of the real self—and those moments make great television" (quoted from Sella 2000).

For the sensation-seeker, the "real self" is something hidden behind the surface that reveals itself in short bursts when the masks of civility are dropped. For those who have assimilated the lesson of phenomenology, on the contrary, human reality is something continuously produced and presented to others, something that arises from the interaction between a subject and an environment. Human reality, if it could be mapped, would be the sum of all the possible selves that we create in all possible situations. This reality emerges no less from the confrontation of individuals with a made-up environment than from their insertion in a naturally occurring one.

Ramona, the chemist who was voted out in the early weeks of the show, aptly described the situation when she called it "a Petri dish for conflict." The stage may have been designed to maximize the chances of interpersonal friction, since audiences want drama, and drama needs conflict, but once they entered the closed world of the island, the participants wrote their own character by interacting with their social and natural environment. *Survivor* can be compared in this respect to an experiment in artificial life—with the emphasis on life rather than on artificiality. As N. Katherine Hayles (1999a) describes it, artificial life is the name given to computer programs that create a complex self-organizing system by placing a number of digital objects, each endowed with specific behaviors, in a closed environment. The dynamics of the interaction between these silicon-based creatures causes them to evolve and to develop new behaviors that weren't scripted in the original software. They are alive in the sense that they achieve autonomy with respect to their creator. As in all artificial life environments, the evolution of *Survivor* depended on the initial conditions of the system, namely, the personalities of the characters: "Casting the people for *Survivor* was as much fun as I've ever had—and it'll be the same with *Big Brother*," said Leslie Moonves, president of CBS. "You get the chance to speculate about whether, say, these two people here will have conflict. Or that this girl and this guy might get together. Sometimes you are right and sometimes you're so far off you can't even imagine" (quoted from Sella 2000).

In contrast to Christof in *The Truman Show,* who insisted on an absolute control over his creature (and whose show was destroyed when the creature rebelled), and to the producers of *Big Brother,* who tried to intervene when the ratings began to fall,[3] the gods of *Survivor* kept a relatively light hand on the development of the show. They set up the stage, selected the actors, appointed a host who functioned as narrator (Jeff Probst), but they let the plot evolve at least partially by itself. Nowhere does the autonomy of the creatures with respect to the creator express itself more forcefully than in the subversion of the game by some of the participants. The idea of the game was to let the voting process select the most deserving player, the one with the best combination of social and survival skills. Voting was supposed to eliminate those troublesome individuals who posed a threat to the cohesion of the group, even though the group had been created for the sole purpose of being methodically dismantled one member at a time. But two participants decided to play by their own rules. Sean opted for randomness, by voting out people in alphabetical order, while Richard Hatch, who eventually won the game, opted for strategy. As already mentioned, the "alliance" he organized from the very beginning with Rudy, Kelly, and Susan stipulated that they would all vote for the same person, in order to maximize their chances. He and his co-conspirators took their fate into their own hands, rather than leaving it to others and to chance. The subversion of the voting process from popularity contest to the protection at all costs of personal interests allowed some of the stronger, but also more abrasive participants to survive until the final round, thereby preserving the narrative interest of the show, for every good story needs a villain. Whereas the plot of *Big Brother* lingered on in love and harmony because the jury (a real-world audience) systematically voted out unpopular players, Richard Hatch became the bad guy everybody loved to hate. By helping to maintain the ratings, the small rebellion of the alliance-mongers eventually served the interests of the producers as well as their own. The gods seem indeed to have learned something from their creatures, for the advertisement to the sequel of *Survivor,* filmed in the winter of 2001 in the Australian outback, extolled the ability to control group dynamics through clever maneuvers: "Surviving social politics, it's what the game is all about."

As an allegory of our media-crazed society, *The Truman Show* leaves us with a bitter taste, a feeling only alleviated by the demise of the show. The prospect of an absolute and complete truth about a human being is more disturbing to the contemporary mind than the lies and fabulation for which media have traditionally been blamed. *The Truman Show* inscribes itself in a long tradition of fear of new media, but it also demonstrates the displacement that the object of this fear has undergone since the early age of print and the birth of the novel. The main threat to our ability to relate to the world and to its members no longer comes from escapes into the fictional, as it seemed to be the case in the days of *Don Quixote* and *Madame Bovary,* but from the transformation of life itself into a spectacle. Whereas Don Quixote and Emma Bovary innocently lived fiction as if it were life, we are now so jaded that we watch the representation of life as an entertaining fiction, mindless both of the violence done to the individual whose privacy is being invaded and of the life we sacrifice when we live vicariously through televised hyperreality. We are more alienated from the real by its supposedly exact copy than by the worlds openly made up by narrative imagination.

Does the popular success of *Survivor* confirm these fears? Has the idea of human life as spectacle become so well accepted that we no longer notice its revolting implications? It is not my intent to analyze the psychological and cultural roots of our society's fascination for voyeur Web sites and reality TV. But I would like to advance one argument in defense of *Survivor* and its relatives. These shows make no secret of being artificially designed environments, but they are designed in such a way as to encourage emergent behaviors. In *Truman,* life becomes a spectacle that oppresses life. In *Survivor,* by contrast, as in Artificial Life programs, the spectacle breeds life. Without putting the two on the same pedestal, couldn't we say that in its best moments, the maligned, lowbrow genre of reality TV shares at least this one feature with art?

4. Narrative in Real Time

Life is lived looking forward, but it is told looking backward. Whether invented or experienced, events are normally emplotted retrospectively. Knowledge of the outcome shapes the narrator's selection and evaluation of the preceding states and events; the crisis to be highlighted determines the exposition and the complication; the point to be made specifies the arguments to be used. While the laws of material causality operate forward, the laws of narrative, artistic, textual, or more generally of communicative causality operate overwhelmingly backward.

Modern literature attempts to reconcile the prospective orientation of life with the retrospective orientation of narrative through the use of the present as primary narrative tense.[1] In many recent novels—especially those told in the first person—the present is more than a historical present, more than the "present of vividness" occasionally found in narrative of personal experience;[2] it is a present with a full temporal meaning, expressing simultaneity between the time of narration and the time of experience. The narrative present imparts to the text an existential dimension: the narrator narrates her life as she lives it, without knowing what comes ahead. At the same time, however, narrative form is ensured by the author, who resides outside the narrated time and shapes the life of the narrator according to the global design of a plot. The layered character of the fictional speech situation, by which the actual sender pretends to be the narrator, allows a paradoxical combination of prospective orientation, retrospective organization, and illusion of simultaneous representation. Because of the dualism author/narrator, present-tense fiction is really a disguised form of retrospective narration.

If genuinely simultaneous, genuinely nonretrospective narratives exist at all, they are found in nonfiction. A relative simultaneity occurs in chopped-up narratives such as diaries and news reports. The diarist lives her life and tells it at the same time, as she recounts in discrete entries the stories of the day past. Tomorrow will not only bring new individual stories; tomorrow will continue a lifestory whose end will remain forever unknown to its chronicler. In a similar vein, the news reports of a daily newspaper recount the latest episode in an ongoing story—wars, trials, scandals, political campaigns—whose coverage will be continued until its resolution. These texts are simultaneous on the macrolevel, if one regards as "text" the sum of the daily installments covering the same topic, but they are retrospective on the microlevel.

Of all forms of verbal representation, none comes closer to true simultaneity than live broadcasts, particularly radio broadcasts of sports events. The live broadcast is one of the rare nonfictional contexts in which the use of the present to report a sequence of actions encodes a full temporal meaning.[3] Significantly, Ann Banfield calls this use the "baseball present," as opposed to atemporal uses, such as the present of general truths, or the so-called historical present of retrospective narration. A live broadcast may be compared to a computer program operating "in real time": it is a time-consuming process that receives its input from another process running at the same time. In diaries and news reports, by contrast, the process providing the input is temporary halted, or rather, bracketed out during the operation of the output-generating process. The real-time situation promotes a narrative tempo in which the delay between the time of occurrence of the narrated events and the time of their verbal representation strives toward zero, and the duration of the narration approximates the duration of the narrated: excluding the paratexts of the pregame and postgame shows, the broadcast of a baseball game begins shortly before the first pitch and ends with a terse recap a few seconds after the last out.

But if the sports broadcast is temporally anchored in the present, this does not mean that its discourse is restricted to the present tense, nor that it always focuses on the current action. In this chapter, I propose to study the text of a baseball broadcast with several questions in mind: how variable is the relation between time of occurrence and time of narration; what operations does it take to give narrative form to the game; and more generally: is genuinely simultaneous narration possible at all in real-world communication?

My data are taken from the broadcast of a play-off game between the Chicago Cubs and the San Francisco Giants on October 9, 1989. The announcers, working for the CBS network, are John Rooney and Jerry Coleman. At the time of the game, the Giants were leading in the series three games to one, which means that they could clinch a trip to the World Series with a victory.

Three Aspects of Narrative

As a preamble to the analysis of the broadcast, let me distinguish three dimensions of the narrative text: the chronicle, the mimesis, and the emplotment of events. As a chronicle, a narrative enumerates events and satisfies the audience's curiosity for *what* happened in the reference world. As a mimesis, the text focuses on the *how* and immerses the audience in the action by conferring presence and vividness to the narrated. As a plot, finally, it organizes the narrated in a global design that makes events intelligible to the audience and satisfies its demand for the *why* of the events. Mimesis, chronicle and plot correspond roughly to the three semantic dimensions of the definition of narrative presented in chapter 1: mimesis establishes a world and individuates its members; chronicle describes events that make this world evolve; and plot suggests the connections and motivations that explain these events. Mimesis, however, can also be used for the expansion and mental visualization of the materials that fill my second dimension.

The relative development of chronicle, mimesis, and plot is highly variable among narrative texts and provides an important factor of generic diversity. Some texts are pure chronicle—pure listing of individual events without attempt to give meaning to their sequence. Historical annals and diaries fall in this category: the author's main ambition is to provide a more or less exhaustive enumeration of what happened to a certain individual or in a certain place in a certain time span. Other texts are mostly mimetic, with little chronicle or emplotment: for instance, a short text evoking some memories; a verbal snapshot of a scene or location, as in travel writing; or the profile of a famous personality. In some narrative genres, mimesis and chronicle are well developed, but plot occurs only on the level of individual episodes. This is often the case in biographies, since lives are not plotted by a storyteller, and to a lesser extent in biographical novels, where the life is indeed plotted by the novelist. Chronicle and plot dominate the text, at the expense of mimesis, in the laconic stories of a Kleist, a Borges, or in legends and fairy tales: there are lots of events, they fit into a tightly knotted plot, but the narrative pace is too fast for the reader to develop a sense of spatial immersion in the storyworlds. Of the three dimensions, I regard the emplotment of events as the decisive factor of narrativity. A text does not develop its full narrative potential if it simply describes scenes or reports events. There must be some global scheme, some explanatory theme, some principle of selection—in short, some necessity to the report of events. The fully narrative text is summarized by a statement suggesting a meaningful story arc: not simply "What happened during ten years of the life of Marcel," but rather: "How after seemingly wasting his life Marcel is led to understand that lost time can be recaptured through art." Through this emplotment, the meaning of the text is no longer reducible to the sum of the chronicled events.

The Broadcast as Chronicle

Of the three narrative dimensions mentioned above, the chronicle is the dominant one in the baseball broadcast. Mimesis may be embryonic, plot may be nonexistent, but chronicle is a mandatory ingredient. As a largely nonselective enumeration of events, the chronicle presents a special affinity for the real-time situation: it requires no retrospective point of view, no global design, and consequently no teleological principles. Since the audience of the live broadcast is mainly interested in the status of the game (who is winning, what is the current strategic situation), the primary task of the announcer is to report everything that happens on the field as soon as it happens. This ideal must, however, be reconciled with another requirement: the demand for continuous entertainment. The necessity to fill up the entire time of the game with talk limits the simultaneous report of events to less than half of the broadcast. The rhythm of the game is not a steady flow but an alternation of slow periods and sudden outbursts of action. It is only in fiction that time adjusts to the pace of language. In the real-time narratives of the real world, language must play catch with time. The relation between the duration of the narrated and the duration of the narration is rarely comfortable: there is usually either too much or too little time for language to capture the action live.

This imbalance in the availability of time is particularly striking in the microdrama that forms the basic unit of the game of baseball: the duel between the pitcher and the batter. Most of the encounter consists of the same event: the pitcher throws the ball, the batter fails to put the ball in play, the ball returns to the pitcher. This type of event does not decide the fate of the batter—whether he will be safe or out—and it presents therefore the lowest possible degree of tellability. During a broadcast, the routine of throwing a pitch without immediate consequences is repeated on the average about three and a half times for each batter, which means more than 250 times per game. The report of this action takes much less time than the action itself. Here is, typically, how individual pitches are reported:[4]

> ROONEY: The pitch, swing and a miss, 0 and 1. The pitch to
> Sandberg. A ball. Outside. The wind by Reuschel and the 1-1
> pitch. A ball. High. He missed with a fastball.

If the time of narration had to equate the time of the narrated, every pitch would have to be described on the level of detail displayed in this passage:

> COLEMAN: [Bielecki] grabs the rosin bag, steps behind the rubber,
> checks it out, toes the rubber again with that right foot, looks
> at that catcher, sign coming down, he's got it, the 2-and-0 pitch.
> Moving in. Thompson. Fouled it off on the right side.

When the batter finally makes contact there is an onrush of events. Here is what happens on the last pitch of the same confrontation:

> ROONEY: There's a line drive through the gap down in right center-
> field that gets down and rolls out to the warning track and on
> to the wall. In to score Walton. Sandberg has a double, he's
> gonna go for third. Here's the relay from Thompson, and tags
> him out. Sandberg gets an RBI double and then is thrown out,
> trying to stretch it into a triple.

Now suddenly the announcer has to keep track of four simultaneous processes: the flight of the ball, the running of the hitter, the catch and throw of the fielder, and the scoring of the man on base. If the broadcast adhered strictly to simultaneous narration, there would be a blatant discrepancy between the attention devoted to the three preliminary pitches and the emphasis put on the play initiated by the fourth pitch. The main narrative problem to be solved by the real-time broadcast is to create appropriate relief in the reported action by compressing time during events of little importance and expanding time during the decisive events.

In a retrospective narrative, the compression of time is accomplished through an acceleration of the narrative pace. The dead moments in the lives of characters are either deleted or summarized. The narrative camera simply "fast forwards" until the next tellable situation: "Ten years after these events, Emma was walking on the beach, when suddenly . . . " When the narrative discourse operates in real time, this option is not available. The language of the live broadcast has three choices for coping with a lack of tellable events.

The first option is to stay with the present and to adjust to the slowing down of the action. Staying with the present means filling the time with any kind of information about the current situation, such as enumerating the cast of secondary characters (coaches and umpires), describing for the umpteenth time the defensive line-up, or chronicling in painful detail the gestures of the players, as in the description quoted above: "[Bielecki] grabs the rosin bag, steps behind the rubber, checks it out," and so on.

Rather than staying with an empty present, the broadcast may escape toward the past—either the past of the game in progress through recaps:

> COLEMAN: And the beat goes on, it's all even at one, Cubs got one in the third, Giants tied in the seventh.

or the past of the players through background information:

> ROONEY: Here's Ryne Sandberg. He's 6-of-17 for the series. He has a couple of doubles, a triple, a home run, three RBIs, one on a sacrifice fly. He's been on three times with walks.

Both of these strategies present the advantage of killing time while fulfilling another function in the economy of the broadcast: recaps update the listener who joined the action in progress (for, unlike literary narratives, the broadcast welcomes those who want to begin in the middle), while the use of background information serves the purpose of character presentation. The display of the batters' statistics may be compared to the summary of the past life of a character newly introduced in a novel. The statistics were gathered during a time-span larger than the history of the game, but they are presented for the sake of their predictive value for the current pitching duel.

The most radical departure from real-time reporting is a widening of the context from the chronicle of the game in progress to casual conversation about baseball in general, such as gossip, reminiscences of seasons past, or didactic expositions of the finer points of baseball strategy. The broadcaster who starts a digression runs, however, the risk of a resumption of the action before the point is made. This happens in the game analyzed here when Coleman and Rooney launch into a lengthy discussion of the art of pitching. When the dissertation is completed, a new batter has stepped to the plate and already taken a few pitches. To catch up with the present, the broadcasters must skip the ritual introduction and summarize the missed pitches in the past tense.

The Broadcast as Mimesis

When an important play finally happens, the live broadcast cannot expand time by slowing down the narrative pace, as is customarily done in the novel. Increasing the level of detail in the description would put language behind in its race to keep up with the present. This in turn would create a conflict with the goal of informing the audience of events as soon as they happen. As already mentioned, the primary interest of the audience is for the *what* and not the *how* nor the *why* of the action. When a decisive play is chronicled in the present of real time, the emphasis is placed on the outcome, not on the description of the play. The main clue to the importance of the play is the rise in the tone of voice—the only type of signal that does not result in a loss of time. Once the audience is informed of the *what,* however, a curiosity develops for the *how* and the *why.* For the spectators at the stadium, this curiosity is satisfied by instant replays on the scoreboard. In the radio broadcast, the replay is performed by retellings in the past tense.

Retellings serve two functions. The first is to signal the key events and to create narrative relief. The retelling of events establishes their tellability. Most of the plays deciding the fate of the batter receive some kind of retelling; the most crucial sequence in the game (the scoring of the winning run) is retold on six different occasions.

The second function of retelling is to complete the live report with details that enable the audience to visualize the play. Consider this passage:

> ROONEY: *There's a swing and a ground ball up the middle fielded in back at second by Thompson. The throw not in time. An infield hit.* Thompson did not get a really good grip on the ball and his momentum was carrying him off left field. And it was tough to throw Walton out after that.
>
> COLEMAN: I think we got the story all the way. Walton did *not* get down the line the way he could when he was running well. He just made it and Thompson bobbled the ball a little bit, held on to it and almost got him anyway. But Walton is *not* the runner he was six weeks ago.
>
> ROONEY: Real good range by Robbie Thompson going back at second base. But he knew he had to hurry the throw and he could not get a good grip on the ball.

The simultaneous narration in the present tense takes only twenty-five words (those in italics)—about the time needed to catch and throw an infield hit. It states the essential facts for the fan who wants to keep score: where the ball went, who fielded it, whether the batter was out or safe. The report is fully objective and free of evaluation. The retrospective narration adds details to this skeleton and enables the audience to form a mental picture of the action. In Rooney's retelling, we see the second baseman struggle to grip the ball and get his balance for the throw. In Coleman's version, we see the runner barely making it to first base, and the fielder bobbling the ball. The third retelling by Rooney adds an evaluation ("real good range") and the representation of a mental event ("he knew he had to hurry the throw"). In the simultaneous version, by contrast, the telling was strictly limited to the report of physical events. The retrospective retellings add a *how* and a *why* to the *what* and turn it into a story. Or rather, into a pair of contrasting stories. One of them is about Thompson struggling with the ball and being nearly successful at a difficult task; the other, about an injured Walton running too slowly and almost failing an easy task.

The Broadcast as Plot: Emplotment and Thematization

In this last example, retelling not only develops a mimetic dimension but also demonstrates the strategies of emplotment. The raw facts of the play are turned into a microstory through three basic operations:

1. The retelling selects a hero and an opponent, and it adopts the side of the hero in its presentation of facts.
2. An event is put into focus as the key to the play: Walton reaching base or Thompson bobbling the ball.
3. The text suggests an interpretive theme that subsumes the events and links them into a meaningful sequence. The theme of the Thompson story is "near success despite unfavorable circumstances"; the theme of the Walton story is the opposite: "near failure despite a lucky break."

As Paul Ricoeur observes: "A story should be more than an enumeration of events in a serial order, it should organize these events into an intelligible totality, so as to make it always possible to ask: what is the theme of the story" (1983, 102; my translation).

As a competitive game, baseball instantiates the most basic narrative pattern: the fight of the hero and the antihero. Every game, consequently, has an elementary story, the story of which team overcame the other. Yet baseball is not a literally narrative game, because, as we will see in chapter 8, its constitutive events, such as throwing, hitting, and catching balls, or running around bags disposed in a diamond pattern, are not the kind of actions that we perform in real life to pursue our personal interests, nor are they symbolic representations of such actions, as are the events of a video game in which the player wages a war against evil aliens or builds a civilization. The plays of the baseball game are abstract events intrinsically deprived of human interest, and it is only because they have been conventionally associated with winning and losing, outcomes that do provoke emotional reactions, that they matter to the players and spectators. If the broadcaster describes all the plays in the game, he will produce a chronicle, not a fully developed story. By contrast, if the spectator of a movie reports the action on the screen to a blind friend sitting next to her, she will produce something much closer to a story, even if she has not seen the movie before, because the film is narratively scripted. To emplot a baseball game, then, the broadcaster must add something that, as Hayden White (1981) observed, is not inherent to the physical events: he must give them significance, by connecting them to themes of human interest. One could imagine a speech-generating machine that would chronicle a game in response to information concerning the states and events of the game (so that the automaton would know the count of balls and strikes, who is on base, how many are out, and when the ball is put in play), but narrative emplotting can only be performed by a creative mind. In a game-report merely concerned with the outcome of the game, such as this AP report: "Expos 4, Mets 1: At New York, Montreal's Tony Batista hit a tie-breaking two-run homer in the eighth inning" (July 23, 2004), the players are mere pawns on a game board, and it does not really matter to the reader (unless he is a fan of Tony Batista) who hit the game-winning home run. In a thematized version, by contrast, players become characters with distinctive identities, and their fate and actions carry an exemplary value. This is why the emplotment of sports games often involves a moral lesson.

In literary narrative the repertory of available themes is as diversified as human experience: it ranges from the interdictions, violations, revenges, deceits, and broken promises of myths and fairy tales to the identity crises, sexual awakenings, and social revolts of contemporary novels. The choice is much more limited in the tightly ruled universe of baseball. The narrative themes relevant to baseball are the scripts, or scenarios, that describe interesting ways of winning or losing: *the incredible come-from-behind victory, the fatal error, the heroic feat, the lucky-break victory, the unlikely hero, the inevitable collapse, overcoming bad luck, persistence that pays off.* These themes acquire existential significance through the metaphorical assimilation of victory to life and defeat to death. The broadcast is narrative to the extent that it configures the game by activating a script on the basis of some events, thereby marking these events as key plays in the game.

Reporting in real time, the announcer lacks, however, the temporal distance that allows the selection of key events and the development of narrative themes. Plot is a global design—and a global design necessitates a comprehensive apprehension of facts. This apprehension is only available from a retrospective point of view. The announcer is therefore in the strange situation of a narrator ignorant of the plot. His perspective combines the situations of reader and storyteller: like the storyteller, he transmits information, but like the reader, his apprehension of the plot is purely speculative. He reads the game as it goes on, trying to discover patterns of significance, reassessing past events, projecting events to come on the basis of the developing themes, and testing several different themes that organize the game into different possible plots.

The Broadcast as Plot: The Story of the Game

As every true baseball fan will immediately recognize by looking at the line score below, the game between the Giants and the Cubs was a dramatic one. Whoever wrote the script had a keen sense of narrative suspense and knew the Aristotelian principles of plot configuration. The first two innings form the exposition, the middle innings develop a conflict, the eighth leads to the crisis, and the ninth brings the denouement.

	1	2	3	4	5	6	7	8	9	Runs	Hits	Errors
Cubs	0	0	1	0	0	0	0	0	1	2	10	1
Giants	0	0	0	0	0	0	1	2	x	3	4	1

Here is the story of the game, as told in real time. In the first inning, the contest is prospectively thematized as *do or die for the Cubs* (or, *the Cubs' last chance*):

COLEMAN: I have to believe, John, most of the Cubs players are really tense in this one. I don't care what to say. Even though you're down 3 and 1 you have to say the worse you can do is lose. They have to win it to keep it alive. The pressure is definitely on the Chicago Cubs.

Through this prospective thematization a point of view is established and a side is selected. Even though Coleman and Rooney are in principle neutral announcers (the CBS broadcast is intended for a national audience), they will report most of the game from the perspective of the Cubs.

Until the third inning, the game is dominated by the pitchers, and the broadcasters complain about the lack of tellable events: "John, you keep waiting for something to happen, and so far, nothing is happening." At this very moment, however, the first decisive event occurs. A fly ball by Jerome Walton of the Cubs is dropped for an error by Giant outfielder Kevin Mitchell, and Walton scores on the next play. It turns out that Mitchell forgot to flip down his sunglasses and lost the ball in the sun. This blunder activates the theme of the *fatal error*:

COLEMAN: He better get a good answer to that one: why didn't
you pull [your glasses] down?, if that has anything to do with
the winning or losing of the ball game. Well it could be a very
controversial decision before this is over. If this run holds up,
Kevin may have some explaining to do.

In a comment like this, the emplotment of the game combines a
retrospective interpretation with the prospective evocation of a possible outcome. A whole game is projected on the basis of the play
just completed—a game in which the score stands as it is, and the
future adds nothing to the story. This projected game presents all
the components of narrativity: a main protagonist (more antihero
than hero), Kevin Mitchell, a key event and turning point, Mitchell
forgetting to flip down his sunglasses, and the dominant theme of
the *fatal error*.

In the middle innings, the Cubs put several batters in scoring
positions, but they all get stranded and the score remains the same.
In keeping with the reputation of the Cubs as perennial losers unable to reach the World Series, the announcers shape the story of
the game as a tale of *futility* and *wasted opportunities*:

COLEMAN: Bielecki may have to throw a shutout to win. Chicago
simply can't get the base hit to get them in . . . Too many opportunities lost, so Bielecki better be sharp. You've got to say
that, when it's all over and done with, no matter how this thing
ends up, if the Cubs don't win this ball game they have no one
to blame but themselves. They had their chances.

The futility of the Cubs contrasts with the *opportunism* of the
Giants, who will eventually score three runs on only four hits, while
the Cubs, with ten hits, manage only two runs:

COLEMAN: So far the difference between the Cubs and the Giants
with a runner at third they get a fly ball to score them. The Cubs
had two runners at third and couldn't get them in.

The sense of impending doom for the Cubs materializes in the sev-
enth inning, when the Giants tie the score. This run not only erases
the theme of the *fatal error*; it also activates the theme of *redemption*, since the run scores on a sacrifice fly (appropriately named)
by the same Kevin Mitchell who was guilty of the error.

The comedy of futility versus opportunism turns into tragedy in the bottom of the eighth inning. Like a good drama, the game reaches an obvious climax, and the climax is strategically located shortly before the end. This lucky timing guarantees that the plot won't run out of twists before the book is full. The dominant theme of the eighth inning is the *downfall* of the Cubs' pitcher, Mike Bielecki. Until now he has been portrayed as a lonesome hero, keeping his team in the game without help from his offense. Now the hero runs out of strength: after easily retiring the first two batters, Bielecki cannot put his pitches in the strike zone, and he ends up walking the next three batters to load up the bases. The *downfall of the hero* is recorded step by step in these observations:

> COLEMAN: Bielecki visibly tiring now right now. Taking lots of time in between pitches, and that's usually to restore your energy after you let go, trying to get it back, so you can throw the next one just as hard. . . . Bielecki at the start of the ball game was ahead of every batter, but he has lost some of that sharpness now.
>
> Again Bielecki, taking a lot of time . . . And Bielecki suddenly has lost the plate.

At this point there is no attempt by the broadcasters to fill up the dead moments with gossip. When the pitcher takes time between pitches, they remain silent, and the listener can hear in the background the roar of the crowd sensing the kill. This timely violation of the rule of constant entertainment expresses better than words the intensity of the situation.

With the bases loaded and two outs, Bielecki is finally removed from the game and replaced by a reliever. The contest now becomes a *confrontation between a hero and an antihero*. The hero is Will Clark, the best batter of the Giants; the antihero is relief pitcher Mitch Williams, described several times as an "erratic left-hander." The climactic character of the situation is forcefully stressed by the broadcasters. There is no need anymore to emplot past or future events: the action is NOW, the game is on the line. The fate of the Cubs hangs on the outcome of the duel between Clark and Williams. The first three pitches create a clear advantage for the pitcher, but on the verge of striking out, Will Clark hits a single to centerfield, scoring two runs, and the confrontation ends in *the triumph of the hero*.

After the climax of the eighth inning, the ninth brings the denouement. The broadcasters reactivate the theme of the *doomed*

Cubs by describing their imminent defeat and elimination as a fait accompli, but against all expectations the Cubs manage to put two men in scoring position. This activates a classic theme of sports narrative: *it ain't over till it's over.* With two outs the Cubs drive in a run, and they are just one hit away from tying the game. But as soon as the possibility of the miraculous comeback is suggested, the doom of the Cubs is consummated. The next batter grounds out, and the game is suddenly over.

> COLEMAN: Cubs hanging tough . . . Another base hit, don't go away, it's still alive. . . . Out of nowhere the Cubs are back in it. Sandberg waiting, watching, here's Bedrosian, pitch on the way to Ryne, ground ball to second, Robbie Thompson grabs it, play to first, the ball game is over, and the Giants win the National League pennant.

Real Time *versus* Retrospective Telling

The themes of this real-time telling would receive various degrees of emphasis in a retrospective narration of the game. Some would rise to the highest level of prominence, becoming the theme(s) of the macrostructure; some would sink to lower levels; some would survive in a modified version (*fatal error,* no longer verified, may become *error and redemption* on the microlevel), and a few might disappear altogether. If I had to retell the game from the point of view of its outcome, I would come up with a version emphasizing the theme *opportunism overcomes futility*:

> The Cubs really had a chance to win, they got a great performance from their pitcher, and they put lots of men on base, but they could not score, and when Bielecki finally collapsed in the eighth, they put in this wild reliever Mitch Williams with the bases loaded, and boom, the amazing Will Clark did it again—he slapped a single to win the game.

Does the text proposed above capture a plot inherent to the broadcast, or is it my own emplotment of the game, using the broadcast as data? The answer lies halfway in between. In the text of the broadcast, the potentially plot-functional elements form only a subset of the total information. Every action is chronicled, but only some of the plays are retold and thematized. When the broadcast concludes abruptly with the report of the last out, the elements of a number of possible plots may have been sketched, some of them more forcefully than others, but none has been etched in stone. One of these plots will be solidified in a retrospective construct—by the broadcasters in the postgame show, or by the listener, who stores the game in memory by constructing a game-story. The retrospective retelling is guided by the emplotment proposed in real time, but not limited by it. Listeners construe the game-story by making their own selection among the themes, heroes, antiheroes, and key events proposed by the broadcast. Exploiting the background of the complete chronicle, they may also create their own game-plot by selecting another hero, regarding as key play an event chronicled but not emphasized by the announcer, or rationalizing the game through a different system of themes. Like unmediated life experience, the real-time broadcast is a quarry of narrative material, an open text encapsulating many potential stories.

When plot-functional units must stand out from the general background of a near-complete chronicle, as is the case in the live broadcast, their signalization tends to be more forceful than in a situation that gives the narrator time to choose which events to narrate. In a standard retrospective narrative, key events are usually told only once, and their thematic significance is often conveyed implicitly. This is particularly true of literary narratives. The reader does not need to be told, "this event was a fatal error, this one was a revenge." She comes to these conclusions through a private interpretation. Because the narrated events are carefully selected by the storyteller, a sense of plot can be conveyed by a mere enumeration of unevaluated events. In the live broadcast, by contrast, the strategic importance of events is established through multiple retellings, and the narrative themes are signaled through a more or less explicit narratorial interpretation. Listed below are some examples of the exact textual expressions that prompted my identification of the narrative themes. Even when the themes are not explicitly named in the text, I did not have to stretch my imagination to find descriptive labels:

Do-or-die: They have to win it to keep it alive.

Fatal error: He better get an answer to that one—why didn't you pull them down?—if it has anything to do with the winning or the losing of the ball game.

Wasted opportunities: Too many opportunities lost

Redemption: Mitchell kind of redeeming himself

Doom (of the Cubs): [Giant's victory] almost seems a fait accompli
   the way things have been going for the Cubs.
It ain't over till it's over: Don't go away, it's still alive.

Thanks to the formal features described above, listening to a baseball broadcast is like visiting a factory of plot. Retrospective narration only displays the result of the process of emplotment, but real-
time narration offers a glimpse at the process itself. Since every play
is chronicled, but only some plays are emplotted, we can study the
criteria for the selection of narrative elements, and we can assess the
relevance of the plot with respect to the game it purports to capture.

   This raises the question of what makes a version of the game-
story acceptable to the audience—besides the intrinsic tellability
of the script (a factor to be determined by a poetics of plot). Is
the validity of an emplotment assessed entirely on the basis of its
truthfulness to the data, as is, according to the scientific position,
the case in historiography, or do other criteria enter into consideration? Consider the game-story according to which the game was
lost by the Cubs' inability to take advantage of opportunities. This
version of the game ignores an important piece of data, namely, the
fact that the Cubs displayed considerable opportunism in scoring
their first run: it occurred on a key hit, after a Giant error put a
runner in a scoring position. The game-story is a simplification of
the chronicled material, but the audience is nevertheless likely to
accept it (if I can judge by my own reaction) because it confirms
a stereotype: the reputation of the Cubs as perennial losers and
lovable patsies. The acceptability of an emplotment is not simply a
matter of truthfulness to the chronicle but also, and perhaps more,
a matter of conformity to baseball lore and to the loyalty of the
audience. This is why most game-stories are told from the point
of view of the home team, casting the local players in the role of
protagonists. A defeat of the home team is much more likely to be
presented as a case of futility of the protagonist than as a heroic
deed of the opponent—unless the opposing pitcher is officially recognized by baseball lore as a future Hall of Famer. These biases
suggest that cultural norms and the values of the recipient community are no less influential on the emplotting of baseball games
than on the interpretation of literary texts.

II
Narrative in New Media

5. Toward an Interactive Narratology

In *Cybertext,* a book whose contribution to digital textuality truly deserves to be called ground-breaking, Espen Aarseth attempts to analyze two types of digital texts, hypertext fiction and text-based adventure games (also known as interactive fiction) according to the parameters of what he calls the "communication model of classical narrative" (1997, 93): a transaction involving a real author, an implied author, a narrator, a narratee, an implied reader, and a real reader.[1] He suggests some adjustments, such as redefining the relations between the parameters for hypertext (the author no longer controls the narrator, the reader no longer identifies with the narratee), or renaming the parameters for interactive fiction (intrigue for plot, intrigant for implied author, and intriguee for narratee), but he declares himself unsatisfied with these patches. In his more recent work, Aarseth turned his back on narratology and forcefully rejected the idea that computer games, and by implication interactive fiction, form a species of narrative. Implicit to this move is the belief that existing narratological models are the definitive word on the nature of narrative. But the narrative theory invoked by Aarseth, which we may call "classical narratology" (Herman 1999), was designed for standard written literary fiction based on the illocutionary act of "telling somebody that something happened." The communicative model of classical narratology does not work for the mimetic mode of film and theater, and one should not expect it to describe narrative modes even more removed from the standard case than dramatic enactment.

In contrast to Aarseth, I regard narratology as an unfinished project, and if classical narratology fails the test of interactive textuality, this does not necessarily mean that interactive textuality fails the test of narrativity. It rather means that narratology must expand beyond its original territory. In this chapter I propose to investigate what needs to be done to allow narratology to deal with interactive digital texts. Needless to say, the development of a digital narratology will be a long-term collaborative project, and I can only sketch here what I consider to be its most urgent concerns.

Before embarking on this investigation, let me enumerate the properties of digital systems—other than the fundamental feature of programmability, that is, algorithm-driven operation—that I regard as the most relevant for narrative and textuality:

- Interactive and reactive nature: the computer's ability to take in voluntary or involuntary user input and to adjust its behavior accordingly.
- Volatile signs and variable display: what enables bits in memory to change value, causing pixels on the screen to change color. This property explains the unparalleled fluidity of digital images.
- Multiple sensory and semiotic channels: what makes the computer pass as the synthesis of all other media.
- Networking capabilities: the possibility to connect computers across space, bringing their users together in virtual environments.[2]

This list focuses on properties inherent to computer systems and therefore avoids features of digital objects that result from the proper exploitation of these properties. This is why it does not include immersivity, a feature that some authors list as distinctive of digital media (for example, Schaeffer 1999, 310). As I argue elsewhere (Ryan 2001), literature, film, and painting can also produce immersive experiences, though the digital medium, thanks to the above-mentioned properties, has taken immersion to new depths. I also restrict my list to features that do not derive automatically from the basic property of programmability and were added only progressively to computer systems. In the early days of computing, users had to key-punch code on cards and feed the stack of cards to a reading machine connected to the computer. An eternity later—or so it seemed—the machine would spit out a striped white-and-green piece of paper with the output of the program, or, more frequently, a list of syntax errors. This type of system, known as batch processing, lacked interactivity (the user could not communicate with the machine during the run of the program), multimedia capabilities (all the computer could output was alpha-numerical text), volatility of inscription (both input and output were on paper), and networking capabilities (the machine, which served multiple users, had no remote terminals and would not let users communicate among themselves).

Of all the properties listed above, I regard interactivity as the most important. Not all digital texts are interactive, but those that aren't could usually be taken out of the computer and played by an-other medium.[3] The term has been under attack by cybertheorists for being too vague, especially after advertising language fell in love with it and started promoting everything under the sun as interactive,[4] but when interactivity is associated with narrative, its meaning is unambiguous.[5] As game designer Chris Crawford ob-serves: "it mandates choice for the user. Every interactive applica-tion must give its user a reasonable amount of choice. No choice, no interactivity. This is not a rule of thumb, it is an absolute, un-compromising principle" (2002, 191).

Yet if interactivity is the property that makes the greatest differ-ence between old and new media, it does not facilitate storytelling, because narrative meaning presupposes the linearity and unidirec-tionality of time, logic, and causality, while a system of choices involves a nonlinear or multilinear branching structure, such as a tree, a rhizome, or a network. Narrative meaning, moreover, is the product of the top-down planning of a storyteller or designer, while interactivity requires a bottom-up input from the user. It will con-sequently take a seamless (some will say miraculous) convergence of bottom-up input and top-down design to produce well-formed narrative patterns. This convergence requires a certain type of tex-tual architecture and a certain kind of user involvement. It would be of course easy to constrain the user's choices in such a way that they will always fit into a predefined narrative pattern; but the aes-thetics of interactive narrative demand a choice sufficiently broad to give the user a sense of freedom, and a narrative pattern suf-ficiently adaptable to those choices to give the impression of being generated on the fly. The ideal top-down design should disguise itself as an emergent story, giving users both confidence that their efforts will be rewarded by a coherent narrative and the feeling of acting of their own free will, rather than being the puppets of the designer.

Interactive narratology does not have to be built entirely from scratch, since it involves the same building blocks as the traditional brand: time, space, characters, and events. But these elements will acquire new features and display new behaviors in interactive environments. To account for the pragmatics of the interactive text, it will also be necessary to expand the catalog of modes and to devise alternatives to the classical communication model. In chapter 1 I address this need by proposing a simulative, an emergent, and a participatory mode. Among the issues new to interactive narratology will be the types of architecture that lend themselves to choice without compromising narrative logic, the various modes of user involvement, and the means and types of interaction. Under means I understand such tools as the link, the menu, the map, and simulated real-world objects that interactors can pick up and use, and under types, whether the interaction is blind or purposefully selective, and whether it counts as a concrete action in the virtual world or remains purely abstract. As for the object of interactive narratology, it includes not only "literary" hypertext fiction, but also text-based adventure games (to be discussed in more detail in chapter 6), interactive drama (chapter 7), some single-user video games (which ones, exactly, will be discussed in chapter 8), and multiple-user online role-playing games.

A complete overview of all the expansions of classic narratology required by interactive digital texts would far exceed the frame of this chapter. In the discussion to follow, I will focus instead on what I regard as the most prominent concerns of interactive narratology: the structures of choice (textual architecture), the modes of user involvement (types of interactivity), and the combinations of these parameters that preserve the integrity of narrative meaning.

Textual Architecture

Textual architecture, in both traditional and interactive narrative, is a building composed of a story and a discourse level. Stories (or plots) are mental constructs of such complexity that it will take many different types of two-dimensional diagrams to represent their various dimensions. In Figure 1 I propose four partial representations.

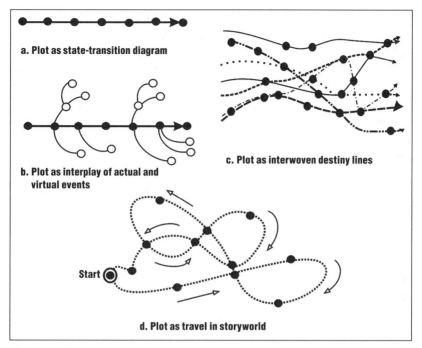

a. Plot as state-transition diagram

b. Plot as interplay of actual and
   virtual events

c. Plot as interwoven destiny lines

Start

d. Plot as travel in storyworld

Figure 1. Plot graphs

In all these diagrams, the temporality of plot is symbolized through an oriented line. In Figure 1a, the most basic plot diagram, the horizontal axis stands for a timeline punctuated by the events that change the global state of the storyworld, while the vertical axis could be used for the description of the individual states. Here the plotline is reduced to the collective destiny of the storyworld, and its representation of events is limited to what actually happens. But the virtual, that which could have or still might happen, plays an important role in the decisions of both life and narrative. In the course of a story, each of the characters faces several decisions points, in which many choices offer themselves. Figure 1b contrasts the actual life story of a character with the virtual paths that the character did not or could not take. While Figures 1a and 1b capture semantic aspects of story that are common to all narratives, Figures 1c and 1d describe specific types of plot structures. 1c shows plot as a weave of different destiny lines—one for each character. The lines that traverse a circle indicate which characters participate in this event. This model provides an efficient mapping for narratives that interleave the lives of a large cast of characters into numerous subplots and concurrent story lines, such as television soap operas. As for Figure 1d, it represents plot as an itinerary through the geography of the storyworld. The two axes of the diagram stand for the east-west and north-south coordinates of a map, the black dots for the various locations within the storyworld, and the oriented line for the journeys of the hero. This type of diagram is particularly useful for narratives of travel, such as the *Odyssey* or James Joyce's *Ulysses*.

In traditional narrative, discourse can be represented by the same type of diagram as 1a, but the order of the events may differ on the story and the discourse level. Assuming that story is sequentially ordered 1-2-3-4-5, etc., a narrative beginning in medias res will, for instance, present events in the order 7-1-2-3-4-5-6-(7)-8-9. Or a narrative may return many times to the same state or event, presenting a sequence as 7-1-2-7-3-4-7-5-6-7-8-9. It would be very artificial for a braided narrative of type 1c to stick to a strictly chronological order, especially since the exact temporal relations between events of different strands (that is, what precedes what and what occurs simultaneously) are usually left indeterminate. The most natural discourse sequence in this case will follow a character for a while and then jump to the life story of another, but multistrand narratives will usually avoid moving back and forth in time along the same strand for fear of confusing the reader with excessive fragmentation.

If, as I argue in chapter 1, "story" is a cognitive structure that transcends media, disciplines, and historical as well as cultural boundaries, the plot diagrams that describe traditional narratives are also valid for interactive narratives, or to be more precise, for the output of each of the individual runs of their underlying program. But if we look at interactive narratives as productive engines, they will also present patterns that are unique to their mode of operation. Figures 2 and 3 show several different types of structural patterns for interactive narrative.[6] The diagrams in Figure 2 correspond to different ways to navigate through a fixed, predetermined story, while the diagrams in Figure 3 represent patterns of choices that result in different stories.

Figure 2a, the network, is a graph that allows loops and makes at least some of its nodes accessible though different routes. Networks are very efficient models for communication systems, because they

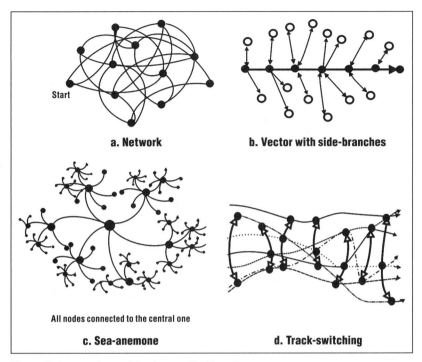

Figure 2. Interactive architectures affecting discourse

make it possible to reroute information when a path is blocked, but the feature that allows rerouting is a major obstacle to the generation of coherent plots. A story is an action that takes place in time, and time is irreversible. Any diagram that allows a return to a previously visited node cannot, consequently, be interpreted as the model of a chronological succession of events, because the same event never occurs twice. Moreover, if the nodes represent events, and if the arcs are interpreted as temporal succession, a network would allow the reader to pass though incoherent sequences: for instance through a node that describes a character's death, then through a node that shows her alive; and then again through the death node. But if networks cannot model the temporality of narrative without running into inconsistencies (unless they represent dreamworlds, which follow a different logic), they can model the temporal unfolding of discourse. In this interpretation, the reader's choices at every decision point determines not what will happen next in the storyworld but the order of presentation of the events.

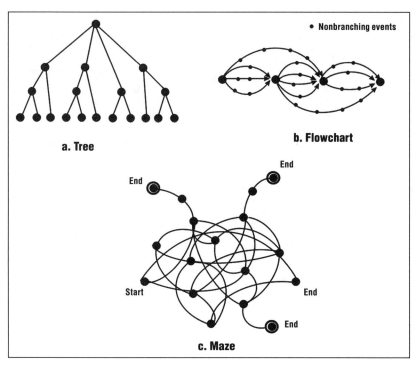

Figure 3. Interactive architectures affecting story

The network is the most common pattern for discourse-level interactivity, but it is not the only one. Figure 2b, the vector with side-branches, takes the reader through the story sequentially, but every episode offers an opportunity to branch toward external materials or optional activities that enrich the story. The radiating structure of 2c, also known as "sea-anemone," allows information to unfold recursively from a main menu into a variety of submenus.[7] From each point on the diagram, the user can return to the main menu in one jump. Widely used in informational Web sites, the radiating pattern has no special affinities for narrative, but as I will show in chapter 7, it can be put in the service of what Raine Koskimaa calls "archival narratives": stories that the reader reconstructs, not through random travel through a network but by consulting a well-organized database of documents. Figure 2d shows how a braided narrative such as 1c can be made interactive through a track-switching system. Every strand is linked to every other strand at certain decision points, but the links follow the temporal flow of the story and never take the reader back in time.

The various patterns are easily combinable: for instance, a radiating pattern could contain on a lower level a vector with side-branches, or the tips of its branches could be structured as networks; a track-switching pattern for braided narrative could combine with a radiating menu reachable in one click, which would give the reader easy access to previous episodes; and the nodes of a network could embed the closed loops of linear stories that return to their point of origin without offering any choice on the way.

For a diagram to represent multiple variants on the level of story, it must be able to capture the flow of time. On the tree-diagram of 3a, branches grow in a steady direction, are kept neatly separate, and do not allow returns to a previous point. These properties allow the vertical axis to represent a temporally organized sequence of events, while the horizontal axis stands for the splitting of the storyworld into parallel worlds with distinct histories. Tree-shaped diagrams are particularly efficient at modeling the decisions that await characters at various moments in their lives. The diagram of virtualities shown in Figure 1b is in fact a tree lying on its side. All it takes to turn the system of possibilities that underlies all stories into an interactive narrative is to let the user make the decisions for the characters at every branching point. The main drawback of the tree as architectural model for interactive narrative is the exponential growth of its branches and the necessity to preplan each branch separately. A tree with many decision points would quickly lead to unmanageable complexity, and the structure is therefore most efficient for stories with long stretches of noninteractive narration.

The flowchart of Figure 3b offers a more efficient management of choice, because the strands of plot are allowed to merge, thereby limiting the proliferation of branches. Here the horizontal axis stands for time, and the vertical axis for different ways to reach a certain point. But the horizontal axis could also receive a spatio-temporal interpretation: the user progresses from site 1 at t1 to site 2 at t2, by performing certain actions. To respect narrative logic, the flowchart should not allow different strands to join when the past actions of characters cast a shadow on their future. For instance, the path of the hero of a Proppian fairy tale who arrives at the dragon's lair with a magic aid obtained from the donor does not merge with the path of his older brother who reaches the same location without the magic help, because the two brothers do not have equal chances of success in their fight against the dragon. Since plotlines can only come together when the past is erased, a narrative with several endings that depend on the user's past actions would have to branch when the decisive action is taken, even if the strands leading to the various outcomes present similar events beyond the decision point. This kind of diagram is therefore most efficient at representing computer games organized into self-sufficient episodes and discrete levels.

Figure 3c, the maze, can only be viewed as a plot diagram if it represents the topography of the virtual world, as does Figure 1d. The user wanders across this topography, trying to reach certain locations that correspond to the liberation from the labyrinth, while avoiding other endpoints that represent failure. The maze thus traces a spatial narrative with several endings, and every itinerary of the user represents a different adventure in the virtual world. In the network variant, there is no end point to the story. In this type of architecture, each site offers different challenges, and the plot is written by the actions performed at every location, as the user travels from site to site. What neither the maze nor the network diagram can show, however, are the modifications to the system of connections that take place during the user's visit to the virtual world. Some links may be created and others severed, some sites may become reachable and others inaccessible as a result of the user's actions. It would take a series of discrete network diagrams to capture the dynamics of this architecture. The same serialization may in fact be necessary for networks that operate on the discourse level: the link structure of the text may be affected by the user's choices, and it will take several temporally ordered snapshots to capture these changes.

As was the case for discourse patterns, the various types of plot maps can combine into more complex architectures. The patterns of the macrolevel will then embed microlevel patterns of a different type. For instance, the possibilities of action attached to the nodes of the network could be quests that implement the pattern of the flowchart; while to progress along a flowchart, the user may have to solve a maze. This is indeed what happens when the levels of a computer game consist of "new maps." A textual architecture can even combine choices that affect discourse with choices that affect plot. As I have shown elsewhere (Ryan 2001), in the interactive movie *I Am Your Man,* for instance, the user can chose at certain points which character to follow, but this decision has no effect on what happens in the storyworld: it only determines what the user gets to see. At other moments she makes decisions for the characters that affect their destinies and lead to different endings.

While the diagramming of narrative possibilities constitutes an important design tool, it cannot describe all types of interactive architecture. A plot diagram, in contrast to a discourse diagram, presupposes that every path has been foreseen by the designer. But the richest storyworlds allow meaningful narrative action to emerge in the real time of user-computer interaction. In this type of system, the designer populates a world with agents capable of diverse behaviors, and the user creates stories by activating these behaviors, which affect other agents, alter the total state of the system, and through a feedback loop, open new possibilities of action and reaction. When the world contains a high number of different objects, and when these objects offer a reasonable variety of behaviors, the combinatorial possibilities are so complex that the designer cannot anticipate all the stories that the system can produce. This emergent quality is raised to a higher power when the user interacts not only with system-generated agents of limited intelligence but with human partners capable of far more imaginative and diverse behaviors, as is the case in multiplayer online virtual worlds.

Types of Interactivity

Interactivity is an umbrella category that covers a wide variety of relations between a user and a text. I propose here to distinguish four strategic forms of interactivity based on two binary pairs: internal/external and exploratory/ontological. These two pairs are adapted from Espen Aarseth's typology of user functions and perspectives in cybertexts (1997, 62–65), which is itself part of a broader cybertext typology.[8] But I use different labels that shift the emphasis toward the user's relation to the virtual world. In addition to the four types described below, there is also a metatextual interactivity that doesn't combine with any other type, because it involves a modification of the code and cannot therefore be exercised during the actual performance of the text. The manifestations of this metatextual activity include adding new links and nodes to a hypertext, creating new maps and new levels for a game, and building permanent objects for an online virtual world.

Internal versus External Interactivity

In the *internal* mode, users projects themselves as members of the virtual world by identifying with an avatar, who can be shown from either a first-person or a third-person perspective.[9] In the *external* mode, users are situated outside the virtual world. They either play the role of a god who controls the virtual world from above, or they conceptualize their own activity as navigating a database.

Exploratory versus Ontological Interactivity

In the *exploratory* mode, users navigate the display, but this activity does not make fictional history nor does it alter the plot: users have no impact on the destiny of the virtual world. In the *ontological* mode, by contrast, the decisions of the user send the history of the virtual world on different forking paths. These decisions are ontological in the sense that they determine which possible world, and consequently which story, will develop from the situation where the choice presents itself. But since fate-deciding decisions require a knowledge of the world, which is acquired in part through exploration, texts either allow both types of interactivity, in which case they belong to the ontological category, or they limit themselves to the exploratory kind.

The cross-classification of the two binaries leads to four combinations. Each of them is characteristic of different genres, prefers certain types of architecture, and offers different narrative possibilities.

External-Exploratory Interactivity

The external-exploratory mode is predominantly represented by text-based hypertext fictions, though it also includes multimedia works and even purely visual ones, such as the visual hypertext *Juvenate,* discussed in chapter 7. In the texts of this group, the user is external to both the time and space of the virtual world. There are no time limits to the user's actions; these actions do not simulate the behavior of a member of the virtual world; and interactivity is limited to the freedom to chose routes through a textual space that has nothing to do with the physical space of a narrative setting. The implicit map of the text represents a system of connections between fragments (or lexia, in George Landow's terminology), not the geography of a virtual world. The cult of nonlinearity and complexity of contemporary aesthetics has made the network of Figure 2a the preferred architecture of literary hypertext, but it could implement any of the configurations shown in Figure 2, as well as the maze of 3c if it leads to one or more endings.

In classical hypertext, the network is usually too densely connected for the author to control the reader's progression over significant stretches. Randomness sets in after one or two transitions. Once it escapes the control of the author, the order of discovery of the lexia can no longer be regarded as constitutive of narrative sequence, because it is simply not possible to construct a coherent story out of every traversal of a reasonably complex network. The only way to preserve narrative coherence in this type of architecture is to regard it as a construction kit for assembling a world and a story. Approaching hypertext like a jigsaw puzzle, the reader should feel free to rearranges its elements mentally, so that a fragment encountered at t1 in the reading sequence may be assigned time slot t22 in the reader's final reconstruction of the plot. If we conceptualize reader involvement as exploratory, the path of navigation affects not the narrative events themselves but only the way in which the global narrative pattern (if there is one at all) emerges in the mind. Similarly, with a jigsaw puzzle the dynamics of the discovery differ for every player, but they do not affect the structure that is put together. Moreover, just as the jigsaw puzzle subordinates the image to the construction process, external/exploratory interactivity deemphasizes the story itself in favor of the game of its discovery. This mode is therefore better suited for self-referential fiction than for textual worlds that hold us under their spell for the sake of what happens in them. It promotes a metafictional stance, at the expense of immersion in the virtual world. This explains why so many literary hypertexts offer a collage of literary theory and narrative fragments.

Though the links between the nodes of hypertext are not necessarily used to facilitate narrative comprehension, the study of the possible relations between interlinked lexia and of the cognitive operations required of the reader to grasp these relations represents the major expansion of narrative (and literary) theory required by hypertext fiction. The list below, which outlines some of the major semantic dimensions and textual functions of links, is indebted to the work of Mark Bernstein, Susana Pajares Tosca, Jeff Parker, Stephanie Strickland, and Scott Rettberg. While informational hypertexts will be dominated by links of type 2, 3, and 5, literary ones can be expected to offer a more diversified combination of link functions.

1. *Spatial links.* The concept of spatial form was proposed by the literary critic Joseph Frank to describe textual networks of contrasts and analogies between themes, images, and episodes. These networks run against the grain of the temporal development of narrative and reorganize the text into formal patterns that can only be apprehended by contemplating it from a synchronic perspective; hence the label "spatial form." In print texts spatial patterns remain implicit, and they may or may not be noticed, but hyperlinks force them to the reader's attention, challenging her to arrange the connected elements into meaningful structures. Through their propensity to create metaphorical relations, spatial links impart a lyrical quality to the text.

2. *Temporal links.* Recognizing such a function may seem to contradict what I write above about the impossibility of interpreting networks as representations of the flow of time; but if their loops prevent this interpretation on the global level, there is no reason why at least some of the links of a hypertextual network could not suggest that the events described in the connected lexia succeed each other in time. Many hypertexts present default links or single links that move the plot forward. It would indeed be nearly impossible to reconstruct a narrative out of a hypertextual network if it did not offer some fragments of story that come in the proper order. In a jigsaw puzzle, the equivalent of chronologically connected lexia would be groups of pieces that were never broken up. A temporal interpretation of at least some links is unavoidable in hypertexts with multiple endings that implement the architecture of the maze shown in 3c. As soon as the reader reaches a path that leads to an exit, the events along this path will be automatically interpreted as the end of the story, and the links between these events as representations of chronological sequence.

3. *Blatant links, or "Choose Your Own Adventures" links* (Jeff Parker's term). The labels of these links give the reader a preview of the content of the target lexia, enabling her to make an informed choice among many plot developments in a structure of type 3a: "If you want Cinderella to leave the ball at midnight, click here; if you want her to stay at the ball, ignoring her Godmother's warning, click there." Mark Bernstein (2000) dismisses blatant links as too legible: they allow readers to skip the links that they don't want

to follow. This would be an advantage in informational hypertexts, but a drawback in literary ones, at least for those, like Bernstein, who associate literariness with opacity, ambiguity, and difficulty. But if they give away the *what* of the story, blatant links retain the ability to arouse curiosity on the level of the *how*.

4. *Simultaneity links.* In narratives with the braided pattern of 2c, these links allow the reader to jump from one plotline to another, in order to find out what different characters in different locations are doing at the same time. The effect can be ironic. In an example provided by Jeff Parker (from his own hyperfiction *A Long Wide Smile*), the text highlights the words "knowing *what kind of things she does*" in the interior monologue of a man thinking about his fiancée. Clicking on the link will show what the fiancée is doing at this very same time—something that the man could never have anticipated.

5. *Digressive and background-building links.* These opposite functions suspend momentarily the development of the story. Both of them presuppose the vector-with-side branches structure of 2b. A variant of this type of link could provide alternative versions and discarded drafts that showcase the genealogy of the text and the dynamics of the writing process.

6. *Perspective-switching links* (Parker's "portal links"). These bidirectional links take us into the private worlds of different participants in the same episode. When the characters are also narrators, the contrast between these private worlds may expose their unreliability. In Parker's example, a first-person narrator reports his fiancée as asking one of her friends (who is also her lover), "*Did you ever ride ponies?*" When the reader clicks on this link, she gets the same scene narrated by the lover: "'*Did you ever write rhyming poetry?*' she said." Obviously one (or both) of the two narrators has misunderstood the words. Here the links themselves express a perspective that cannot be attributed to either narrator—the meta-textual perspective of the (implied?) author.

Internal-Exploratory Interactivity

The texts of this category transport the user into a virtual body inside a virtual world, either by projecting her as a character or by displaying the virtual world from a first-person, horizontal perspective that reflects the point of view of one of its members. But the role of the user is limited to actions that have no bearing on the evolution of the virtual world, nor on the personal destiny of the avatar: actions such as traveling around the virtual world, looking into its nooks and crannies, picking up objects, examining them, and looking for Easter eggs. To make exploration interesting, the space of the virtual world should be structured as a diversified architecture of either contiguous or embedded subspaces, and to make exploration challenging, the passageways between these subspaces—doors, windows, tunnels, and hidden openings—should be difficult to find. Internal-exploratory participation is particularly well suited to a type of narrative that I will call the "go through a portal and discover another world" story: down the rabbit hole or through the looking glass of Lewis Carroll's Wonderland, inside the wardrobe that leads to C. S. Lewis's Narnia, or up the fairy-tale bean stalk with Jack. This exploration cannot present danger, otherwise the destiny of the avatar would be at stake. It proceeds therefore at a leisurely pace, within the time of the virtual world, but not in a race against the clock.

Of the four modes of participation discussed in this chapter, internal-exploratory is the least common, at least in a pure form, because it imposes severe restrictions on the agency of the interactor. The internal-exploratory mode is best represented in early digital texts with limited technological resources, such as *The Manhole* (1988), an interactive environment designed by Robyn and Randy Miller, who later became famous as the authors of the *Myst* series of computer games. Structured as a series of still pictures activated by clicking on invisible hot spots, *The Manhole* invites the user to explore a fantastic world populated by strange creatures and full of secret passages that lead into new worlds. In contrast to standard computer games, *The Manhole* has no puzzles, no goals, no obstacles, and no endings: the user travels freely across its space, and the reward lies entirely in the journey. The network architecture of *The Manhole* prevents it from developing a sustained plot, but its individual screens are teeming with potential stories that kindle the imagination: a pink elephant rowing down a canal, or a walrus guarding a library full of books on subjects ranging from fantasy to deconstruction. Exemplifying the indeterminate mode of narrativity, *The Manhole* provides the illustrations, and challenges the user to create the stories.

Through its emphasis on travel, internal-exploratory participation lends itself particularly well to narratives that invest in the imaginative appeal of their spatial setting. This could be an electronic version of *Alice in Wonderland,* where Alice, the player's character, would explore Wonderland, stumble into the lives of its inhabitants, overhear conversations, gather gossips, and watch the unfolding of the story of Wonderland like a live spectacle. But not all narratives that foreground the experience of space fall into the exploratory category. If Alice travels across Wonderland in the attempt to fulfill a mission of some significance for the virtual world, as is the case in the computer game *American McGee's Alice*, the user's participation will be internal and ontological.

Another type of digital text that relies on the internal-exploratory mode is what Henry Jenkins calls the embedded narrative (2004, 126). This structure, which covers any attempt by the interactor to reconstitute events that took place in the past, connects two narrative threads. In a detective story, the prime example of the genre, these threads are the story of the murder and the story of its investigation. The story of the murder is determined by the author and follows a fixed internal sequence, while the story of the investigation is "written" by the actions of the user, who may discover the facts in a wide variety of different orders, as he wanders across the virtual world in search of clues.

The Aristotelian plot of interpersonal conflict leading to a climax and resolution does not lend itself easily to active participation because its strength lies in a precise control of emotional response that prevents most forms of user initiative. Its best chance of interactive implementation resides therefore in a VR simulation that places the user in the role of a semipassive witness or minor character. In this type of production, the user would exercise her agency by observing the action from various points of view, by mingling corporeally with the characters (who would be played by synthespians, that is, computer-simulated actors), and perhaps by exchanging an occasional word with them, but she would remain what Thomas Pavel (1986, 85) calls a "non-voting member" of the virtual world. If interactive narrative is ever going to approach the emotional power of movies and drama, it will be as a three-dimensional world that opens itself to the body of the spectator but retains the top-down design of a largely fixed narrative script.

External-Ontological Interactivity

In this type of text, the user plays god to a virtual world. Holding the strings of the entities that populate this world, and sometimes selecting these entities, but not identifying with any of them, she specifies their properties, makes decisions for them, throws obstacles in their way, alters the environment, launches transforming processes, and creates events that affect the global evolution of the virtual world.

The prime example of external-ontological interactivity is the simulation game, whose representatives include *Simcity, Simlife, Caesar,* and *The Sims* (CD-ROM, single-player version).[10] In these games, which exemplify the type of structure described above as emergent, players rule over a complex system, such as a city, an ant colony, an empire, or a family. The range of possible developments at any given moment depends on the possibilities of action offered by the various objects and individuals within the virtual world. For instance, a computer in *The Sims* affords two types of action: play games or look for a job. The choice of one of these affordances affects the life and the options of several members of the virtual world. In one possible scenario, the user may decide that Betty in *The Sims* will use the computer to get a job. When Betty earns money, she will be able to buy a wider variety of commodities, and this may affect Bob's feelings for Betty. The possibilities of action evolve during the run of the program, and since affordances are determined by the global state of the system, as well as by the nature of the objects, the user's choices will always produce a coherent narrative development.

Simulation games do not follow a scripted narrative path, but they do present a global design that gives a general purpose to the actions of the user. This built-in design is a broad evolutionary theme that allows a wide variety of particular instantiations: themes such as suburban life and the pursuit of happiness *(The Sims),* human development *(Babyz),* the management of a city *(Simcity),* or the building of civilizations *(Civilization).* But the user can sometimes subvert the built-in theme: *Sims* players have been known to create all sorts of catastrophes for their characters rather than supporting a crassly consumerist philosophy that makes happiness dependent on the accumulation of commodities. (I believe, however, that the game pokes fun at this philosophy rather than uncritically promoting it, for instance, by offering ludicrous objects for sale.)

Since evolution is a never-ending process, the narratives of this group never come to a resolution, unless this resolution is the total destruction of the system by a catastrophic event that the user cannot prevent. In *Simcity,* for instance, an earthquake could destroy the town, and in *The Sims,* a fire could kill the whole family. These catastrophic events, which are thrown in by the system, demonstrate the limits of the power of the user. She may play god to the virtual world, but far from being omnipotent, this god must accept the laws of the virtual world. In contrast to the rules of board games, these laws are not spelled out to the player before the game begins but discovered during play by interacting with the gameworld.

Because they are evolving entities, the worlds of external-ontological interactivity exist in time, and the user must learn to act in a limited time span. In *The Sims,* a clock is continually running and rules the life of the characters. They must eat, sleep, and go to the bathroom at regular intervals. The clock of the virtual world and the clock of the real world do not run at the same pace; for instance, it may take ten minutes of the player's real-world time to manage twenty-four hours in the life of the Sims. The difference between these two times parallels the standard narratological distinction between "time of the narrated" and "time of the narration." The temporality of the virtual world means that the user has only a limited time span to perform certain actions. If Betty gets a job, the player must take her to the curb in front of her house at eight o'clock to allow her to catch the bus that will take her to work. If she misses the bus she may be fired. But the user can stop the clock to perform actions that necessitate the consultation of a menu of possible options, such as such as buying goods and decorating the house. Whereas internal-exploratory interactivity takes place in a time frame that I have described as leisurely, the external interactor has a choice between an inexorably running time and a suspended time.

The external position of the user with respect to the virtual world is suggested by a visual display that shows this world from above and at an angle, in a perspective typical of a type of map known as panoramic. In *The Sims,* for instance, the display is a compromise between a plan view of a house taken from a vertical perspective and an elevation view taken from a horizontal perspective. The panoramic map allows items to be easily recognized, but its vertical projection prevents objects from hiding each other, thereby offering an omniscient apprehension of the virtual world that can only belong to a disembodied eye. Floating high above the world, the user encounters no obstacles to navigation. In contrast to the horizontally experienced space of internal participation, which is structured as a collection of subspaces of problematic accessibility, the obliquely projected world of external participation can be easily explored by scrolling the display. The space of simulation games is not a series of problems to be solved, as it is in narratives with internal participation, but a container for objects capable of diverse behaviors, and its design is supposed to facilitate the manipulation of these objects.

Internal-Ontological Interactivity

Here the user is cast as a character situated in both the time and space of the virtual world. His actions determine the fate of the avatar, and by extension, the fate of the virtual world. Every run of the system produces a new life, and consequently a new life story for the avatar. This narrative is created dramatically, by being enacted, rather than diegetically, by being narrated.

If the mythical Holodeck of the TV series *Star Trek* could be put into operation, it would be the fullest possible implementation of internal-ontological interactivity. The Holodeck is a kind of VR cave, to which the crewmembers of the starship *Voyager* retreat for relaxation and entertainment. In this cave, a computer runs a three-dimensional simulation of a fictional world, and the interactor becomes in make-believe a character in a digital novel. The plot of this novel is generated live, through the interaction between the human participant and the computer-created virtual characters. As Janet Murray writes: "The result is an illusory world that can be stopped, started, or turned off at will but that looks and behaves like the actual world. . . . The *Star Trek* Holodeck is a universal fantasy machine . . . a vision of the computer as a kind of storytelling genie in the lamp." It enables crewmembers to "enter richly detailed worlds . . . in order to participate in stories that change around them in response to their actions" (1997, 15).

As we wait for AI and VR technology to become sufficiently sophisticated to implement the Holodeck, we will have to satisfy our desire for internal-ontological participation in virtual worlds with screen-based projects that use the keyboard rather than the whole body as interface. At the present time, the closest to the Holodeck is *Façade,* an AI-based project in interactive drama by Michael Mateas and Andrew Stern that truly makes narrative action the center of interest because the user's participation is not motivated by winning a game. This project will be discussed in chapter 7. But by far the most common form of internal-ontological interactivity is represented by computer games that project the player as an individuated character who must accomplish missions in a world full of danger. The best examples of this type of game are first-person shooters *(Doom, Quake, Half-Life)*, and medieval fantasy games inspired by J. R. R. Tolkien's *Lord of the Rings (Morrowind, EverQuest,* and *Ultima Online).*

The player of a game is usually too deeply absorbed in the pursuit of a goal to reflect on the plot that he writes through his actions, but when players describe their sessions with this type of computer game, their reports typically take the form of a story. (See chapter 8 for Espen Aarseth's narrative of his adventure in *Morrowind.*) It may be objected that creating a narrative is not the point of adventure/action games. Computer games are mainly played for the sake of solving problems and defeating opponents, of refining strategic skills, and of participating in online communities, and not for the purpose of creating a trace that reads as a story. The drama of most games is only worth experiencing as an active participant; it is meant to be lived and not spectated. Yet if narrativity were totally irrelevant to the enjoyment of games, why would designers put so much effort into the creation of a narrative interface? Why would the task of the player be presented as fighting terrorists or saving the earth from invasion by evil creatures from outer space, rather than as "gathering points by hitting moving targets with a cursor controlled by a mouse"? The narrativity of action games functions as what Kendall Walton (1990, 21) would call a "prop in a game of make-believe." It may not be the raison d'être of most games, especially not of those games that rely on the physical skill of eye-hand coordination, but it plays such an important role as a stimulant for the imagination that many games use lengthy film clips, during which the player can only watch, to enrich the plot. Yet the fact that it is necessary to temporarily remove control from the user to establish the narrative frame is a further indication that interactivity is not a feature that facilitates the construction of narrative meaning.

Generally modeled after the nondigital role-playing games *Dungeons and Dragons,* worlds of this type almost invariably implement the archetypal pattern of the quest, as described by Joseph Campbell and Vladimir Propp. In a quest narrative, a hero is given a mission, passes many tests in order to fulfill this mission, and defeats a villain, thereby ensuring the triumph of good over evil. The main deviances from the archetype are the possibility for the hero to lose, the virtually never-ending character of the adventure, and an occasional dissociation of the hero-villain dichotomy with the forces of good and evil: the avatar of the player can be a bad guy, such as a hired killer or a car thief. As was the case with Propp's corpus of Russian fairy tales, individual games mainly differ from each other through the concrete motifs that flesh out the conventional structure. When quest games speak to the imagination, it is usually through motifs that express elemental fears and desires, as do fairy tales and other texts of popular culture.[11] Their lack of variety on the level of plot structure can be explained by the inherent difficulty to create truly interactive narratives, but, as Andrew Darley has observed, it also owes to the fascination of designers and customers with the spectacle of technology. As long as new games can offer better graphics, faster action, and more realistic representation of movement ("game physics"), why should developers bother to develop new narrative formulae? The game *Doom III*, released in 2004, is visually and kinetically far superior to its predecessors *Doom I* and *II*, and it induces a far stronger sense of horror (even some hard-skinned players find its dark corridors, repulsive monsters, and gory display of blood downright frightening), but the plot is basically the same. We may have to wait for the improvement of graphic representation to hit a ceiling to see game designers devote more attention to narrative.

No matter how the narrative pattern is thematically concretized, its progression depends chiefly on two types of action: moving around the virtual world and shooting. This feature may be attributed to a cultural fascination with violence, especially among teenage males, and to the reluctance of developers to move away from established audiences, but it also reflects the properties of the medium. Computer games offer two ways of performing actions: selecting them from a menu, which requires a stopping of the clock and a temporary de-immersion from the virtual world, and performing them within the gameworld by manipulating control devices, a much more immersive mode of operation, because it doesn't break the flow of the action. The first type dominates games with external interactivity, while the second type is the preferred mode in internal participation. Of all types of actions, none are better simulated by manipulating a control device than moving and shooting: the movements of a cursor on a screen imitate travel, and clicking a mouse or pushing a button on a joystick imitates the pulling of a trigger. For an action game to simulate life as a constant engagement with the world, the opportunities for action must be frequent, and for the game to be worth playing, the actions must have an immediate effect: nothing is more irritating than clicking and seeing nothing happen. When the player chooses a direction, he sees his avatar move immediately, and this provides the sensation of a high degree of control. Shooting gives an even greater feeling of power because of the instantaneous and dramatic result of pulling the trigger: shattered objects, gushing blood, and "fragged" bodies. It is not my intent to defend the violence of computer games; but the theme of shooting exploits with a frightful efficiency the reactive nature of the medium.[12]

Ontological-internal interactivity combines the types of temporality of the two preceding categories: leisurely time when the user is exploring the world, suspended time for actions that require a selection from a menu, and "real time," or "running clock time" when the player fights enemies. The cut scenes that reinforce the narrative themes operate in an ambiguous temporality: while they move the time of the virtual world forward, they suspend time for the player, since they deprive him of the opportunity to take action. The difference between time of the playing and represented time—what Jesper Juul (2004, 134) calls "mapping"—tends to be much smaller in games of internal participation than in god games, approaching a 1:1 scale. It takes about the same time to click on a mouse and to pull a trigger, while the construction of a power plant in a simulation game, as Juul observes, condenses a lengthy process into an instantaneous event. Online virtual worlds give a sense of their size by making the rate of progress across their space reflect the speed of travel in real geography: it may take several months for an avatar to cross a virtual world from one end to the other. On the basis of this speed, virtual worlds can be given precise "physical" measurement in terms of kilometers, even though they only exist as code whose inscription takes an infinitesimal amount of real-world space.

To give the user the sense of being inside the virtual world, games of this group represent space from a horizontal perspective, but to allow the player to plot his strategy, they may offer the possibility to switch between map view and horizontal view. In a world where the main activity consists of moving, geography must be interesting, and space will therefore tend to be organized into subspaces, as it is in the internal-exploratory group. But in contrast to purely exploratory texts, this diversified space will be full of dangers for the avatar. The preferred spatial structure of shooter games is the labyrinth, because its walls and blind corners allow enemies to hide. Many virtual worlds of this group present a symbolic structure reminiscent of the organization of space of archaic societies, as described by Mircea Eliade. The sacred and profane spaces of religious cosmology become an organization into safe and dangerous zones that may include healing houses for the wounded, shrines where players are protected from their enemies, areas designated for trade and areas designated for socializing, and terrifying sources of power at the center of the universe. It takes indeed a 570-page book to describe the symbolic geography of the online game *EverQuest*. Each region of its virtual world, Norrad, is described in terms of its dangers, benefits, legends, history, and system-generated characters that roam in the area.

Hybrid Categories

Narratology is essentially a taxonomical project, but most taxonomies have to deal with phenomena that do not fit neatly into clear-cut categories, and this one is no exception. Arranging the four types of interactivity on a wheel-shaped diagram (Figure 4) presents them as points on a continuum and makes room for hybrid forms that mediate between the pure types.

In the texts of the southwest corner, the user is clearly external to the virtual world, but the impact of her actions is debatable. Take the case of a story-tree that asks the user to decide whether a certain character should act like a hero or like a coward. Does the user's choice count as the exploration of a predefined narrative branch in a system designed by an author, or does the user decide the fate of the virtual world, here and now, by selecting one option rather than the other? The answer depends on whether or not the choice is blind, and whether or not the user has several shots at the system. If the text cannot be replayed (a purely theoretical possibility, since it is hardly ever implemented), and if it presents clearly defined options, the user will see herself as playing god to the virtual world, but if the choices are random, and the text can be played over and over again, allowing the textualization of all the possibilities, she may conceptualize her role as exploring a data-

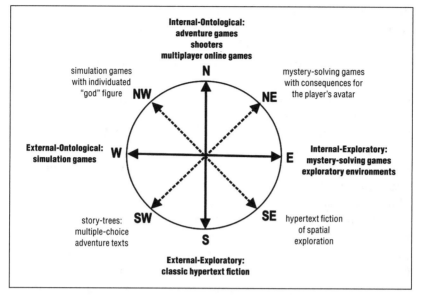

Figure 4. Types of interactivity

base. When the user identifies with the main character, as could happen in a *Choose Your Own Adventures* story, tree-shaped texts will belong to the northeast corner.

The northwest pole is represented by simulations that individuate the god figure of the external-ontological category and tie his fate to his performance as manager of the virtual world. In the game *Caesar*, for instance, the user is the ruler of the Roman Empire; in *Simcity*, the mayor of the city; and in *Babyz*, she has to raise a child. The mayor will be voted out of office if his administration of the city does not please his constituents, Caesar will be dethroned if the barbarians invade his empire, and the baby will never learn to walk and talk if she is neglected by her mother. But these avatars are not truly internal to the virtual world, because they do not exist on the same plane as its regular members, and they do not interact with them on a truly personal basis. (*Babyz* may be an exception: users develop emotional relations to their babies, to the point of proudly posting their picture on the Web.)

We have seen above that the main representatives of the internal-exploratory category are texts that cast the user into the role of an investigator of past events. As long as the story of the investigation and the investigated story remain strictly separate, the role of the user is clearly exploratory, but when the result of the investigation has a lasting effect in the virtual world, the two narrative threads will merge into an ontologically meaningful development. This hybrid situation occupies the northeast corner of the diagram. In the game *Myst,* for instance, the user discovers events that took place in the past, but the story lines formed by these events extend into the present, and the user's actions determine both his own fate and the fate of the characters: in one ending, he frees the good wizard Atrus and imprisons his villainous sons in a book; in the other ending, he himself ends up as prisoner of the brothers. Another type of interactivity that occupies the northeast corner of the diagram is what I call fake ontological participation. Because interactivity depends on the execution of code, and because code is invisible, users can never be completely sure that the system truly listens to their input. In the Web-based narrative On-line Caroline, as Jill Walker has discovered (2004), the program creates a character who exchanges e-mail with the user, and the user is under the impression that his personal relation with Caroline will affect her behavior, but no matter what the user tells Caroline, her life story remains exactly the same.

At the southeast pole, finally, are texts that lend themselves to different acts of imagination. Depending on the propensity of the reader for immersion, she may see herself as located inside or outside the virtual world. Take, for instance, the case of Deena Larsen's *Marble Springs,* a hypertext that invites the reader to explore a Colorado ghost town. The reader navigates the textual network by navigating the map of the town or of the cemetery. If she clicks on a house on the city map, she gets a poem that relates to its female inhabitants; if she clicks on a gravestone on the cemetery map, she gets the inscription. Some readers will see themselves as the external operator of a textual machine, as they do in standard hypertexts, while others will identify with a traveler to Marble Springs. These readers will interpret the cursor on the screen as the representation of their virtual body in the virtual world.

Some Myths about Digital Narrative

If we compare the field of digital textuality to other domains in the humanities, its most striking feature is the precedence of theory over the object of study. Most of us read novels and see movies before we consult literary criticism and cinema studies, but it seems safe to assume that a vast majority read George Landow's *Hypertext 2.0* before they read any work of hypertext fiction. Or, to take another example, we read full descriptions of what virtual reality technology would mean for our lives and for art long before VR became reality (if it ever did!). This advance theorizing has put into circulation a number of myths about digital narrative. Switching from the descriptive stance of narratology to the prescriptive stance of poetics, I will conclude this chapter by issuing a warning against the uncritical acceptance of three of these myths.

1. *Digital narrative is about choice, and the more choice you give to the user, the more pleasurable, or the more aesthetically valuable, the textual experience.* Here digital narrative could learn a lesson from another field. It used to be an axiom among economists that choice is good and more choice is better, but this theory has recently come under fire. As Steven Perlstein (2004) writes in a review of *The Paradox of Choice: Why More Is Less* by Barry Schwartz, "at some point there gets to be so many options about what to buy or what career to go into or which mutual fund to invest in that many people make worse decisions than they would if they had fewer choices—or simply put off making a decision at all." In the domain of interactive narrative, an overabundance of choices is more likely to lead to confusion, frustration, and obsession with the missed opportunities, as well as to logically inconsistent sequences of events, than to give the user a sense of freedom and empowerment. The best protection against these dangers is to place limits on the agency of the user, either by orchestrating periods of user activity and periods of system control or by narrowing down the choices in the case of constant interactivity. It is the successful assimilation of this lesson by designers of shooter games that allows players to respond quickly and efficiently to new situations.

2. *Narrative can be produced through a random combination of elements, and by permuting a finite set of textual fragments, it is possible to create a nearly infinite number of different stories.* I call this idea the myth of the Aleph, after a short story by Jorge Luis Borges, in which the scrutiny of a cabbalistic symbol enables the experiencer to contemplate the whole of history and of reality, down to its most minute details. The Aleph is a small, bound object that expands into an infinity of spectacles. The experiencer could

therefore devote a lifetime to its contemplation. The kaleidoscopic effect of recombinant objects works very well with visual elements, because pictures do not need to represent anything, and to a certain extent with poetic language,[13] because the predominently symbolic and metaphorical meaning of poetry leaves much more interpretive freedom to the reader than texts whose meaning depends on chronological or logical sequence. Narrative not only relies on sequence; it also builds a literal, rather than symbolic, model of human experience. As an attempt to make sense out of life and to overcome the randomness of fate through purposeful action, this model simply cannot be generated through aleatory processes. The computer may throw in random events in a simulation game, but the response of the system to these events must be rational, if the run of the program is to be interpreted as a story.

3. *Becoming a character in a story is the ultimate narrative experience.* This idea is suggested by the Holodeck, whose simulation of Victorian novels was proposed by Janet Murray as a model of "the future of narrative in cyberspace." The viability of this model is questionable for a number of reasons: technological, algorithmic, but above all psychological. What kind of gratification will the experiencer receive from becoming a character in a plot patterned after a novel or drama? In the scenario discussed by Murray, Kathryn Janeway, the commander of the starship *Voyager,* sneaks into the Holodeck and becomes Lucy, the governess of the children in an aristocratic household. Lucy falls in love with the father of the children, Lord Burley, and they exchange passionate kisses, but the very responsible Kathryn realizes that this love for a virtual human is detrimental to the fulfillment of her duties in the real world, and she eventually orders the computer to delete the character. It is as if narrative, whether print or digital, were only good for those readers who throw the text away midway though their reading.

The personal experience of many fictional characters is so unpleasant that users would be out of their mind—literally as well as figuratively—to want to live their lives in the first-person mode. If we derive aesthetic pleasure from the tragic fate of literary characters such as Anna Karenina, Hamlet, or Emma Bovary, if we cry for them and fully enjoy our tears, it is because our participation in the plot is a compromise between identification with the character and distanced observation. We simulate mentally the inner life of these characters, we transport ourselves in imagination into their mind, but we remain at the same time conscious of being external witnesses. But in the interactive drama of the *Star Trek* Holodeck, which is of course an imaginary construct, the interactor experiences emotions "from the inside," to use a concept proposed by Kendall Walton (1990, 28–29). Just as not every novel can be successfully adapted to film, not every type of character and consequently not every type of plot lends itself to the first-person perspective of interactive drama. Given the choice, would we want to share the subjectivity of somebody like Hamlet, Emma Bovary, Gregor Samsa in *The Metamorphosis,* Oedipus, and Anna Karenina, or would we rather enter the skin of the dragon-slaying hero of Russian fairy tales, Alice in Wonderland, Harry Potter, and Sherlock Holmes? If we pick a character from the second list, this means that we prefer identifying with a rather flat but active character whose participation in the plot is not a matter of emotional relation to other characters but a matter of exploring a world, solving problems, performing actions, and competing against enemies. There may be a good reason why computer games overwhelmingly favor certain types of plot and user experience. If interactive narrative wants to expand the rather limited emotional repertory of games and develop complex characters who undergo truly poignant experiences, it may have to limit user participation to a largely observatory role, rather than placing the user in the role of the experiencer.

6. Interactive Fiction and Storyspace Hypertext

We all know that computers are programmable machines. This means, technically, that they execute commands, one after the other, in a tempo controlled by the pulses of an internal clock. This also means, in the domain of artistic expression, that the behavior of digital objects is regulated by the invisible code of a program. This program often plays a double role: it presides over the creation of the text, and it displays it on the screen. If we regard dependency on the hardware of the computer as the distinctive feature of digital media, then the various types of text-creating and text-displaying software (also known as "authoring systems") should be regarded as the submedia of digitality. It is evident that developments on the level of hardware had a crucial impact on the features of digital texts: for instance, faster processors and expanded storage capabilities allowed the integration of text, image, and sound, while the creation of large computer networks allowed communications between multiple users and the collaborative construction of the text. But the form and content of digital texts, as well as the reader's experience, are also affected by the underlying code.

In this chapter and the next, I propose to revisit the evolution of digital narrative over the past twenty-five years, presenting it as the story of the relations between software support and textual products and asking of each authoring system: what are its special affordances; and how do these affordances affect the construction of narrative meaning? I will limit my investigation to texts composed by individuals or small groups, as opposed to texts produced by corporate teams working with a large budget. This means that I will ignore commercial video games, one of the most productive domains of narrative activity in digital media.

In chapter 5 I define four basic properties of digital media: interactivity / reactivity, volatility of inscription, multiple sensory channels, and networking, singling out interactivity as the most prominent. A text that takes advantage in a narratively significant way of one or more of these properties is a text that thinks with its medium. This attention to the properties of the medium can go in two directions: starting from an idea and looking for the medium that will best serve this idea; or starting from a medium and asking: what can I do with it. The second direction is the most common because very few people are proficient in more than one medium. With "old media" the artist can seek inspiration from an established tradition, but with recently developed media, the discovery of the language of the medium (or its invention) is an integral part of artistic activity. But whether or not a text thinks with its medium is ultimately a value judgment rather than an objective observation. This judgment acknowledges the text's ability to create an original experience that cannot be duplicated in any other medium, an experience that makes the medium seem truly necessary. Thinking with the medium is not the overzealous exploitation of all the features offered by the authoring system but an art of compromise between the affordances of the system and the demands of narrative meaning. Nor is thinking *with* the medium synonymous with thinking *about* the medium, a formula that describes the currently fashionable habit of sprinkling digital texts with theoretical comments on the nature of digital textuality. A work that truly thinks with its medium does not *have* to think about it, because it inspires readers to do the thinking themselves.

Interactive Fiction

The first narrative genre that grew and ran exclusively in a digital environment was a hybrid of game and literature known as Interactive Fiction (henceforth abbreviated as IF). The classics of the genre are the games produced by the now defunct company Infocom, especially the *Zork* adventures (1980), but the literary minded will mostly remember *Mindwheel* (1984), a so-called electronic novel written by the poet Robert Pinsky. Born in the early eighties, when personal computers first made their appearance, IF is a dialogue system in which the user, manipulating a character (henceforth referred to as the avatar), interacts with the machine not through the selection of an item from a fixed menu but through a relatively free production of text: the user can type whatever he wants, though the parser associated with the system will understand only a limited number of verbs and nouns. Nick Montfort defines interactive fiction as "a program that simulates a world, understands natural language text from an interactor, and provides a textual reply based on events in the world" (2004, 316). "In this genre of fiction," says the Web site of Inform, the authoring system most commonly used nowadays for the production of IF, "the computer describes a world and the player types instructions like touch the mirror for the protagonist character to follow; the computer responds by describing the result, and so on until a story is told."

All narratives can be said to describe a world, but the engine that operates IF goes one step further, in that it not only evokes a world through visible text but also constructs a *productive* model of this world through computer-language statements that the player never gets to see. These statements specify the general laws that define the avatar's range of options and determine the results of his actions. For instance, if Coca-Cola is described as both liquid and toxic in the computer's world-model, and if the avatar drinks a can of Coke, the action will result in his death. When the player takes an action, the system updates its model of the current state of the fictional world, for instance, by canceling the attribute "alive" of the avatar after he ingests poison. When the attributes of an object change, so do the various actions to which the object lends itself. Characters, for instance, are objects linked to scripted behaviors that enable them to move, to talk, or to die. When their attribute "alive" is turned off, their affordances are dramatically altered: their corpse can still be seen, picked up, or moved around by the player, but they are no longer able to act on their own. The system is a simulation, rather than a mere world-description, because the world-model allows not just one but a large number of different narratives to unfold. Video games added sensory channels to IF, and they allowed users to interact in real time rather than in suspended time through keyboard input that simulates physical action, but they owe much of their popularity to a common narrative formula, and they operate according to the same principles: building a dynamic model of a fictional world.

The coherence of the stories generated by the system is guaranteed by the world-rules, and by the fact that every episode involves the player's character. When the world-rules are inconsistent with each other, or with common world knowledge, the narrative becomes illogical or unpredictable. For instance, if Coca-Cola is not defined as liquid, the system will block the avatar's attempt to imbibe the substance with the message "you cannot do that." In a standard narrative there is no need to mention that Coke is liquid, because the reader will make the inference on the basis of real-world experience; but in IF, every relevant property must be specified in the invisible code, since the proper development of the narrative depends as much on the knowledge-base of the computer as on the reader's inferential capabilities.

The interactive fiction engine supports two main types of narrative. The first, and most widely represented, is the puzzle-based quest, a type that also dominates the video game industry. In this archetypal pattern, the player-hero receives a mission and sets out on a journey through the fictional world, during which he visits various places and passes various tests with the help of objects or information gathered along the way.

The importance of travel across space in the quest narrative means that the design of this type of IF begins with the creation of a geography made up of distinct sites (or "rooms," in the jargon) connected by a network of passageways. As Henry Jenkins observes: "Game designers don't simply tell stories; they design worlds and sculpt space" (2004, 121). The underlying map of the fictional world specifies what sites are adjacent to every location, and what objects are contained in the various areas. From the cave of the robbers, for instance, it may be possible to go east to the forest, or to crawl west through a narrow shaft to the secret room that holds the treasure, but the player cannot go through the wall to the north or to the south unless she picks up a magic pebble on the floor of the cave. To play the game efficiently, the player must construct a mental map, and sometimes a graphic map, of the fictional world. The various locations within game geography are usually associated with certain objects, some useful to the quest, the others false leads or mere decoration. The narrative logic of IF and of computer games in general is closer to the mode of operation of detective novels than to the logic of drama, in that a gun shown hanging on the wall will not necessarily fire, contrary to Chekhov's prescription for a well-constructed play. In a game narrative, it is indeed part of the player's task to sort out what will fire and what will not.

Though the world-model allows different narratives to unfold— in principle a new one for each game-session—these narratives are not all equally satisfying to the player: some end with the fulfillment of the mission, others lead to the death of the avatar. To parody Tolstoy, we can say that the unhappy narratives are unhappy in many different ways, while the happy narratives all follow the same route. It is, however, important to distinguish the variable stories created by the player's actions from the predetermined "master narrative" (or narratives) written into the system as the solution(s) of the game. As P. Michael Campbell argues (1987, 82), the variable stories of the avatar's life differ from each other through what Roland Barthes (1977) calls "satellite" elements, but they all traverse the same "kernels." Whereas one player will make ten unsuccessful attempts to open the door that leads to the treasure, another will use the right tool right away. The adventures of these two players (or rather, of their avatars) in the gameworld will produce different sequences of events and bring different text to the screen, but both players will eventually perform the same actions to complete the master plot. As Nick Montfort observes, "winning" is getting the whole story; "losing" is causing the story to end prematurely (online, 6). The master plot thus functions as the player's reward for allowing his avatar to fulfill his mission. Whether the player wins or loses, however, the story achieves closure when the system is no longer able to modify the state of the fictional world (Montfort online, 11).

Reading (and playing) for the master plot is not the only way to approach IF, or computer games in general. For the true connoisseur, one of the special pleasures of the genre lies in trying to evade the control of the game-designer, in the best tradition of deconstructive reading. A world-model in which every law, as well as every property of every object, must be specified is bound to present inconsistencies and fatal omissions. The subversive reader will engage in an active search for these bugs, in the hope of coaxing unplanned stories or delightful nonsense out of the system. Espen Aarseth (1997, 123–24) describes a particularly amusing bug in Marc Blank's *Deadline* (1982), a mystery story in which the player must find the murderer of a wealthy businessman, Mr. Robner. If the player maliciously decides to interview Mr. Robner himself, the system will forget that he is dead, and the player will be able to strike up a conversation with him. The system will not allow the player to arrest Mr. Robner for his own murder, invoking insufficient evidence, but if the player shoots Mr. Robner, the system will declare the mystery solved and will send the player to jail. Clever designers may of course anticipate the reader's subversive game by purposefully introducing interesting bugs or opportunities for misreading into the program. As P. Michael Campbell observes, the game master in Pinsky's *Mindwheel* tries his best to distract the reader from his quest and to coax him into spending more time chatting with an entertaining bum who happens to be Gil Hodges, the former second baseman for the Brooklyn Dodgers. "Here, in *Mindwheel*, . . . the 'misreading' process has been at least somewhat incorporated into the text. It's OK to play around in the story; the story will play along" (1987, 79).

By inviting the user to play with the system, rather than focusing exclusively on advancing in the game—a contrast that I will describe in chapter 8 as *paidia* versus *ludus*—*Mindwheel* anticipates the second form of IF narrative: a conversation with a system-generated character (chatterbot, in the jargon) reminiscent of ELIZA, the landmark AI program that began its distinguished psychoanalytical career in 1966. In this type of IF there are no puzzles and no geography: the entire action takes place in the same room, and the only problem to be solved is eliciting interesting confessions from the character. Narrative in these texts appears on two levels: one constituted by the stories told by the participants—mostly the character but occasionally the player—during their conversational turns, and the other created by the evolution of the relations between the player and the character in the course of the exchange.

One of the best examples of this type of IF is Emily Short's *Galatea*. In this text, you play the role of a visitor to an art gallery who comes across a statue by the famous Greek sculptor Pygmalion.[1] According to legend, Pygmalion fell in love with Galatea, and in answer to his prayers Aphrodite gave life to the statue. But not in Short's version: here Pygmalion loved the lifeless statue, but he is upset when Galatea wakes up because she is no longer a passive (sex?) object. Frustrated in his desire to possess her entirely, he sells her to a collector and later commits suicide. Out of this common narrative core, the text develops several different stories. In one version Galatea confesses her unhappy love for Pygmalion; in another, she plays psychoanalyst to the player, like her model ELIZA; in yet another, the player tells her that she is an AI-created agent, and she is so mad at being called a machine that she strangles him; in still another version, a spoof of Internet romances, the player discovers that she is an avatar manipulated by a rather dumpy female who inspires none of the feelings that the player experiences for the beautiful statue. (This is only a partial list.) Winning in this literary game means unraveling one of the stories written into the system and reaching the words "the end," but there is considerable pleasure in just conversing with Galatea, for she has a lot to say about important subjects: love, art, the gods, feminism, and of course herself. (In one of the stories, she can even be made to be preoccupied with something other than her own person!)

Getting the statue to tell stories is not an easy task, because the player must formulate queries in a way that will be understood by the parser. In the ELIZA program, users could type whatever they wanted, and Eliza always had a canned response, though these responses were rarely to the point: the chatterbot just grabbed a keyword from the user's input and built it into a sentence of her own. When she was at a loss for a response, she turned the player's input into a question. It was left to the user's imagination to make the conversational inferences that would lend coherence to the exchange. In *Galatea*, the parser accepts only a small number of queries, but this limitation pays off in two ways: it allows the system to provide much more relevant answers than ELIZA could offer; and it also makes it possible to keep track (at least to some extent) of the flow of the conversation. The same input by the user will elicit different reactions from Galatea, depending on what mood she is in—a mood determined by the user's previous actions. Most attempts to get her to kiss you will fail:

PLAYER: Galatea, kiss me
SYSTEM: Either she doesn't hear the suggestion, or she deems it unworthy of response

But if you have properly courted her, you will get your reward, though it may not be clear to you why Galatea cooperates in one case and refuses to come down from her pedestal in the other: statues (especially statues of beautiful women) are unpredictable!

PLAYER: Galatea, come down

SYSTEM: "Er . . .?"

PLAYER: Galatea, kiss me

SYSTEM: She turns so that she is looking at you straight on—level
gaze, smoky eyes, brows pale and washed out in the light. Not
her more beautiful angle, which might be why she avoids it. Her
eyes meet yours, a swift flicker of darkness. She puts a hand on
your shoulder for support, leans down—

After a moment you disentangle your fingers from her hair. "Come
on," you say. "There are things we should talk about, and this
is not the place."

The End

Another difference between *Galatea* and ELIZA is that ELIZA
makes no assumptions about your identity, while *Galatea,* a
narrative-oriented program, scripts the role and persona of the
user within the developing plot. Through his gazing at Galatea,
his attempts to receive a kiss from her, his dejection when he sees
the dumpy female who speaks through her, the user is projected in
most versions as male, though I don't want to exclude the possibility of a queer reading. The scripting of the user is particularly
evident when you try to tell something about yourself to Galatea,
and the system rewords and expands your query:

PLAYER: tell parents

SYSTEM: "My parents died when I was fairly young," you say. "So
I don't remember them well. Mostly just images. My mother
played the violin, and I remember her getting ready to go play
for a Scottish dance group. She was all dressed up and about to
go, but she stopped to play one tune for me and my sister before
she left."

A pause. "We didn't see her again, though something tells you
she's already guessed as much."

Though *Galatea* is not really an AI program and stands little
chance of winning the Turing award, the system can sustain a re-
markably coherent conversation if the user cooperates. ELIZA always had a response in stock, because the program picked words
from the user's input or abruptly changed the subject, but Galatea,
a much more discriminating conversationalist, limits her responses
to relevant topics. The best way for the human user to get Galatea

to talk is to adopt ELIZA's own strategy: choose a key word from the statue's previous turn and ask her about it. By selecting only current topics, this approach respects the philosopher H. P. Grice's cooperation principle for conversation: "Make your conversational contribution such as required, at the stage at which it occurs, by the accepted purpose or direction of the talk in which you are engaged" (Grice 1975, 47). If you fail to focus your contributions on relevant topics, you may get the conversation-killing response: "Galatea doesn't know what you are talking about." This can lead to humorous effects, for instance, when you ask her about truth.

For the narratologist, IF is a gold mine of illocutionary situations, discourse modes, and interplay of diegetic levels that expands significantly the technical repertory of language-based narrative. Usually told in the second person and in the present tense, IF is one of the rare narrative forms where the use of "you" enters into a truly dialogical rather than merely rhetorical relation with an Other, and where "present" denotes narrow coincidence between the time of the narrated events and the time of the narration. Rather than imaginatively preexisting the act of narration, the events of the fictional world are made to happen at the very moment of their description through the performative force of the discourse that appears on the screen.

The most distinctive narratological features of IF, when compared to either print narrative or to the other digital forms discussed in this chapter, is the construction of the story through a movement that leads in and out of the diegesis—in and out of the fictional world. Standard narrative fiction adopts a unified, world-internal point of view. But in IF, some utterances can be attributed to a narrator situated within the fictional world, for instance:

PLAYER: Kill Mr. Robner

SYSTEM [as narrator]: With a lethal blow of your hand, Mr. Robner falls dead. Your mind becomes confused amidst strange screaming, yelling, and the pangs of your conscience. "How could I have done it?" you ask yourself, as you hear the distant sound of police sirens. Sergeant Duffy and two other officers enter and grab you rather unceremoniously.

(Mark Blank, *Deadline*; quoted from Aarseth 1997, 123–24)

while others (marked in italics in the example below) represent an external voice, the voice of the system that produces the story in collaboration with the player:

SYSTEM [as narrator]: A plain metal door faces you to the east, near the alley's end. It's firmly shut.

PLAYER: Open door

SYSTEM: *You don't see how.*

PLAYER: Scream in despair.

SYSTEM: *That's not a verb I recognize.*

(From Plotkin, *Spider and Web*)

These interventions of the system all concern input that cannot be processed. In this example the unrecognizable verb is signaled by stepping out of the fictional world; but in a dialogue system such as *Galatea,* the problem can be handled intradiegetically by presenting the misunderstanding as part of the conversation. The character may simply say "I don't understand what you are saying" without stepping out of role, or the report of the miscommunication can be turned over to a narratorial voice: "She clearly doesn't know what you are talking about" *(Galatea).* In this case the misunderstanding involves the character and the player's avatar, and it takes place in the fictional world, while in the *Spider and Web* example it is located on the level of the real-world interaction between the player and the game.

A similar differentiation between intradiegetic (world-internal) and extradiegetic (world-external) utterances can be found in the player's input. When the player dialogues with a character, he speaks in the name of his avatar within the fictional world, and his input is an integral part of the narrative. For instance:

SYSTEM: Interrogation chamber [You are imprisoned in a chair, facing a man behind a desk].

SYSTEM [as character]: You're going to start by telling me how you got through that door. Do you understand me?

PLAYER [to the character]: Yes.

SYSTEM [as narrator]: The man nods briefly—a man satisfied with the least important detail.

(From Plotkin, *Spider and Web*)

On the other hand, when the player makes his avatar perform an action, usually through a two-word sentence, his input is not treated by the system as part of the narration but as a command external to the text. Rather than telling the story himself, the player dictates to the system the development of the story, as would a child asking a parent: "Tell me a story about a unicorn that marries a dragon." The system fulfills the command by expanding the player's input into a more vivid description of the event, and by detailing its consequences:

> PLAYER [to the system]: Kiss Gil.
> SYSTEM [as narrator]: You purse your sensuous lips and give one of the bums a medium-long, fairly wet kiss.
> Fine—while your civilization totters on the brink of utter destruction, you managed to kiss, in splendid fashion, one of the bums but your quest for WHEEL OF WISDOM has not advanced.
> (From Pinksy, *Mindwheel,* quoted from Campbell 1987, 78)

Much, arguably too much, has been made of the creative role of the reader in digital environments. The fact that the system of IF rewrites most of the player's input seriously dampens the claim that interactivity turns the reader into a coauthor: even though the player interacts through language, most of her contributions are treated as paratext, and she does not participate directly in the writing process.

Storyspace Hypertext

In the late 1980s two factors contributed to the commercial demise of interactive fiction.[2] For lovers of games, the fatal blow was dealt by the development of graphic interfaces. The textual screen of the earlier *Zork* episodes looked rather bleak, compared to the visually rendered gameworld, the film clips, and the talking characters of the later installments. Meanwhile, for lovers of literature, IF was out staged by hypertext, a new digital genre that burst onto the scene with a blaze of theoretical publicity. How could a mere game compete in intellectual sophistication with a genre that was heralded as "a vindication" (Bolter 1992, 24) of the ideas of Barthes, Foucault, Derrida, Deleuze, Guattari, and Kristeva on the nature of textuality?[3]

Most of us associate digital textuality with hypertext, and most of us associate hypertext with texts composed from the late eighties to mid-nineties with the authoring program Storyspace: works such as Michael Joyce's *afternoon: a story,* Stuart Moulthrop's *Victory Garden,* and Shelley Jackson's *Patchwork Girl,* all sold by Eastgate Systems. The developers of Storyspace were Jay David Bolter, a classics scholar turned media theorist; Michael Joyce, a novelist; Mark Smith, a programmer; and Mark Bernstein, the owner of

Eastgate Systems. The program was designed with a certain type of text in mind, and for many readers this model has come to pass as the canonical form of hypertext fiction: *afternoon,* and to a lesser extent *Victory Garden* and *Patchwork Girl* are indeed regarded as the classics of the genre. But Storyspace was not exclusively meant as a tool for the construction of literary texts. A major influence on the developers was the vision of Ted Nelson, a computer scientist who coined the term "hypertext" in 1965. Nelson dreamed of a giant computer network called Xanadu, through which millions of texts would be gathered and interlinked. These links would not only facilitate the retrieval of documents; they would also promote creative thinking by blazing associative trails through the database. Xanadu was going to be "a universal data structure to which all other data may be mapped" (quoted by Bolter 1991, 102). Nelson's vision eventually came to life as the World Wide Web, though the linking system that Nelson had in mind for Xanadu is more sophisticated and versatile than the html links of the Web (Wardrip-Fruin and Montfort 2003, 441).[4]

In keeping with Nelson's encyclopedic vision, the authors of Storyspace envisioned the program as a tool for the organization of complex networks of ideas. Since the units of Storyspace work best with relatively small chunks of text, Storyspace projects tend to require vast systems of links and nodes. To take an extreme example, Stuart Moulthrop's hypertext *Victory Garden* has no less than 993 nodes (lexia, in the jargon) connected by 2,804 links—far more than even the most dedicated reader will be able to visit in a reasonable time. This level of complexity would not have been practically feasible without the feature of the bookmark, which allowed users to save readings.

Compared to the Inform engine, Storyspace is a very simple program. There is no need to write code, and the composition process is only slightly more complicated than writing with a word processor. While Inform fictions enable the reader to communicate with the machine through language, Storyspace responds exclusively to the clicking of the mouse.[5] And while Inform constructs a world on the basis of rules that can be regarded as a rudimentary artificial intelligence component (it knows, for instance, where the avatar is in the fictional world and what objects he is carrying), Storyspace limits its operation to the mechanical combination of textual fragments, without any knowledge of their content. Instead of keeping an internal representation of the evolving state of the fictional world, and of sifting a database of logical rules to decide what episode can follow another, Storyspace only needs to perform jumps to certain memory addresses and to display their data when the user clicks on a word designated as link. This makes Storyspace hypertexts much more deterministic in their mode of operation than interactive fiction.

A Storyspace hypertext is a network of links and nodes, also called lexia. The lexia correspond to units of text, the digital equivalent of the page, though the program also allows nodes to be filled with graphic and sound files. But multimedia capabilities were very limited in the early versions of Storyspace, and the classic hypertexts make little or no use of pictures. *afternoon,* for instance, is entirely verbal. When the user clicks on a link, the system displays a new page on the screen. Since there are usually several links on a page, the reader can activate several different lexia, which means that the order of presentation of the lexia is variable. This property of hypertexts is generally known as nonlinearity, though multilinearity would be a better term, since the reader's choices inevitably result in a sequential order. In most hypertexts the words that serve as anchors to the links are marked with special fonts, to make them visible to the reader; but this feature is optional. In *afternoon,* for instance, the links remain hidden. This turns the reader's exploration of the text into a blind navigation, or into a search for Easter eggs—the Easter eggs of what Joyce calls "the words that yield."

One of the most distinctive features of the Storyspace system is the possibility of placing conditions on the activation of links. This feature, known as guard field, prevents a link from being followed until a specific node has been visited.[6] The use of guard fields enables authors to exercise a secret control over the itinerary of the reader through the text, but this control is always limited, because the networks are far too large, and the links far too numerous, for the designer to take into consideration all the possible actions of the reader. A good example of a clever use of a guard field is found in *afternoon:* as J. Yellowlees Douglas observes (2000, 100), readers cannot reach a lexia that suggests the narrator's responsibility for the accident that (maybe) killed his son and ex-wife before they visit another lexia that describes a therapy session with a psychologist. This sequence suggests that the dialogue with the therapist unlocked guilt feelings in the narrator or led to a more lucid self-awareness.

To help authors keep the complexity of the database under control, Storyspace generates a map (Figure 5) that shows the current state of the developing network of links and nodes. Some of the finished products, for instance *Patchwork Girl,* make these maps available to the reader as part of the interface, while others, such as *afternoon,* keep the map hidden. The possibility to consult the map enables the reader to bypass the system of links designed by the author. In *Patchwork Girl,* you can indeed reach any node visible on the map by clicking on its image. But because the networks of Storyspace hypertexts are much larger than what can be shown on a screen, maps cannot be displayed in their totality, unless they represent subsections of the text. The map idea works therefore best when the text is structured in layers. In addition to system-generated maps that appear as part of the interface (which means that they are always available), Storyspace hypertexts may place externally produced maps (artworks) within one of their nodes. In this case again, clicking on the various items on the map will take the reader to the corresponding area in the text. These maps are harder to consult than the system-generated maps, because the

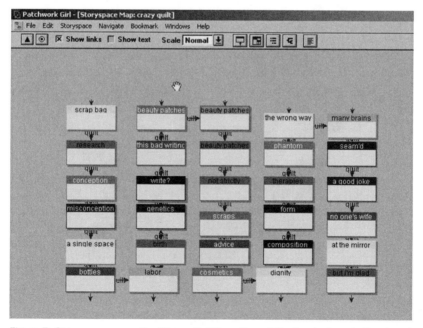

Figure 5. Storyspace map: the "Crazy Quilt" section of Shelley Jackson's *Patchwork Girl.* Reproduced by permission of Eastgate Systems Inc. http://www.eastgate.com.

reader must first find the node in which they are contained, but their function is usually more emblematic than navigational: most of them provide an image of the text that fixes its identity in the mind of the reader. In *Victory Garden,* the "artwork" map looks like a garden with benches and paths; in *Patchwork Girl* (a text that includes both system-generated and artwork maps), like an anatomical drawing of the brain (Figure 6); and in Deena Larsen's *Marble Springs,* like the plan of the Colorado town whose collective story is told in the text.

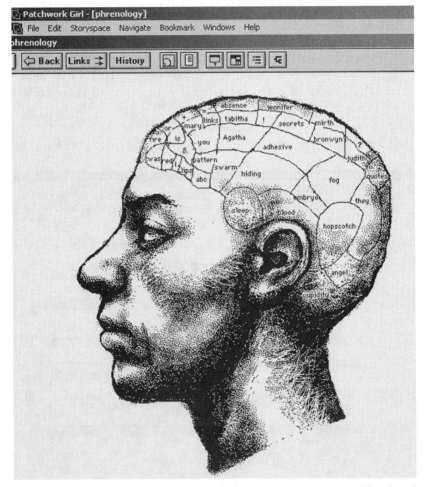

Figure 6. A non-system-generated map for the "Phrenology" section of *Patchwork Girl.* Reproduced by permission of Eastgate Systems Inc. http://www.eastgate.com.

The maps of the Storyspace toolbox account for what has become the most lasting legacy of the system—a legacy also suggested by its name: the conceptualization of hypertext narrative in terms of spatial metaphors, such as the labyrinth or the Garden of Forking Paths. Let me take a closer look at the metaphor of the Garden of Forking Paths, which comes from a short story by Jorge Luis Borges, because it is widely regarded as an emblem of the type of narrative that only hypertext can deliver. "The Garden of Forking Paths" is not only the title of a story by Borges but also the title of a novel described in the story. In this novel, the metaphor refers to branches in time and not in space:

> In all fictional works, each time a man is confronted with several alternatives, he chooses one and eliminates the others; in the fiction of Ts'ui Pên, he chooses—simultaneously—all of them. *He creates,* in this way, diverse futures, diverse times which themselves also proliferate and fork. Here, then, is the explanation of the novel's contradictions . . . In the work of Ts'ui Pên, all possible outcomes [of any action] occur; each one is the point of departure for other forkings. Sometimes the paths of this labyrinth converge: for example, you arrive at this house, but in one of the possible pasts you are my enemy, in another, my friend. (Borges 1962, 26)

In Borges's story, Ts'ui Pên's novel remains virtual, described, but not written. The embedding tale is a suspense story with a traditional linear development. J. David Bolter claims that Borges simply lacked the proper medium to realize the idea: the Garden of Forking Paths can only be implemented in "an electronic space, in which the text can comprise a network of diverging, converging, and parallel times" (1991, 139).[7] I believe, however, that there is only a superficial resemblance between the spatial organization of hypertext and the structure of Ts'ui Pên's novel, and that Borges's idea of the Garden of Forking Paths is no more feasible in hypertext than it is in print, even if it is limited to a subset of the infinite field of the possible, because the metaphor contains a serious inconsistency.

In both hypertext and Borges's story, the spatial image of the Garden of Forking Paths stands for something that is not literally spatial, but the similarity ends there. Relying on a metaphorical process fundamental to human cognition, Borges invokes the spatial image of the forking paths to describe a fundamentally *temporal* phenomenon.[8] In possible worlds theory, this phenomenon would be described as the splitting of a world into parallel worlds with different destinies (and therefore, histories) every time this world is faced with the possibility of a change of state. If time is finely divided, this splitting of worlds and time occurs continually, since accidental interruptions of current processes can happen at every moment in a world's existence.[9] Most of these splittings have no impact on our personal fate, but sometimes we reach decision points in life that affect our long-term destinies. The forks in time that matter existentially to us are the subject matter of narrative. But even when lifestories take one of the forks, relegating the other(s) to the domain of the counterfactual, the experiencer or interpreter cannot forget the paths not taken, because the significance of the actualized events is relative to their alternatives. The consideration of the could-have-been is an integral part of narrative comprehension.

In his spatial metaphor of time, however, Borges forgets that once worlds and their histories have taken diverging courses, they cannot come together again.[10] When you arrive at my house, you can be my friend or my enemy, but this does not create a merging of destiny lines, because the field of future possibilities depends on our relationship, which itself depends on past events. If you are my friend you can expect to receive food and shelter, but if you are my enemy you should be prepared for a far worse treatment. If you receive food and shelter from somebody who is your enemy, this is a significantly different event than being treated in the same way by somebody who is your friend. Models based on the concept of possible worlds explain this situation through the concept of counterpart relation: you do not arrive at the same house in the same world through different temporal paths, but rather, you reach different houses in different worlds that occupy corresponding spatial coordinates within their respective world. It is only in physical space that you can reach the same location via different routes. If the splitting of worlds and time is irreversible, the graphic representation (the map) of the forking paths of life is not a network with loops, as are most hypertext maps, but an arborescent diagram whose branches never intersect with other branches and do not allow circuits. A literal rendition of Borges's vision would therefore only be possible in a fiction based on a tree.

While the space of Borges's garden is a metaphor of time, the space of Storyspace is a metaphor for the organization of the signifieds. The maps represent the arrangement of lexia, not the geography, and even less the temporal development of the fictional world brought to mind by the signifiers. The vaunted spatiality of hypertext is therefore nothing more than the two-dimensionality of the text map, which itself is the graphic representation of the network of links and nodes that underlies the text. That this space is not a physical geography is demonstrated by the fact that readers can click and drag the nodes to other locations on the screen without altering the system of relations that connects them—without, in other words, making the map less faithful to that which it represents.[11] In a map of physical space, by contrast, this operation would be unthinkable: moving London south of Paris would result in a blatant inaccuracy. The space represented on Storyspace maps is purely virtual, because the text itself is stored in computer memory as a one-dimensional string of zeroes and ones. There is nothing inherently spatial about computer organization: as Alan Turing has demonstrated, all computers can be simulated by a machine that reads an infinitely long tape.

On a map of accessibility relations between lexia, the situation described by Borges would be represented by a root node, "x meets y" splitting into "x and y become friends" and "x and y become enemies." Both of these lexia would then contain a link leading to "x arrives at y's house." To maintain narrative consistency, the text should prevent the reader who reaches the house-lexia from the path "x and y become enemies" to move on to "y greets x warmly and offers food and shelter." This could be done by means of a guard field: only those readers who have traversed "x and y become friends" can be directed toward "y greets x warmly." But imagine that the reader later on traverses "x and y become enemies," an event that the text should allow if it is to represent multiple possibilities. Narrative logic would then require the removal of the original guard field and its replacement with a new condition, which would direct the reader toward "y slams the door on x." But Storyspace does not allow the dynamic adding and removing of guard fields during reading. Moreover, the guard field option only works when used sparingly, because the device is based on previously visited nodes, a rather primitive condition, and not on the semantic description of the fictional world. It would be very difficult for Storyspace authors to handle a complex system of dependencies between nodes, especially since the system-generated maps do not show the guard fields. This is why the metaphor of the jigsaw puzzle is a less utopian description of the cognitive processing of hypertext than the idea of a recombinant text whose elements tell a different story with every reading. In the jigsaw puzzle model, the connections between lexia need not represent a logical and temporal order, because the reader can rearrange them mentally into a (more or less) coherent picture. The plot (or plot-versions) is an image that the reader constructs by traveling through the virtual space of the text, collecting narrative fragments at every stop, and trying to assemble these fragments into a meaningful pattern. The main difference between puzzles and Storyspace hypertext lies in the fact that, faithful to postmodern aesthetics, hypertexts may prevent the formation of a complete picture, or they may lead to the construction of many conflicting partial images.

How then can one put the combinatorial features of Storyspace, a program that does not build a world model, in the service of narrative meaning? Since the author cannot control what the reader knows and does not know at every moment of the reading experience, narrative effects that depend on the calculated disclosure of information are incompatible with the medium. We shouldn't expect thrillers, suspense stories, dramatic curves of rising and falling tension, nor immersion in the flux of time in hypertext fiction. Thinking with the medium means in this case finding other functions for links than progressing in narrative time or moving around in the fictional world, though these functions cannot be entirely discarded if the text is to preserve some degree of narrativity. What are the alternatives?

Combine different linking logics. Allow the reader to follow a story chronologically, at least for a while, through linear stretches of lexia with obvious continuation links, but make these stretches intersect at certain points with other storylines, so that the reader can switch from one narrative possibility to another. Within each of these linear sequences, offer links that jump laterally to other lexia on the basis of nonchronological relations such as thematic analogies, expansion of an idea, metatextual comments, or different narrating voices offering alternative versions of the same events. Variations on this approach are found in *Victory Garden* (Stuart Moulthrop), *Patchwork Girl* (Shelley Jackson), and *Califia* (M. D. Coverley).[12] All these texts comprise sequences that move a story forward in time, but they surround these sequences with links to other parts of the story, to other narrative possibilities, or to nonnarrative materials.

Work with "little stories" that fit within one screen. For instance, *True North,* by Stephanie Strickland, is a collection of largely autonomous poems, some of which evoke projects in language development by two nineteenth-century figures, Willard Gibbs and Emily Dickinson. Through allusions to these figures (as well as to others), the poems achieve some degree of micronarrativity. Lexias are also arranged by links and color-coded words into cycles or thematic groups that form broader figures on the macrolevel. Another example of this approach is Deena Larsen's *Marble Springs,* a text described in chapter 5.

Present the text as a simulation of mental activity—dreams, memory, stream of consciousness—rather than as a representation of external events. The links will then stand for the associative processes that bring images, ideas, and recollections to the conscious mind, and the succession of lexia will represent the flow of inner life, rather than the actual chronology of the events that occupy the thoughts of the cognizing subject. In this model, looping back to an already visited lexia will not be interpreted as flashbacks in time, nor as a return to a certain location, but as the obsessive recurrence of a certain thought. As for lexia with contradictory content, they will stand for conflicting interpretations of events, rather than for contradiction within the fictional world itself. This approach is best illustrated by two works by Michael Joyce, *Twelve Blue* and *afternoon.*

Thinking with the medium in hypertext also means giving meaning to the reader's activity. In computer games, this meaning derives from the player's identification with the avatar and from the tasks to be fulfilled in order to win: tasks such as acquiring goods for the avatar, defending the earth against evil aliens, or stealing cars. But in hypertext, as I argue in chapter 5, the reader's involvement in the fictional world is external and observatory, and the significance of her activity cannot come from playing the role of an individuated member of the fictional world. It must therefore be metafictional rather than fictional. The metaphor of the jigsaw puzzle cannot provide a satisfactory interpretation of the reader's involvement, because it does not take into consideration the particular themes of the text. Any picture can be cut up, boxed, and sold as a puzzle. From a literary point of view, the best hypertexts are those that manage to present the reader's activity of moving through the network and reassembling the narrative as a symbolic gesture specific to the text, a gesture whose interpretation cannot be predicted by reading the medium as a built-in message, as McLuhan's famous formula[13] advocates. Here are two examples of hypertexts that, in my view, successfully customize the significance of the reader's activity.

The short story *Twelve Blue* by Michael Joyce contains several narrative subworlds, each inhabited by different characters but connected by common themes. (Foremost among them is the theme of drowning.) An interface of colorful threads, which suggests destiny lines, dangles the promise of stories. By clicking on a thread of a given color the reader is able to follow the life of a certain character for a limited time, but the thread eventually decays, and the reader is switched to a different plotline, as if memory had failed, or as if the synapses of the brain had suddenly fired in another direction. The whole process resembles stream of consciousness, except that the stream runs through the minds and private worlds of many characters. The random activity of clicking and bringing text to the screen thus mimics the mysterious functioning of memory, the fluidity of dream, and the operation of a collective consciousness. But it is only because the colored threads can keep us for a while in the world of the same individual that we become familiar with the inner and outer lives of characters and learn to care for them. Joyce has successfully streamlined navigational choices to enhance narrative interest.

In Shelley Jackson's *Patchwork Girl*, the reader's clicking symbolizes the activity of sewing a crazy quilt from different of pieces of material cut out from old garments. The quilting theme allegorizes the postmodern practice of constructing a text out of disparate elements, including recycled quotes. Faithful to this practice, *Patchwork Girl* abounds in intertextual allusions and includes both narrative fragments and theoretical considerations on the nature of its medium. But the reader's symbolic stitching also simulates the activity of two female figures: the heroine, Mary Shelley (a fictional counterpart of the author of *Frankenstein*), who assembles a female monster by sewing together body parts collected from different women; and the author, Shelley Jackson, who constructs a narrative identity for the monster from the lifestories of these women.

Patchwork Girl is one of the last major hypertexts written with

Storyspace, and its general design hints at a departure from the complex labyrinths for which the Storyspace toolbox was conceived. The text is divided into semiautonomous components that irradiate like the spokes of a wheel from a central page: a "graveyard" (containing the stories of the monster's body parts), a "journal" (Mary's diary), a "quilt" (made of theoretical reflections on the hypertextual reading experience and its putative configuration of subjectivity), a "story" (the monster's life after leaving Mary), and "broken accents" (more observations on the writing process). The general linking system is rather economical, with one or two links leading out of most nodes. The narrative episodes, for instance, either fill a single lexia (the stories of the women who provided the monster's body parts), or they offer a simple, almost linear linking structure that enables the reader to catch the flow of the story, rather than having to assemble the storyworld from scrambled elements. In a gesture of user-friendliness, this linking strategy belies the thematics of dismembering that permeate the text. In contrast to the endless looping of *afternoon* or *Victory Garden*, the reader develops a good sense of having reached the end of the stories. Though the voices of Mary and of the monster are occasionally interwoven, differences in typographical presentation make it easy to identify the speaker. The clear separation of the major constituents of the text, as well as the absence of hidden tricks in the linking strategy—no use is made of guard fields— allows for the type of goal-oriented navigation that we find in well-designed Internet Web sites. Abandoning the metaphor of the labyrinth so prominent in early Storyspace hypertexts, *Patchwork Girl* looks toward a narrative structure that will flourish under a new generation of computers systems and authoring programs: the structure of an open archive.[14]

7. Web-Based Narrative, Multimedia, and Interactive Drama

In the early to mid-1990s, computer systems underwent two developments that deeply affected digital textuality: the ability to encode and transmit visual and aural data efficiently; and the ability to connect personal computers into a world-spanning network. The textual consequences of these new features are publicly posted on millions of Internet pages. Though Web pages implement the same hypertextual architecture as Storyspace fiction, they differ significantly from the latter in their linking philosophy and graphic appearance. From a visual point of view, the major design characteristic of Web pages is what Bolter and Grusin have called their "hypermediated structure": the division of the screen into separate areas, or windows, containing different types of data. As a multimedia text, a Web page is not constructed through a single authoring program but assembled from elements generated by a variety of sources: word processors, drawing programs, photo-manipulation programs, sound-manipulation programs, and animation software. The majority of Web pages have an informational function to fulfill, and in contrast to experimental literature, they make it a positive value to be easy to search. This goal translates into a linking strategy that enables the reader to make informed choices of destination rather than clicking blindly on hidden links or mysterious words. The typical structure of a Web site is not a maze that exposes visitors to running in circles, but a sea-anemone (Figure 2c), or radiating structure, that connects every page to the center, so that the visitor can always return in one click to the home page, no matter how far she has wandered along the arms.

Archival Narratives

When it is put in the service of narrative meaning, the radiating structure facilitates the dynamic unfolding of storyworlds. Narrative texts do more than chronicle actions and events; they also provide background information that situates these events within a concrete environment. As they follow the life of the main characters, they also pick up the destinies of the secondary characters, together with their spatial surroundings. These lifestories may branch into other stories, which lead into yet other environments. All narratives must eventually limit this accumulation of space and time, though some authors—Dostoevsky and Laurence Sterne—do it rather reluctantly. With a digital database, the decision to stop the spatial and temporal growth of a textual world no longer needs to be made by the author. It is the reader who decides how far she wants to follow trails into new narrative territories.

Lev Manovich has argued that "narrative and database are natural enemies" because narrative presupposes a cause-and-effect trajectory, while a database, particularly a digital one, "represents the world as a list of items, and it refuses to order this list" (2001, 225). Yet if the database is properly structured, and if its contents are appropriate, the unpredictable probes and always incomplete exploration of the reader will not prevent the emergence of narrative meaning. The reconciliation of database and narrative is facilitated when the following conditions are met:

1. A storyline with which readers are already familiar. When the global coherence of the story is not problematic, readers can bring a magnifying glass to certain parts without losing sight of the whole plot.
2. A very modular narrative, whose individual parts are themselves more or less autonomous stories.
3. A narrative that foregrounds the setting, so that learning about the world in which the story takes place is at least as important to the reader as following the narrative events proper.
4. A database design and a linking philosophy sufficiently transparent to enable readers to aim with precision at the elements of the story that they want to expand.

As an example of a narrative database that meets these conditions, consider the huge online archive devoted to the Lewis and Clark expedition, Discovering Lewis and Clark. The Web site develops the story—and the world—of Lewis and Clark to truly encyclopedic dimensions. For instance: we read in the diary of Lewis and Clark that music was often performed in the evening by a fiddler named Pierre Cruzatte. A link takes us to a page that tells everything known about Cruzatte. We can even see a movie clip of a Cruzatte impersonator performing popular tunes of the time. Or we may click on the fiddle and get the history of the violin. From there we can go to a page on Thomas Jefferson as a violinist, where we learn that he owned a bow by François Tourte, a master bowmaker of the time. This in turn leads to a lecture on bow design that describes the innovation introduced by Tourte. Readers who do not care about music may branch instead toward Indian tribes of the Northwest; toward early-nineteenth-century cartography; or toward food on the expedition. Since this is a Web site, new materials are posted every month. With its documentary subject matter and practical design, the Lewis and Clark archive makes no claim to offering an "artistic" navigational experience. Yet there is no reason why a text with literary ambitions and a new story to tell could not be structured as a user-friendly archive with reasonably accessible documents.

A step in this direction is M. D. Coverley's heavily multimedia hypertext *Califia* (2000), a text written with the SuperCard program of the Macintosh operating system and sold by Eastgate Systems (Figure 7).

A visual delight—each page combines text boxes, pictures, and iconic buttons into stunning collages—*Califia* abandons the "Garden of Forking Paths" metaphor that dominated the first generation of Storyspace hypertexts in favor of a simpler navigational design: go North, then East, then South, then West. Each of the four stories (narrated by one of the three main characters, Augusta) can be followed linearly, and the itinerary actually leads to an end, a rare occurrence in hypertext. But the reader can always switch along the way to the "trails" of the other two protagonists: Kaye, who gathers star charts, Indian lore, and other spiritual guides; and Calvin, who maintains an archive of documents about California and family history: diaries, letters, photos, and topographical maps. The text chronicles a treasure hunt, and though

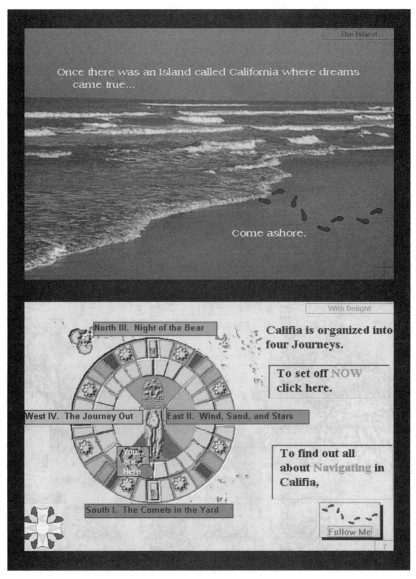

Figure 7. Screen shots from M. D. Coverley's *Califia*. Reproduced with permission of Eastgate Systems Inc. http://www.eastgate.com.

the treasure-seekers are the main characters, the reader feels that the success of the search depends on her ability to decipher the documents in the archive. As Raine Koskimaa writes: "We readers are in a sense put to an equal position with the fictional characters, as users of the same archival program they are using" (2000, 135). *Califia* is actually a fake game, not only because the treasure is never found but mainly because the reader can reach the end without solving any problems, not even running a maze. But the sense that the success of the enterprise depends on connecting the present to the past motivates the reader to explore the database. The encyclopedic information provided by the text may seem at times as tangential to the quest as bow design to the Lewis and Clark expedition, but by unearthing the rich cultural heritage that lays buried under the freeways and parking lots of Southern California the reader eventually gains a sense of place—the true treasure of Califia. At the end of the trip west, as the heroes stand at the edge of the ocean with nowhere to go, they understand that their quest has not been in vain: *"Granted we did not find the riches of which we had been told, we found a place in which to search for them."* The riches are found by simply connecting with the land.

Early Web-Based Narrative: HTML Frames

The development of the Internet had another consequence for electronic literature. While early works were sold as diskettes or CD-ROMs by Eastgate, the current generation of digital fiction or poetry is primarily distributed for free on the World Wide Web. Since downloading is still slow, and people have limited patience with reading on a screen, this encouraged the creation of short texts meant to be read in one session. One of the landmarks in the transition from classical hypertext fiction to Web-based forms of literature is a text written with the Frames feature of the HTML mark-up language, *My Boyfriend Came Back from the War* by the Russian author Olia Lialina (Figure 8). This text, which dates back to 1996, has achieved cult status on the Web and inspired multiple adaptations in other authoring systems,[1] thereby serving as anchor in a new form of textuality that Katherine Hayles calls "the work as assemblage": a "cluster of related texts that quote, comment upon, amplify and remediate each other," "cycling through diverse [sub] media in exuberant and playful performances" (2003, 277, 280). Yet if the various adaptations illustrate the diverse resources of their supporting systems, none of them achieves the simple yet powerful eloquence of the original.

For the reader who likes to explore a text systematically, one of the most frustrating aspects of the densely connected networks

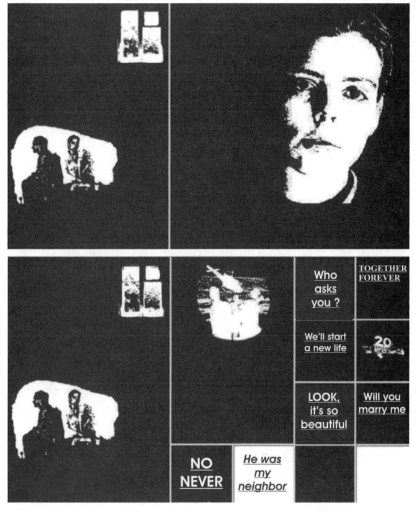

Figure 8. Screen shots from Olia Lialina's *My Boyfriend Came Back from the War,* slightly modified to enhance readability of text. Reproduced with permission.

of classical Storyspace hypertext is the difficulty to follow several routes simultaneously, or to move back and forth between these routes. Once the reader selects one of many links out of the same page, he can only explore the other alternatives if the path curves back toward the intersection; but since many other choices will present themselves in the meantime, there is no reliable way to return to the decision point from within the link system of the text (that is, without using the alternative modes of navigation offered by the interface buttons).[2] In *My Boyfriend Came Back from the War*, Lialina proposes a clever solution to this problem—or rather a clever alternative to what is usually a deliberate design philosophy—by exploiting a feature of HTML which makes it possible to divide the screen into separate areas, or frames. In contrast to Storyspace windows, which correspond to distinct pages and partially hide each other when several of them are opened simultaneously, HTML frames are subdivisions within the same page, and their entire content is visible all the time, thereby affording the reader a panoramic view of the text. Frames can be manipulated and explored individually by the user, and they can be nested within other frames, though the fixed size of the screen sets limits on how many frames can be efficiently used at once.[3]

The text begins with a unified screen displaying the phrase "My boyfriend came back from the war; after dinner they left us alone." The first click divides the screen into a pair of windows showing, respectively, two dejected people looking in opposite directions and the self-referential image of a window frame, which suggests that the lovers, far from being left alone, are placed under surveillance by the reader and the family. The next click further splits one of these windows in two, and so on until the screen is partitioned into seventeen distinct spaces (1 + 16) that contain either text or a black-and-white still picture whose lack of gray tones suggests the binarism of stereotyped gender roles (male vs. female) and of the discourse of war (us vs. them, good vs. evil). When the reader reaches this bottom level, text replaces itself in each window, telling a linear story through a broken dialogue. When a window has been exhausted, it turns black, telling the reader that its narrative thread has come to an end. Reading the text thus becomes a game of creating as many frames as possible and then erasing the white marks of their content. While the reader explores a window, the others remain visible on the screen, offering alternative stories, and the reader can always switch from one window to another by clicking on another frame. This feature makes the use of an external text map superfluous; or rather, the text functions as its own map, showing at any given time which frames hold content to be explored, and which ones have been exhausted. By clicking on the frames, the reader "digs" deeper into them, leaving the other frames in their current state. The exploration of the text thus represents a vertical activity of unearthing content, in contrast to Storyspace hypertext, where clicking on links is a lateral sliding to another node and to another area of the map. Whereas lateral movement is an endless journey that allows travelers to loop back to previously visited places, the vertical exploration of *My Boyfriend* eventually reaches bottom.

From a thematic point of view, the splitting of windows suggests the multiple possibilities that arise when a soldier returns to his girlfriend after a long separation, but the successive divisions of the screen also symbolize the division that war involves, the growing apart of the lovers, and the failure to communicate that takes place in most scenarios. Only two of the threads end on a positive note: "Together forever"; or "Look, it's so beautiful" / "kiss me"; but they are the shortest, and they may represent no more than wishful thinking. Other scenarios show the stalling of the boyfriend when asked to set a date for the wedding ("Will you marry me?"; "TOMORROW"; "No, better next month after holidays and the weather must be better. Yes next month. I'm happy now."), the girlfriend being questioned by her lover about her faithfulness during his absence ("You don't trust me, I see"; "But it was only one. Last summer . . . And if you think . . . Why should I explain? . . . Don't you see"), or the boyfriend sheepishly breaking up with a lame excuse and a vacuous promise ("All guys change; don't worry; I'll help you").

Told in a halting, minimalist dialogue that leaves large gaps to be filled in by the reader (let's not forget that it was written in English by a Russian speaker), *My Boyfriend Came Back from the War* powerfully captures the emotional drama of a long-awaited moment that fails to deliver the happy ending required by the conventions of the romance. Through its choice of a simple yet poignant story tailored to the size of the screen, its efficient visual interface to the idea of multiple narrative possibilities, and its all too rare combination of human interest and creative exploitation of the affordances of its supporting software, Lialina's text proposes a powerful demonstration of what it means to think with the medium.

Approaching *My Boyfriend* from the perspective of the cinema, Lev Manovich comments: "The result is a new cinema in which the diachronic dimension is no longer privileged over the synchronic dimension, time is no longer privileged over space, sequence is no longer privileged over simultaneity, montage in time is no longer privileged over montage within a shot" (2001, 326). But why should the point of reference for the originality of this work come from the cinema? We could just as well regard Lialina's text as a remediation of print; then we will be sensitive to what Manovich calls montage in time, namely, the dynamics of frame replacement as the reader clicks on various parts of the screen. Or better, we could read *My Boyfriend* in the context of narrative Renaissance paintings. As Wendy Steiner has shown, these paintings often partitioned their space with architectural or landscape features and represented different moments of a story in each of these frames. Though *My Boyfriend* resorts to the same technique of partition, it uses its medium to display evolving content within each frame, and rather than telling one story dispersed through many frames, it associates each frame with one of the narrative possibilities that branch out from a common situation.

Flash

The major influence on the form of today's digital works is the widespread adoption of a program named Flash produced by Macromedia that allows what is called the "streaming" of information: when the user downloads a Flash movie—as the products are called—from the Web, the movie can start playing on the user's screen before all the data have been downloaded. The label of "movie" that designates Flash products underscores the program's major difference from Storyspace: a shift in emphasis from spatial navigation to temporal dynamics. As a machine that executes instructions sequentially, regulated by the pulses of an internal clock, the computer has always operated in a temporal flow; but this flow can be easily stopped by the software. This is exactly what happened with Storyspace and the Infocom engine: the program performs a series of jumps to specific addresses, displays their contents on the screen, and waits for user input before taking another jump and displaying the content of other addresses. In Flash and other programs of its generation, time is liberated, and the screen can rewrite itself without user action.[4] Many Flash texts play indeed like movies, foregoing interactivity. These texts use the medium primarily for the convenience of building animated multimedia displays and for making themselves widely available over the Internet.[5]

The forward movement of the movies allows animation effects, but the designer can control the flow of time, for instance, by making the movie stop on certain frames until the user activates a button or by looping back to a previous frame. Sometimes the Flash movie imposes its tempo on the user; sometimes the user is able to determine how much time she wants to spend on a certain frame. This possibility to alternate between the leisurely reading experience of books and the forward movement of cinematic movies is what makes interactive digital texts, and Flash texts in particular, truly unique among media.

The emphasis of the program on temporal dynamics does not mean that Flash products neglect spatiality: the author works with a two-dimensional display, called the *stage,* as well as with a temporal one, the *timeline.* But space in Flash means primarily the *visual space* of the stage, rather than the *topographical space* of a fictional world, as it does in IF games, or the *structural space* of the text, as it does in Storyspace hypertexts. The author creates a Flash movie by placing various objects on the stage, by attributing scripted behaviors to these objects, and by connecting them to sequences of frames on the timeline. When the frames are played, the objects associated with them appear, disappear, and perform their script like actors on the stage.

A program of superior multimedia capabilities, Flash can handle a wide variety of objects: text, bitmaps (for imported pictures), vector graphics (for pictures generated within the program), and sound files. Some of these objects function as buttons: when the user clicks on them, or simply mouses over, the system performs an action that modifies the display. Hypertextual effects are created by programming the system to perform a "goto" another frame on the timeline and to display the text or the images linked to this frame. It may seem that Flash replaces the spatiality of Storyspace with a purely linear protocol, but its movement back and forth along the timeline is similar to the mode of operation of Storyspace on the level of machine-language instructions. Unlike Storyspace, however, Flash does not generate a spatial diagram of the system of links. Since it is left to the author to keep track of what happens when the user activates a certain button, the underlying transition networks of Flash movies tend to be much simpler than those of Storyspace hypertexts.

An important feature of Flash is its layered structure. The stage does not consist of a single image but of many graphic levels whose superposition creates an impression of depth. Since the layers of this palimpsest are independent of each other, objects can move inside the foreground while the background remains stable. An object on a close layer can hide an object on a distant layer, or layers can be made invisible when certain condition are met, thus revealing the contents of a deeper layer. One of the most productive effects of this lamination is the possibility of making images emerge from the depth of the digital palimpsest when the user mouses over certain "hot spots," which are themselves active objects hidden on the deepest layers. While visible action buttons make Flash movies interactive, hidden hot spots make them reactive, since they respond to involuntary user actions.

The programming language of Flash allows designers to associate objects with custom-designed behaviors and to diversify the actions triggered by the buttons. In Storyspace all the buttons were links, the only mode of activation was clicking, and all that clicking could do was display another lexia. In Flash buttons can make an object change color and shape, move around the screen, or be replaced by another object; they can stop the forward movement of the movie or, on the contrary, set it again in motion; and like Storyspace links, they can trigger jumps forward or backward along the timeline. These behaviors can also be made conditional on variables internal to the program, which means that they will be activated independently of user control. In contrast to IF systems, the programming language of Flash is generally not used to build a world model attributing lifelike properties to objects but to regulate their purely visual behavior. Whereas IF may contain code that says "if x is a lock pick, it can be used to open a door," Flash code will typically be made of statements such as "On mouse-enter (= when the cursor moves over an object), make the object disappear." Because of the programmability of the system, the author can control how fast the movie will play, how long images or text will remain visible, what transformation they will undergo, and how much time the user will have to perform a certain action. With Flash, timing becomes a new source of meaning.

It is difficult to predict where narrative is headed in the age of Flash. Most applications so far have been minigames, purely visual works, random combinations of sound, text, or picture fragments known as "remixes," "theoretical fictions" that privilege meta-textual comments at the expense of narration,[6] concrete poetry, or visual adaptations of print poems. All we can say at the present time

is that Flash narratives, because of the length restriction, will be neither the complex labyrinths of Storyspace nor the time-consuming
quests of IF. In the narrative domain, Flash has been used for both
traditional stories and postmodern experiments in antinarration.
An example of a traditional story is *Arloz the Little Rhinoceros,* a
parody of the children's classic *Babar the Little Elephant,* in which
Flash animates the illustrations of a text that reads linearly. The anti-
narrative use is illustrated by Judd Morrissey's *The Jew's Daughter,*
a text-only work in which part of the screen replaces itself without
visible mark when the mouse passes over highlighted words, so that
the reader cannot tell what is new and what is old. Needless to say,
this makes it impossible to follow the development of a story. The
text is only readable on the metanarrative level, as an allegory of
the instability of meaning, or perhaps as a simulation of the dynamics of the writing process—the replacement standing for corrections
and for the technique of cut-and-paste.

   Can Flash be used to produce a middle ground between *Arloz*
and *The Jew's Daughter*—texts that are both formally innovative
and readable as stories? The best examples of works that achieve
a viable compromise between these somewhat conflicting goals
come from a form of poetry that is beginning to emerge on Web
sites devoted to Flash art as an alternative to the concrete (visual)
poetry, code poetry, and computer-generated texts that currently
dominate the scene of digital poetry. This new form explores the
relations between words and images by combining a short, often
linear text evoking some aspect of human experience with an interactive graphic illustration that puts into play the design resources
specific to Flash. Insofar as the reader's manipulations affect neither discourse nor story, these are interactive texts without being
interactive narratives.

   In Ingrid Ankerson's and Megan Sapnar's poem "Cruising"
(Figure 9), the text is reduced to a line, and this line is integrated
into a frieze made of distinct pictorial frames that runs from left
to right in a closed loop. On the first iteration, the text is read
aloud, and most readers will just listen. Then the text becomes
interactive. (Actually, the reader can interact from the very beginning, but the human voice captures too much of her attention
to let her think about anything else.) By moving the cursor, the
reader can make the text and its graphic background grow or
shrink, move left or move right, and move at different speeds. The

Figure 9. Screen shots from "Cruising," by Ingrid Ankerson and Megan Sapnar. Reproduced with permission.

goal is to get a combination of size, speed, and direction that allows the text to be deciphered; for most of the time, the letters
are too small, and they move too fast for the eye to make out the
words. The user's control of the speed and direction simulates
the driving of a car; and indeed, driving a car is what the text is
all about: "I remember cruising Main Street with Mary Jo and
Joanie, the heat pumping full blast, windows down, night rolling
through Mary Jo's father's station wagon like movie credits." The
looping of the text mimics the repetitive aspect of the favorite
activity of small-town teenagers: up and down, up and down the

same street, the only difference between two runs residing in the speed of the car and in the resulting legibility of the landscape framed by the car window. At low speed we see distinct images, and we can read their details, while at high speed the images look like the frames on a strip of film, except that the frames do not blend into each other to form a moving picture. As a simulative mechanism, the interface enables readers to participate vicariously in the experience described in the poem, while as a comment on the medium, it underscores the hybrid status of digital poems between text that we can read at our own pace and film that rolls before our eyes. What literary critics once hailed as "the unity of form and content" has become in this work the triple unity of interface, theme, and image.

Whereas "Cruising" keeps a balance between textual appeal and programming virtuosity, my second example, "Nine," by Jason Lewis, clearly tips the scale toward the second feature. A literary game, "Nine" (Figure 10) presents itself as a digital version of the nine-tile puzzle. This puzzle, which most of us remember from our childhood, consists of a frame holding eight tiles and an empty space arranged in a 3 by 3 grid. The purpose of the game is to slide the tiles until a certain pattern is created: for instance, arranging the numbers 1 to 8 in ascending order or reconstituting a picture. Thanks to the volatility of inscription of its medium, "Nine" adds a new dimension to the game by associating each tile with multiple image fragments: twelve in this particular case. As the player holds down the mouse button on a tile, the twelve images fade into each other in a continuous loop. The task of the player is therefore twofold: get all the tiles to display fragments of the same image; and then slide the tiles to unscramble the image. For inexperienced players, the puzzle is nearly impossible. But solving the puzzle is not the point of the text, and, in fact, it goes against its symbolism.

"Nine" creates a new twist on the classic game by associating it with a narrative. Every time the player moves a tile, a fragment of a story appears in the empty square. Rather than ascribing a specific square on the grid to every narrative fragment, the program displays the first fragment in the square left empty after the first move, the second fragment in the square vacated after the second move, and so on. This means that no matter how the reader plays the game, he will read the text in the same order. The variable, fragmented,

Figure 10. Screen shots from "Nine," by Jason Lewis, slightly modified to enhance readability of text

problematic aspect of the text thus resides entirely on the visual level. As the author describes it: "'Nine' is a dynamic poem presenting images from the lives of the artist, constantly shifting them in-and-out of focus, in tension with, and making something of a mockery of the clean linear story told by the text which winds through them."

With its twelve layers of images that smoothly blend into each other, the version of the game of nine implemented in this text is an impressive programming feat, but how does the game relate to the narrative? An autobiographical text, "Nine" tells about the attempt of the author, the son of a Cherokee woman and an "Island man" but raised in a white family, to reconnect with his racial identity:

> born edward guthrie seventeenth december nineteen sixty-seven;
> reborn jason edward lewis twenty seventh july nineteen seventy;
> son of a white family from the foothills of northern california

The narrative retraces the travels of Jason in pursuit of Edward. Wherever he goes, his identity changes: in Berlin he passes as a Turk; in Indonesia, as a "rich guy from Jakarta"; among natives, "I am native." Are these false identities, imposed on Jason/Edward by others because of his brown skin, or is Jason, through their diversity, coming to terms with the very contemporary notion of multiple selves in one body? The cryptic end of the poem does not resolve the ambiguity: "now I hear Edward Guthrie racing to catch up to me, his brothers and sisters from the Islands joining the chase." Would the meeting of Jason and Edward restore Jason to his true, nonwhite self, or would it represent the acceptance of fragmentation and multiplicity as the essence of identity?

Through the attempt to reassemble the images on the tiles, the reader reenacts the identity quest of the narrator. The twelve images include topographical maps of the various places visited by Jason, pictures of the places represented on the maps, and photographs of Jason in these various locations. There are consequently several different Jasons to put back together, each rooted in a different place. But the reader is not supposed to succeed at this task: as the author explains in an accompanying sound file, "Life is a puzzle . . . 'Nine' is a dynamic poem about the impossibility of finishing such a puzzle and the insistent need to keep trying . . . The reader must pursue parallel yet conflicting goals: Assemble a complete image, even as it constantly slips away, and pursue the text as it unfolds, even as it forces you to constantly rearrange the tiles." Through its implicit conception of identity as hopelessly elusive and of the experience of fragmentation as inevitable, this way of reading the text may be symbolically satisfying, but it is unlikely that readers will divide their attention between the story and the game, as the author would like them to do. I read the story first (it can be done in eight moves) and then started playing more deliberately with the tiles. I quickly gave up the hope of reconstructing coherent pictures by playing by the rules, but when I restarted the game, I discovered a trick that makes the puzzle easily solvable without moving a single tile: when you first open the file, the tiles display fragments of different images arranged in the proper order. All that needs to be done to reconstitute the various pictures is to hold down the mouse button on each tile long enough for it to display a fragment of the same image as the other tiles. What should we make of this easy solution, in view of the general theme of the text? Is identity something given at birth that we lose as we begin to play the game of life? Is a return to origins—the initial state of the game—the key to finding oneself? If so, the cheating reader succeeds where the narrator fails—Jason hasn't yet reconnected with Edward at the end of the story, and even if he had, the name "Edward Guthrie" is itself an Anglo name that hides his racial origins. Maybe I am over-interpreting. But the contrast between the virtual reading experience described by Lewis and my actual reading strategy is the inevitable consequence of the tendency of authors of avant-garde art to conceive their work, programmatically, as a game whose rules must be spelled out to the reader. If somebody wants to impose rules on us, aren't we free to cheat?

Director

Another Macromedia product, Director, is more popular than Flash for large, CD-ROM–based projects. The description of Flash given above applies, in its broad lines, to Director as well. But whereas Flash has a full range of animation effects for both text and images, Director seriously limits the behavior of objects made of text.[7] With Director, bit-map and vector graphics can stretch, rotate, fade, and change color, but about all that can be done with alphabetical text, in terms of visual effects, is to make it move across the screen. For this reason, Director does not lend itself as well as Flash to the dance of letters of concrete poetry. (Director, however, can embed small Flash files, so that technically it has all the Flash effects at its disposal.) On the other hand, the features that facilitate the development of large projects make Director into a better narrative tool than Flash because narrative is a type of meaning that needs a reasonably large frame to develop. One of these features is a device called the cast, where the developer can gather all the data-objects—text, images, sound files, and movie clips—that will appear in the product. The cast makes it easy to keep track of a large number of objects and to reuse them in different environments. The other feature is the possibility to embed movies within movies, so that the designer can modularize the project, devoting, for instance, a separate movie to every self-contained episode. One problem with the production of large narrative texts, however, is the absence of a feature that figures prominently in both Storyspace and computer games, namely, the possibility for the user to save a reading or playing session. This means that Director narratives must either be readable in one session or use structures that allow readers to remember easily which part of the work they have already visited and which ones remain to be explored. A well-designed Director text should also offer tools that make it possible to jump quickly to the latter.

Perhaps the most significant contribution of Director (and Flash) to digital textuality is to have made the design of multimedia, sensorially rich texts sufficiently simple and economical to be addressable by a single author or by a small group. In contrast to commercial movies and computer games, which are expensively produced by large designing teams and are therefore enslaved to the tyranny of the market, Director lends itself to individual projects with a do-it-yourself, cottage-industry quality that give free room to self-expression: projects such as building an autobiographical scrapbook, reconstructing a family saga, exploring local history, or preserving cultural memory. It is now possible to tell our personal stories, or the story of our community, through text, music, and pictures without incurring the exorbitant costs of making a documentary movie or publishing a glossy illustrated book.

Though it is the product of teamwork, *Juvenate,* a Director movie produced by Michelle Glaser, Andrew Hutchison, and Marie-Louise Xavier (Figure 11) is permeated with this intimate, personal quality. To call this text a narrative may seem to stretch the

Figure 11. Screen shots from *Juvenate,* by Michelle Glaser, Andrew Hutchison, and Marie-Louise Xavier. Reproduced with permission.

term to its limits, because *Juvenate* does not use language, and its various screens are connected by symbolic, analogical, or contrastive relations—what the critic Joseph Frank has called the "spatial form" of a text—rather than by the specifically narrative relations of causality and temporality. A branching text (it may be called a hypertext) based on a network full of loops and detours that prevents linear progression, *Juvenate* fills its nodes with animated images and sound effects. Verbal text appears only in the paratext of the title and credit screens; on what is written on some of the objects internal to the fictional world, such as the inscription on a paper doll cut out from newspapers; and in the words of children's songs on the sound track. Yet despite renouncing the semiotic code with the greatest narrative power and some of the most fundamental semantic features of narrativity, *Juvenate* constructs a fictional world (divided into the experiential subworlds of illness and childhood); it populates this world with individuals—a sick man, a woman, and their child; and it implies events and at least some fragments of a chronologically ordered lifestory: the man and woman making love, conceiving a child, raising it, and the man contracting a terminal illness and dying. Above all, it captures the poignant experience of a dying man haunted by images of a world from which he is now physically isolated in his hospital bed. The low-grade narrativity of *Juvenate* thus resides in what Monika Fludernik calls "experientiality," and not in the unfolding of a plot.[8]

The paratext of the title screen introduces the general theme of the work as follows:

> Illness removes us from the everyday. Priorities change and perceptions alter. Memories, dreams and reality fly into one another. *Juvenate* offers you a journey through the experience, picking up the stitches of one life via the emotional ligatures of its captive moments.

A quote from Charles Dickens on the exit screen weaves together life and death, suggesting that death is part of the fabric of life but also framing the images of the mental journey of *Juvenate* as the poignant goodbyes of the dying man to the lifeworld and to those he loves: "Life is made of many partings welded together." A Chinese proverb on both the opening and closing screens alludes to the mythical theme of the eternal return: "The beginning and the end reach out their hands to each other." The text concretizes this idea through the interleaved themes of childhood and illness, as well as through the recurrent visual motif of touching or reaching hands: the hand of the child on the face of the father; the hand of the woman on the hand of the man; and the hand of the man reaching out for a sunflower, which will blossom in front of a barbed wire on the next screen in an image of almost too obvious symbolism.

Juvenate takes the user through thirty-seven pictorial screens, each of which corresponds to a separate Director movie. "Heavily textured with supersaturated colors," as the authors describe them on the project's Web site, the images convey "the intense sensory perception experienced by the terminally ill." Almost painful to contemplate, they refuse to aesthetize the experience of the dying. Some of the pictures can be interpreted as sensory perceptions, others as memories, and still others as dreams, visions, and fantasies. Perception focuses on the hospital environment, for instance, through the image of a hand and forearm tied to a blood transfusion system; memory takes us to the domestic world from which the sick man is now exiled: the rooms of the house, the toys and play-ground of the child, and the father playing with his son; dreams and fantasies lead to the world of nature, to visions of death as either the radiant light of the sunflower or as enveloping darkness, and to images of the mother and child that suggest the continuation of life after the man's death.

The user navigates among the pictures through an elegantly simple, natural interface: mouse over the screen until something happens. There is no need to click. For the reader who wants to visit the text systematically, rather than being carried around the inner world of the sick man by the random associations of the mind, a map accessible at any time through a letter key gives direct access to every screen by clicking on its thumbnail image.

The screens of *Juvenate* lack the smoothness and unity of a well-done perspective painting or of a movie frame. This is the result partly of aesthetic design, and partly of the fact that Director images are constructed out of multiple elements superposed upon each other on the various layers of the stage. Objects are cut out from diverse sources, and they do not blend seamlessly with the background. *Juvenate* intensifies this impression of heterogeneous collage by making the light come from different directions, by leaving out shadows, or by resorting to slightly faulty perspective. Erasing distinctions between the foreground and the background, the saturated colors prevent the creation of a sense of depth. This effect is reinforced by the unusual perspective of the photos that form the background: shot at close range, from ground level, or from above, they do not immerse spectators in their space, because they do not represent a familiar point of view. All these features converge to create a spectacle of disparate flatness, of artificial assemblage. This is not a physical space experienced by a mobile body, but an alternative reality created by a feverish mind—the only space left open for exploration when the body is tied to a hospital bed. Here *Juvenate* makes a virtue out of necessity, for it would be impossible in version 7 of Director to simulate movement through a three-dimensional world, as do computer games.

Rather than smoothly unfolding a landscape, then, the user's actions probe the depth of the image and reveal what lies below the surface. Many of these hidden features have to do with the illness inside the body: for instance, mousing over a wrist makes a wound appear; stroking the skin on a forearm makes it translucid and reveals a network of blood vessels. While the flesh of the man decays when the cursor passes over, the scraped knee of the child stops bleeding and forms a scab: healing touch for the son, touch of death for the father. Another interactive effect is the animation of already visible objects. Some of these objects can be manipulated in (almost) the same way as their real-world counterparts: the user can turn the pages of a children's book, dial a telephone and release a recorded message about visitation hours in a hospital, read a horoscope by turning a wheel, rewind and release toys, and sprout sunflower seeds. Mouse action can also activate a variety of intradiegetic and extradiegetic sound effects, such as children's voices, children's songs, bird songs, piano music, laughing, humming, flowing water, ambulance sirens, groans of a man trying to defecate in a hospital bed, and recordings of heartbeat by medical equipment. The juxtaposition of sound and pictures creates meanings that neither of these semiotic channels could convey by itself: for instance, a lawnmower sound threatens the radiant beauty of the sunflower.

Last but not least, mouseover activates transitions. Images are suddenly replaced by other images when the cursor passes over certain areas of the screen. Sometimes transitions occur when the user "touches" visible objects, and they can be deliberately duplicated on the next visit to the same screen, but most of the time jumps to other images are triggered by invisible hot spots that leave the user totally out of control. In these moments the text is reactive, rather than interactive.

The journey through the text begins in one of three screens, selected arbitrarily: one entry point shows the head of the sleeping child, watched over by his mother; another the hand of the man with a band-aid on his wrist and the hand of the child trying to reach for it, in a literal illustration of the Chinese proverb; the third juxtaposes ripe pomegranates, symbol of life, with a doll cut out of newspaper; on close inspection, we can decipher the words "in memoriam" on the doll. In addition to three different entries, the text offers two endings. If the interactor mouses over a certain spot on the sunflower screen, she will be taken to the picture of a sundial bearing, through random choice, either the Chinese proverb or the Dickens quote mentioned above, and from there to the credit screen: this is the "life ending" of the text, the one that tells the user that the task has been completed. But the hot spot is hard to find and slow to react, and whether the interactor finds this exit is a matter of chance. (I once found it but could not replicate the feat on subsequent visits.) Almost as difficult to reach is the "death ending," a screen that shows a fuzzy, almost abstract shape standing for a body lying on its side. This screen eventually dissolves into a black background and then returns to opening screen. Like the "death" of computer games, this ending is an invitation to start the journey all over again.

The thirty-seven different screens of *Juvenate* are arranged in a network of variable connectivity. Depending on the number of incoming and outgoing links, some images are difficult to reach but easy to exit; some are easy to reach but difficult to exit; and most are situated between these two extremes. With its bottlenecks and zones of fast travel, the system of connectivities creates what Espen Aarseth (1999) has called (in relation to computer games) aporias and epiphanies: aporias when users are prisoners of a loop that takes them over and over again to the same screens, epiphanies when they break out of the vicious circle and reach a new image.

Though most of the screens are connected to both images of illness and images of vitality (nature and childhood), some of the connections are more difficult to activate than others, probably because of the size or location of the hidden hot spot. For instance, I was long held captive in one of the hubs of the system (at least five incoming links), the image of a hospital room with a telephone by the patient's bedside. I finally discovered that by holding the cursor still for some time on one of the keys of the phone, I could not only get out but actually reach a different screen for every key. The nine outgoing links were just harder to activate than the five incoming ones. Another of the hubs is a loop that connects, through two-directional links, a hand holding sunflower seeds (which can be sprouted on mouseover), a hand reaching for a sunflower, and the already mentioned sunflower blooming in front of barbed wire. Because only two links lead out of the loop (one of them the hard-to-activate link to the "life" ending), it is easy to fall captive to this near-vicious circle of light and hope. I was personally relieved when I escaped to a screen that shows a hand clutching a bottle of aspirin, for the ludic desire to see all the screens takes precedence (at least for me) over the fundamental aspiration to see life triumph over death. I was in fact quite proud of myself when, after visiting 134 screens (with countless returns to the hubs of the system), I finally reached the good night of the death ending. During this particular trip, I left six screens unvisited. Some of them correspond to the dying man's most pleasant experiences, as if the grim reality of the hospital environment hindered access to the brighter memories of life. But on subsequent visits I discovered rare connections to these happy moments, such as the man and woman making love, the image of the child as fetus on an ultrasound machines, or a festive candlelit meal with a sound track of laughter.

The network and the map offer not only two alternative ways to navigate the text but also two complementary ways to experience it. Some readers will regard the text as a labyrinth to solve and will refuse to consult the map; but in their obsession with finding the exit, they may neglect to play with the images or to pay attention to the musical structures of recurrent motifs that connect the various screens: motifs such as the ring, the paper doll, the toy soldier, and the wound on the man's wrist. Other readers will not hesitate to use the map in order to visit the sparsely connected screens. These readers will not experience the satisfaction of solving the labyrinth all by themselves, but they will travel much more leisurely through the network, taking the time to explore each picture in depth, mentally following the chains of visual motifs (even when they do not appear in adjacent screens), deliberately returning many times to some images to study their thematic and network connections, breaking up the journey into small stages, and overall enjoying exploration more than destination. It is the rare merit of *Juvenate* to lend itself to both a gamelike and an aesthetic reading, to reward both the goal-driven action of *ludus* and the free play of *paidia*.[9]

Beyond Authoring Systems: Artificial Intelligence–Driven Texts

With the exception of the IF engine, all the authoring systems discussed so far restrict user participation to the external-exploratory mode. To make participation internal in a visual work it would take a vector-based graphic engine that places the user's avatar inside an environment and lets her explore it from all points of view by manipulating controls, as we find in computer games. Flash and the earlier versions of Director do not support this type of smoothly unfolding, surrounding graphics. To make participation ontological, it would take an artificial intelligence module that builds and updates a world model in response to the user's actions. Though verbal interaction is not a necessary precondition of internal-ontological participation, as computer games demonstrate, the sense of belonging to the fictional world and the variety of the user's contributions can only be enhanced if the system includes a language parser. Once again, Flash and Director do not lend themselves to the extensive programming required by this kind of AI. Those who want to build a narrative environment allowing internal-ontological participation will have to do much of their own programming, both to define and process the actions of the user and to coordinate the various modules, rather than relying on a high-level authoring system to fit together sound, image, and text. My final example, *Façade,* by Michael Mateas and Andrew Stern, a work programmed largely from scratch,[10] goes infinitely further in "narrative intelligence" than any of the projects discussed so far.

The authors' explicit ambition is to fill the gap between the mass audience of computer games and the narrow audience of experimental digital writing that I mention in my introduction. As Mateas and Stern write, "We are interested in interactive experiences that appeal to the adult, non-computer-geek, movie-and-theater-going public" (online, 2; reprinted in Mateas 2004, 29). *Façade* is a work of interactive drama that seeks to create an action patterned according to the plot model recommended by Aristotle: an introduction, leading to a complication, climax, and resolution. This dramatic curve, which has been diagrammed by the Freytag triangle, is condensed into a fifteen-minute action whose goal is to create an intense emotional experience. It should take half a dozen short visits for the player to unravel the narrative variety of which *Façade* is capable, rather than the many hours required by classical Storyspace hypertexts and present-day computer games.[11] Here is how the authors present the project:

> In *Façade,* you, the player, using your own name and gender [though it is possible, and indeed interesting, to switch gender], play the character of a long-time friend of Grace and Trip, an attractive and materially successful couple in their early thirties. During an evening get-together at their apartment that quickly turns ugly, you become entangled in the high-conflict dissolution of Grace and Trip's marriage. No one is safe as the accusations fly, sides are taken and irreversible decisions are forced to be made. By the end of this intense one-act play you will have changed the course of Grace and Trip's lives—motivating you to replay the drama to find

out how your interaction could make things turn out differently the next time. (Mateas and Stern on-line, 2)

Combining serious subject matter and cartoon-style images, in the best tradition of Japanese *animé* film, *Façade* brings Grace and Trip to life through spoken dialogue, facial expressions, and body language (see the screen captures of Figure 12). The superb acting and the variety of modes of self-presentation give the characters far greater human presence than written text alone could do, as I realized in those moments where the sound channel is not yet implemented and dialogue is represented in speech bubbles. (I used a prerelease version; in the final version all dialogue is spoken.) The user's principal mode of interactivity is typing text, but he can also move around the apartment, inspect it from various angles and from various distances, confront Grace and Trip or turn his back on them, and pick up or drop some of the objects that decorate the apartment. From a dramatic point of view, the role of the interactor represents the Northeast point of Figure 4: halfway between passive external witness and emotionally involved participant who

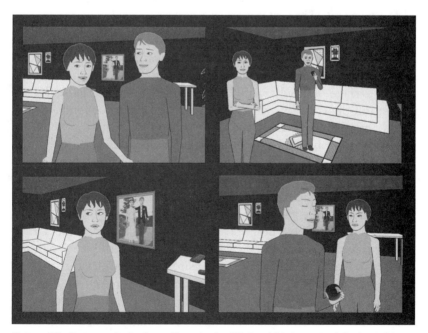

Figure 12. Screen shots from *Façade,* by Michael Mateas and Andrew Stern. Reproduced with permission.

plays out his own destiny. While something minor is at stake for the visitor—the fate of his friendship with Grace and Trip—he is spared the devastating personal experience that Grace and Trip are supposed to undergo. More than an interactive observer, but less than a story protagonist, as the authors describe him (Mateas and Stern 2002, 19), the player of *Façade* is given the role that I recommend in chapter 5 for strongly emotional drama.

While the action permits many variations, it is not a plot with clearly distinct, diagrammable endings but rather an emergent system. The authors describe it as a "middle ground between structured narrative and simulation," meaning by this latter term the multiplicity of possibilities found in games like *The Sims* (Mateas and Stern online, 5). Different runs enact different conversational events in combinations far too numerous to be prescripted, but all the runs follow the same basic pattern:

> *Exposition*: Grace and Trip welcome the visitor to their apartment and engage in small talk with their guest.
> *Crisis*: The small talk turns into an argument between Grace and Trip that exposes the disastrous state of their marriage.
> *Denouement*: The visitor is asked to leave.

Variation takes place not on the level of physical events but on the level of the interactor's assessment of the situation: who, between Grace and Trip, is the most responsible for the deterioration of their marriage, and what will happen after the visitor leaves? This evaluation depends on what is said, which in turn depends on the user's actions. Each run actualizes 30 percent of the total conversational events available, and each selection proposes a slightly different portrait of Grace and Trip, though they retain stable personality features through all the variations: Trip is trying to maintain the image of a successful marriage, Grace is intent on destroying the façade; Trip is vain and wimpy but conciliatory, Grace is aggressive, unforgiving, and impossible to please. In some runs Grace and Trip tell the visitor that "everything will be all right" as they ask her to leave, in other runs the visitor leaves under the impression that the marriage has been irremediably broken, and in yet other runs she may decide that arguing is essential to Grace's and Trip's relation and that nothing will ever change. The user's evaluation of the characters also depends on whether she takes Grace's and Trip's claims at face value or regards them as self-deception. For instance, in some runs Grace presents herself as a frustrated artist who was forced by Trip to give up painting for a lucrative career as a magazine designer; in other runs, Trip describes her as a careerist who poses as an artist but possesses neither the necessary talent nor the dedication to become a painter. The only certainty is that Grace and Trip are doing their best to hurt each other.

The various stories unfold as a variable succession of short scenarios (called "beats" by the designers) selected by the system from a library of some two hundred units on the basis of the current situation and stage of development of the narrative arc. Certain beats will consequently appear early and others will come late. In one beat, Trip draws the visitor's attention to a photo he took during a weekend in Italy that he calls "our second honey-moon." In another, Trip offers drinks to the visitor. In yet another, the phone rings with a message from either Grace's or Trip's parents, but the targeted individual refuses to answer: we hear the message on the answering machine. Each of these scenarios can develop into a variety of ways depending on the state of the system and the input of the user, though it is not necessarily clear to the user how his behavior affects the scenario. For instance, the topic of the Italian photo may be quietly dropped, or it can give Grace an opportunity to complain bitterly about the hassle of flying to Italy just for the weekend. For each situation, the system maintains a list of discourse acts that constitute appropriate conversational responses: acts such as agree, disagree, thank, criticize, hug, comfort, or judge. The textual input of the user is parsed by the system and mapped onto one of the currently available discourse acts; for instance, if the user types "I feel terrible" in response to the question "How are you," the system will interpret her words as "express unhappy." Each discourse act can thus be realized through a vast variety of different inputs. When the system cannot parse the text, it does not interrupt the unfolding of the story to tell the user "I do not understand," as would the IF parser, but instead ignores the input and selects one of the discourse acts appropriate to the current situation. The user cannot derail the smooth run of the system, but the system will often respond incoherently to her input. Here is an example of appropriate system response (Grace has been expressing dissatisfaction with her decoration of the apartment):

GRACE: I bet I can return most of this, and start over again on this
    room . . .

TANIA: Yes, start over.

GRACE: Oh, how nice, I've been waiting so long for someone to
    say that!

TRIP: Wait, what?

GRACE: Trip, our friend has just been refreshingly honest about my
    decorating, which I really appreciate.

And here is an example of wrongly parsed input that leads to an
incoherent response:

GRACE: Trip, have you noticed, we're fighting in front of our
    friend.

TRIP: Grace, come on, it's not helping things for you to say
    that . . .

GRACE: Trip, it's okay if we disagree in front of our friend—

TRIP: Disagreeing?! We're NOT disagreeing. We're, we're not.

TRIP: (frustrated sigh) Sheejus.

TANIA: It's ok to disagree.

GRACE: You don't agree? Okay, well . . .

GRACE: Okay, well, we're all getting along better tonight than
    I thought.

In this second example, the interactor (Tania) tries to calm down
the feuding couple by telling them that disagreeing is a normal part
of life, but the parser jumps on the word "disagree" and relates it to
the discourse act DISAGREE rather than to PACIFY. But then Grace
downplays the disagreement to save the appearance of a conversation serving the social goal of entertaining a friend. Such mis-
understandings are frequents in *Façade,* and this is not too surprising, for general-purpose language understanding is still way out
of reach of even the most sophisticated AI systems. But by sending
the dialogue on a new track, rather than insisting on a processable
input, as would the IF parser, the system handles communicative
failures without breaking narrative flow and without threatening
immersion. This approach is known as "graceful degradation."

A major problem for the interactor is placing a word in the conversation. At the beginning, Grace and Trip try to be polite, and
they ask many questions that give the visitor a chance to express
herself. The system pauses until the player responds. But as the story

develops, Trip and Grace become more and more focused on each other, and less and less on the visitor. They exchange their barbs in such rapid fire that by the time the visitor has finished typing a line and hitting the return key (at which point the input can be processed by the system), Grace and Trip have produced three or four lines of dialogue, and the context has evolved. This timing problem can lead the system to evaluate the interactor's contributions in the wrong context, especially if the interactor is a slow typist.

Yet the difficulty for the visitor to participate in the exchange and to be properly understood does not lead to a serious loss of credibility, because the problem is minimized by the narrative theme, by the personalities of Grace and Trip, and by the number of characters. Thematically, *Façade* is about a conversation that degenerates into an argument. As the philosopher H. Paul Grice has shown, conversation is normally regulated by a so-called cooperation principle that enjoins the participants to "make [their] contribution such as required, at the stage at which it occurs, by the accepted purpose of the talk exchange in which [they] are engaged" (1975, 47). The cooperation principle brings into play a number of "conversational maxims," the most important of which are the maxim of quality ("Do not say that which you believe to be false") and the maxim of relation ("Be relevant"). Insofar as they bring order and civility to conversation, the cooperation principle and the maxims lose their validity when the purpose of the exchange is to express hostility. In a fight, you feel free to interrupt your opponent, ignore his arguments, make false accusations, monopolize the floor, or leave questions unanswered. To fight, in essence, is to be uncooperative. If Grace and Trip fail to respond adequately to the user's input, it is because they are so blinded by their own anger that they become unable to carry on a normal conversation. The limitations of the parser would be much more damaging if the topic were an enlightened intellectual exchange between rational participants, such as a dialogue between Socrates and his disciples. The frequent deafness of the system to the input of the user can also be attributed to the personalities of Grace and Trip: both are extremely self-centered characters who hardly listen to each other. This personality feature can be expected to carry over to their relations to the visitor: Trip only wants to display their fabulous lifestyle, Grace only wants to explore the cracks in the façade of their life, and neither really cares about the visitor. The number of characters, finally, relieves the interactor from the burden of carrying the action. In a two-person dialogue system, such as the IF text *Galatea* discussed in chapter 6, the user spends a great deal of effort getting Galatea to talk. Here, Grace and Trip take control of the events, and the user's input is not indispensable to the development of the story, except when she is asked a question or given a command. But even in those moments where the system pauses to receive the user's input, she remains under the control of the other two characters, because the speech acts of question and command represent a powerful way for the speaker to direct the flow of the conversation.

One way of giving the visitor more initiative without overburdening the parser is to extend the possibilities of physical actions and make the system more responsive to them. Physical actions are much less ambiguous than verbal input because the user can perform them with a mouse click, rather than using a phrase that the parser can understand. For instance, if I you want to leave, it is much more efficient to do so by walking to the door and clicking on the handle (provided a behavior is associated with it) than by saying "Goodbye," "I want to go," and "I've had enough," all phrases that may not be in the parser's repertory. In the version of *Façade* that I tested, the possibilities of physical action are still underdeveloped. For instance, kissing Grace or Trip on the lips elicits no more than a pleasantly surprised or offended look, and the ejection of the visitor if the action is repeated. Here the program is missing some interesting opportunities for narrative development: the kiss could, for instance, introduce a whispering between the user and the other character, the hinting of an affair; or the system could respond differently, depending on whether the kiss involves same-sex or different-sex partners. Similarly, the objects on the shelves present wonderful conversation pieces, and the visitor could easily steer the dialogue in a new direction by picking them up, but so far not much is done with this possibility. Grace should have more to say about her collection of statuettes in the final version. At the present time we have dialogue systems that respond to the user's verbal input, and simulation systems like *The Sims* that do not process language but respond to physical gestures performed through mouse actions and arrow keys. The full potential of interactive drama will only be reached when it combines these two modes of participation.

Espen Aarseth has expressed doubts about the idea of interactive drama because it requires too much cooperation from the user: "Either users will surrender to the playwright's ideas of acceptable behavior and become docile servants of the narrative, or (more likely) they will revolt against the system's narrative goals and turn the 'play' into a subversive metanarrative, with a well-formed ending out of reach" (1997, 138). This dilemma assumes that "becoming a servant of the narrative" cannot be a fulfilling experience; but when we play a game, don't we freely submit to the game rules? When children engage in make-believe, such as playing house or cops and robbers, don't they find pleasure in playing the roles required by a partially prescripted scenario, rather than becoming anybody they want? Aarseth speaks here from the perspective of the hard-core computer game player who delights in finding ways to beat the game (known to insiders as cheats) that haven't been foreseen by the designers. A classic cheat allows, for instance, the player of *The Sims* to access a vast cache of money and to buy whatever he wants for his family. But if subverting the system in a computer game is an enjoyable sport, it is because the rules are so unbending that, precisely, players cannot cheat. Insofar as the rules are implemented by code, not freely accepted, as is the case with nondigital games, the use of cheats is not really cheating but a way to exploit the weak points of the system. In the case of interactive drama, by contrast, the player is given so much freedom (freedom of speech, that is) that derailing the parser is no longer a sport. I personally find much greater pleasure in getting the system to display its narrative intelligence and to produce interesting stories than in causing failure. If we cannot expect a certain degree of cooperativeness from other people, we will have to give up all but the most solitary of pleasurable activities.

The success of interactive drama depends on both medium-free and medium-specific rewards. The medium-free rewards reside in narrative features that we also expect from novels, drama, or film: characters for whom we care, even if we hate or despise them (as I relate to Grace and Trip), and a well-constructed, logically motivated plot. The medium-specific rewards lie in the replayability of the project, which depends on the active part of the system in the construction of the story, and in the sense that the system truly listens to the user. It would be easy to fake interactivity by giving the user a choice between several character names, and by linking each of these names to a fixed scenario. It is only by replaying the program several times, by seeing different story-variants develop, and by receiving intelligent responses to her input that the user will be convinced that she exercises true agency. The aesthetics of interactive drama lie neither entirely in the narrative displayed on the surface of the screen, for if they did we would be better off watching a DVD recording of *Who's Afraid of Virginia Woolf?* than playing *Façade,* nor in the underlying code, for code cannot be seen, but in the interplay between the two. We want to appreciate both the intelligence of the program and the drama on the screen, but more importantly we want to enjoy ourselves in the storyworld.

We may not know how much can be accomplished with the idea of interactive drama until it receives the same financial and technological support as a game like *Doom III.* Academic projects such as *Façade,* which was developed over four years by its two authors, cannot come close to this kind of resources. If the game industry decides that interactive drama is commercially viable, *Façade* will be a preview of things to come; otherwise it may become a nostalgic glance at what could have been.

Depending on whether we think with the medium or think from the more familiar point of view of traditional literature, we will judge the current achievements of digital narrative in two contrasting ways. Some people will say: the electronic medium has produced nothing comparable to Shakespeare's tragedies, to Proust's *À la recherche du temps perdu,* or even to the great classics of the cinema. Digital textuality has failed to become a major force on the literary scene, the computer is no substitute for the book, and there is little hope that this situation will ever change. These people are both right and wrong: right because Proust's novels have nothing to gain by offering multiple choices, nor Shakespeare's tragedies by allowing the spectator to manipulate a character; and because print narrative is not threatened with going out of fashion. But they are also wrong, because, as Peter Lunenfeld has sharply argued about interactive cinema, you don't take something that works and try to fix it. Digital texts should not be expected to be enhanced versions of the novel, of drama, or of the cinema. Their achievements reside in other areas: freely explorable narrative archives; dynamic interplay between words and images; and active participation in fantasy worlds. Digital narrative is only a failure if we judge it by the criteria of the literary canon, this is to say, by the criteria of another medium.

8. Computer Games as Narrative

In this chapter, I propose to revisit a question that has split, but also animated and energized, the young academic discipline of video game studies: is the concept of narrative applicable to computer games, or does the status of an artifact as game preclude its status as narrative? This dilemma has come to be known as the ludology versus narrativism (or narratology) controversy. But the terms are slightly misleading, because the ludology camp enrolls the support of some influential narratologists, while the so-called narratology camp includes both straw men constructed by the ludologists to promote their position and game designers and theorists who use the terms "narrative" and "story" rather casually. My discussion of the controversy will cover three issues:

1. The theoretical question: can games be narratives or possess narrativity? If we answer this question positively (to kill narrative suspense, let me admit right away that I will), two more issues arise:
2. The aesthetic and functional question: what is the role of narrative within the game system?
3. The methodological or practical question: how can the concept of narrative be fruitfully invoked in game studies?

The Theoretical Question

The only feature that objectively and absolutely defines video games is their dependency on the computer as a material support.[1] But if there is a general tendency that distinguishes them from other formalized games (sports and board games in particular), it is their preference for organizing play as a manipulation of concrete objects in a concrete setting—in a fictional world rather than on a mere playfield. In chess, tic-tac-toe, and go, players move tokens in an abstract space structured by lines, points, and squares, and in soccer or baseball they are themselves the tokens that move on the playfield, but in the vast majority of computer games, especially recent ones, players manipulate avatars with human or humanlike properties situated in a world with features inspired by real geography and architecture, such as hallways, rivers, mountains, castles, and dungeons. Insofar as the actions of the player cause this world to evolve, computer games present all the basic ingredients of narrative: characters, events, setting, and trajectories leading from a beginning state to an end state. One may conclude that the unique achievement of computer games, compared to standard board games and sports, is to have integrated play within a narrative and fictional framework.[2]

Most game producers would agree with this pronouncement. Even in the 1980s, when computing power allowed only rudimentary graphics, developers promoted their products by promising a narrative experience that rivaled in its sensory richness the offerings of action movies. The games were packaged in colorful boxes that featured realistic action scenes, as well as text that wrapped the player's action in archetypal narrative themes. Games were presented as being about saving princesses and fighting monsters rather than merely about gathering points by hitting targets and avoiding collision with certain objects, even though the monsters and princesses were usually represented by geometric shapes that bore little resemblance to the fairy tale creatures they were supposed to stand for. Through these advertising techniques, designers asked the player's imagination to supply a narrativity that the game itself was not yet able to deliver. The investment of the game industry in narrative interest was boosted by technological developments that closed the gap between the game and its package, such as more memory, better graphics, higher speed, improved AI—all factors that contribute to more realistic settings and more believable characters, the prerequisites for a rich narrative experience. Here, for instance, is the story that advertises *Max Payne I*:

Three years back a young NYPD cop, Max Payne, came home one night to find his family senselessly slaughtered by a gang of drug-crazed junkies, high on a previously unknown synthetic drug. Now that same drug, Valkyr, has spread through the whole New York City like a nightmare plague, and Max Payne's on a crusade for revenge, out to get even. To Drug Enforcement Administration, DEA, this new drug was evil incarnate, to be stopped at any cost. Max's boss and best friend, the only one who knew his true identity, has been murdered, and Max's been framed for the slaying. Max is a man with his back against the wall, fighting a battle he cannot hope to win. Prepare for a new breed of deep action game. Prepare for pain.

The elective affinity (rather than necessary union) between computer games and narrative frequently surfaces in the talk of designers. In their seminal book *Rules of Play: Game Design Fundamentals,* Katie Salen and Eric Zimmerman devote an extensive section to "Games as Narrative Play" (2003, 376–419). The word "story" recurs like a leitmotif in the interviews with game designers conducted by Celia Pearce for the online journal *Game Studies.*

The pronouncements of game developers and the marketing strategies of game manufacturers weigh however little in the opinion of academic scholars. Dismissing the industry's use of the term "storytelling" as loose, informal talk, the school of game theorists known as "ludologists," whose members include Espen Aarseth, Gonzalo Frasca, Markku Eskelinen, and Jesper Juul, has rallied around an implicit battle cry that I would formulate as "Games are games, they are not narratives." While games may occasionally be dressed (or disguised ?) in narrative garb, "stories are just uninteresting ornaments or gift-wrappings to games, and laying any emphasis on studying these kinds of marketing tools is just a waste of time and energy" (Eskelinen 2001, conclusion). The acknowledged motivation of the ludologists in declaring games and narratives to be birds of a different feather that cannot truly hybridize (though they may engage in a superficial flirt) is the ambition to emancipate the study of computer games from literary theory and to turn it into an autonomous academic discipline. As Espen Aarseth writes: "When games are analyzed as stories, both their differences from stories and their intrinsic qualities become all but impossible to understand." Or: "Computer games studies needs to be liberated from narrativism, and an alternative theory which is native to the field of study must be constructed" (2004b, 362).

The only ancestry for their new discipline that the ludologists recognize as legal is the sociological study of games, as practiced by Johan Huizinga, Roger Caillois, and others. The ludologists believe, with good reasons, that what makes a game a game, and what distinguishes it from other games, is its set of rules, not the themes in which it is wrapped up. Focus on narrative issues would consequently distract the analyst from the heart of the matter. The stated ambition of ludologists is to develop an approach that does justice to the ludic dimension of games by focusing on "gameplay," this to say, on the agency of the player, which they see as a set of strategic options within a range defined by the game rules.

In their campaign against a narrative approach to games, ludologists have struck a surprising alliance with narratologists of the classical school. Narratology developed as the study of literary fiction, and the definitions of narrative proposed by its founding fathers reflect this exclusive focus. The most widely endorsed definitions among literary scholars present narrative as "the representation by a narrator of a sequence of events," or "telling somebody that something happened." Both of these definitions, if interpreted literally, presuppose a verbal act of storytelling and exclude consequently the possibility of mimetic forms of narrative, such as drama and movies. Ludologists (for instance, Eskelinen 2001, 3) are generally partial to the definition proposed by Gerald Prince in 1987, but since modified by its author, as noted in chapter 1:

> Narrative: the recounting . . . of one or more real or fictitious events communicated by one, two or several (more or less overt) narrators to one, two or several (more or less overt) narratees. A dramatic performance representing many fascinating events does not constitute a narrative, since these events, rather than being recounted, occur directly on stage. (1987, 58)

No wonder ludologists regard this definition as gospel: the same criteria that exclude drama from narrative work even better against games. But the trend today is to detach narrative from language and literature and to regard it instead as a cognitive template with transmedial and transdisciplinary applicability. Relying on the definition of narrative proposed in chapter 1, I examine below (and hope to refute) several arguments raised by ludologists against the narrativity of games.

The "Games and narratives are different things because they have different features" Argument

This argument consists of enumerating features of literary narrative and of film that do not occur in games. Here I will review some points that have been invoked by Eskelinen and Juul.

1. Even if games are built on stories, this does not make them narratives, because narratives involve "the presence of narrators and narratees" (Eskelinen 2001, 3). This restatement of Prince's position tells us that only language-based texts qualify as narratives. Anybody who follows the film theorist David Bordwell (as I do) will reject this argument: for Bordwell, narration occurs when signs are arranged in such a way as to inspire the mental construction of a story, and it does not necessarily imply a narratorial speech act. Moreover, this argument is not valid for all games. Just as film can present voiced-over narration, games can have narrators who tell through language what is currently happening. For instance, after a player in *EverQuest* slays a tiger, the bulletin board will say: "You killed the tiger."

2. Games can't be narratives because they do not allow the rearrangement of events that marks the distinction between story and discourse: "Games almost never perform basic narrative operations like flashback and flash forward. Games are almost always chronological" (Juul 2001, 8; see also Eskelinen 2001, 2). Actually, scrambling of chronological order may not be a standard feature of computer games, but it is being increasingly used in cinematic cut scenes. *Max Payne I,* for instance, uses flashbacks showing the character Max Payne watching the murdered bodies of his wife and children—a murder he is determined to avenge. Cut scenes allow no interaction, but I can think of some cases where flashbacks would not be detrimental to gameplay. For instance, if during a game of *Sims* the house of your family catches fire, and you have not bought a phone before the accident, all you can do is helplessly watch the fire consume everything and kill your characters one by one. But if the game offered a flashback option, you could go back to the time before the fire, buy a phone, return to the burning house, save your Sims, and avoid having to start the game from the beginning again.

3. Narrative has fixed order of events, games have open order: "[Plot-lovers] often conceive stories as mere plots or closed sequences of events, in which case they should come to grips with games containing open series of events" (Eskelinen 2001, 4). Yet not all games have open sequences of events: in the type that Juul (2005, 72–73) calls progression games, the player has to fulfill a quest by solving problems in a rigidly prescribed order. The free-floating events (such as the missed attempts at passing the tests) are those that do not propel the game forward. The structuration of games into levels suggests, similarly, a fixed structure on the macrolevel. Moreover, free order is only detrimental to story when it results in incoherent sequences of states and events; but well-designed games guarantee that each new situation will logically develop out of the preceding one by limiting the choice of actions available to the player.

4. Narrative must represent events as past, but games cannot do so. "In a verbal narrative, the grammatical tense will necessarily present a temporal relation between the time of the narration (narrative time) and the events told (story time). While movies and theatre do not have a grammatical tense to indicate the temporal relations, they still carry a basic sense that even though the viewer is watching a movie, now, or even though the players are on stage performing, the events told are *not* happening *now*" (Juul 2001, 7). But in an interactive medium such as games, "it is impossible to influence something that has already happened. This means that *you cannot have interactivity and narration at the same time*" (Juul 2001, 8). The narratologist H. Porter Abbott invokes a similar argument to exclude games from the narrative family (2002, 13, 31–32). For Abbott, narrative always concerns events (or imagined events) that are already "in the book" of history; it is this pastness that enables the narrator to select materials from memory and to configure them according to narrative patterns. Yet if the retrospective stance is the prototypical narrative situation, there are many types of narrative that do *not* look back at past events: for instance, the counterfactual scenarios of virtual history; the promises of political candidates: "If you elect me, this and that will happen"; the Grand Narratives of religion, whose last events, the Second Coming and Last Judgment, are yet to happen; and in their best moments, when they rise above chronicle and create a sense of plot, the narrative in real time of sports broadcasts.[3] Another problem with regarding narrative as necessarily retrospec-

tive is that it cannot account for the experience of film and drama. As many critics have observed, images, unlike language, create the illusion of the immediate presence of their referent. A movie can admittedly flash the titles "England, 1941," "Los Angeles, 1950," or "New York, 2002" *(The Hours),* and the spectator will realize that the events took place at various points in the past. But once the pictures begin to move, the spectator experiences the events as taking place in the present. The same phenomenon occurs in novels. Written narrative uses tense, a device unique to language, to express temporal remove, but immersed readers transport themselves in imagination into the past, and they apprehend it as "now" regardless of the tense used. Even when stories are ostentatiously told by looking backward, they are experienced by readers, spectators, and arguably players by looking forward, from the point of view of the characters. There are consequently only superficial differences, in terms of the lived experience of time, between games, movies, and novels.

But let's imagine that Eskelinen's and Juul's observations present no exceptions: no games have narrators; they place no restrictions whatsoever on the sequence of events; and they do not tolerate tampering with chronological order, while novels, movies, and the theater behave in the exact opposite way. Let's further assume that game players experience the action as happening now, while novel readers and movie or drama spectators always remain conscious of the difference between the time of the narrated events and the time of narration, even though the events never really happened. Would it mean that games cannot suggest stories? No, it would simply mean that they do so in a partly different mode from novels, drama, and movies. As we have seen in chapter 1, every medium capable of narrativity presents its own affordances and limitations; why, then, couldn't video games present their own repertory of narrative possibilities?

The "Games are simulations, narratives are representations" Argument

This argument rests on the observation that games, unlike novels and movies, are different every time they are played: "But traditional media lack the 'feature' of allowing modifications to the stories, even if exceptions happen in oral storytelling" (Frasca 2003, 227). Here Frasca captures an important difference between games and "traditional media narratives," but why should their variable character disqualify games as narratives? Besides oral storytelling, story-generating programs and hypertext novels also produce variable outputs. For Frasca, the variability of games is incompatible with narrativity, because narratives are in essence representations, while variability is the product of a process that he calls simulation: "There is an alternative to representation and narrative: simulation . . . Traditional media are representational, not simulational. They excel at producing both descriptions of traits and sequences of events (narratives)" (223). Frasca defines simulation in these terms: "To simulate is to model (a source) system through a different system which maintains (for somebody) some of the behaviors of the original system" (223). As the term "behavior" suggests, a simulation is a dynamic system that models a dynamic process. A representation may also offer an image of a dynamic process; for instance, a film may show an airplane taking off, but it presents only one image, while a simulation will model multiple instantiations of the same process: in a flight simulator, the airplane can perform many different takeoffs.

Frasca's characterization of games as simulations is appropriate in the case of representational (dare one say narrative?) games, but questionable in the case of abstract games: simulation suggests external referents, but games like chess, Go, or *Tetris* do not model anything outside themselves. As Jesper Juul (2005, 60–61) has shown, the concept of state-transition machine, or finite state acceptor, provides a more general theoretical model of games. A state-transition machine is an automaton made of five elements: a finite set of states; an input alphabet (the possible actions by the user); a next-state transition function, which leads the machine from one current state to another depending on the input; a start state; and one or more end states, interpreted in a game as winning or losing (Savitch 1982, 31).[4] Simulations are technically state-transition machines whose elements depict something external to themselves: state 1 is interpreted as the airplane on the ground, state 2 as the airplane in the air, and the transition is initiated by the player's hitting a certain key. It takes, consequently, a mimetic dimension to turn a state-transition machine into a simulation of something.

While the simulation machine cannot in itself be called a narrative, each of its individual runs produces images of a world that undergoes changes as the result of events. In other words, games may not be stories, but they can be machines for generating stories. English does not make any distinction between a game as a system of rules, and a particular instance of playing a certain game, but if it did (as does French), the narrative status of games would be easier to grasp. "A game" (French: *une partie*) of a certain game (French: *d'un certain jeu*) will produce an output on the computer screen, which may trigger the cognitive template constitutive of narrativity. The open character invoked by Frasca as a significant difference between games and narratives is thus a feature of the game viewed as machine; but each "game of the game" produces a fixed sequence of events that actualizes one of the possible stories allowed by the system.[5]

What is needed to accept games as narrative machines is the proposal that I make in chapter 1: recognizing other modes of narration than "telling somebody that something happened." As we have seen, literary theory already accepts dramatic enactment, or mimesis, as an alternative to representation, or diegesis. My suggestion, then, is to regard simulation as a legitimate member of the paradigm that includes these two modes.

The "Games are like life, and life is not a narrative" Argument

According to Aarseth, the proper model for the gaming experience is life itself, rather than reading novels or watching movies. He bases the analogy of games and life, as opposed to "stories," on several arguments. The first is the personal involvement of the player: "in games, just as in life, the outcomes (winning, losing) are real and personal to the experiencer, unlike in stories" (2004b, 366). But winning and losing are experiences specific to games, at least when winning and losing are pursued for their own sake and determined by strict rules. In real life, by contrast, the outcome of actions is evaluated in terms of practical goals. You do not win or lose the game of life (despite the popularity of this metaphor); you succeed or fail at concrete attempts to satisfy your desires.[6] In abstract games such as chess and *Tetris,* the values of winning and losing are arbitrarily attributed to states that would not matter to the player if it weren't precisely for the emotions attached to winning and losing. In the type of game that I call narrative, on the other hand, winning and losing are linked to the kinds of event that matter *intrinsically* to the experiencer, such as acquiring valuable objects, averting dangers, and fulfilling missions, but the experiencer is the avatar and not the real-life persona of the player. In other words, players win or lose because avatars reach their concrete goal or fail to do so. It is precisely because all the unpleasant experiences that occur during games—killing, getting hurt, or dying—do not count in the real world that games are enjoyable. Inverting Kendall Walton's claim that literary fiction is like games because it involves make-believe, we can say that the reliance of video games on make-believe brings them closer to the narratives of literary and cinematic fiction than to life itself.

Another of Aarseth's arguments invokes the player's relative freedom of action: "In a game, everything revolves around the player's ability to make choices." Choice is also a feature of life, while novels and movies are entirely pre-scripted. But why couldn't the player's choices be interpreted by the player in narrative terms? Aarseth anticipates this objection through an argument borrowed from Ragnild Tronstad: the game experience is a matter of engaging in a quest, not of receiving a story (2004b, 368–69). While narrative involves constative acts, the quests of games as well as the quests of life belong to the order of the performative: the player's actions makes events happen, rather than describing them. But if the player's input counts in the game-world as the performance of actions, these actions are replayed on the screen through constative acts of the system. These constative acts may take the form of verbal retellings, for instance, when the bulletin board of *EverQuest* flashes the message "you killed the tiger," but most of the time they consist of animated visual sequences. Without this possibility of watching an image of the game-world, players would have no idea of the consequences of their actions, and they would not be able to play the game intelligently. This means that players are not only agents but also spectators of their own pretended actions. The game experience is therefore halfway between living life and watching a movie. Moreover, game action operates on symbols, within a designed environment, whereas real-life action operates on material objects within a world thrown together for no obvious purpose.

We must concede to Aarseth that the interactivity of games brings them a step closer to life than do movies and novels, but the ontological divide between unmediated and mediated experience, between working on things and working on their images, between an objectively existing world randomly put together and an imaginary world designed for a specific purpose, outweighs the divide between choice and no choice, because in the case of games, choice concerns only pretended actions without durable consequences for the player. If games were actual life, players would be responsible for their actions in games, and most of them would end up in jail. The opposition of games and life to the various forms of narrative is therefore fallacious; rather, there is life on one side, and its various modes of imitation on the other, including the diegetic narration of novels, the mimetic enactment of drama, and the interactive simulation of games. (See Figure 13 for a comparison of games, life, and traditional forms of narrative.)

Telling Stories about Games

When players of computer games recount their experience, they frequently do so by telling a story. For instance, a lengthy passage of Espen Aarseth's essay "Methodological Approaches to Game Analysis" consists (ironically) of a narrative of his experience in the fictional world of *Morrowind*:

> With an unlimited supply of money, I could buy the training and weapons I wanted, and become a master fighter, the scourge of *Morrowind*. No monster too dangerous, no quest too hard. I could explore freely, and I could enter the most dangerous places I could find, such as the volcano at the center of the world. There, in a dungeon, liven a demon named Dagoth, and this, finally, was an opponent worthy of my might and magic. (2003a, 5)

Is this retellability of games evidence of their narrativity? Janet Murray thinks so: "Games are always stories, even abstract games,

	Designed for a certain purpose	Relevance of winning and losing	Choice of action	Perceived events affect the life of the experiencer
Life	–	–	Unrestricted	+
Games	+	+	Restricted by design	–
Novels and film	+	–	None	–

Figure 13. Comparison of life, games, and standard narrative media

such as checkers or *Tetris*, which are about winning and losing, casting the player as the opponent-battling or environment-battling hero" (2004, 1). To prove this claim, Murray tells a story about *Tetris*, perhaps the most abstract of computer games: "This game is a perfect enactment of the overtasked lives of Americans in the 1990s—of the constant bombardment of tasks that demand our attention and that we must somehow fit into our overcrowded schedules and clear off our desks in order to make room for the next onslaught" (1997, 144). For Murray, games and stories share an important structure: "the contest, the meeting of opponents in pursuit of mutually exclusive aims." This structural analogy leads Murray to wonder: "which comes first? The story or the game? For me, it is always the story that comes first, because storytelling is a core human activity, one we take into every medium of expression, from oral-formulaic to the digital multimedia" (2004, 1).

These are the kind of statements that fan the antinarrativist fire of the ludologists. They would reply to Murray that it is possible to tell stories about anything; but this does not make "everything" into a narrative. Aarseth might argue that his retrospective account of his adventures in the world of *Morrowind* differs as much from the actual game experience as being raped differs from reading about rape in J. M. Coetzee's *Disgrace*. For the ludologists and their allies in the narratology camp, retellability is not a sign of narrativity, because, as H. Porter Abbott has argued (2003, 33), games are like life: they provide materials for stories, but they are not stories in themselves.

I would like to defend an intermediary position between Murray's extreme narrativism and the ludologists' rejection of the concept of narrative. For me some games have a narrative design and others do not. For a game to lend itself naturally and effortlessly to retelling, its narrative design must be more developed than the general analogy between competitive games and the rivalry of the hero and the villain in archetypal narratives: it must reside in the concrete surface structure, and not merely in the abstract deep structure. Chess, for instance, is a classical example of warlike, competitive deep structure, and it is one of the most complex and fascinating games in existence, but it is also one of the most resistant to narration. Chess games are reported in terms of precise moves on a grid (A3 to A4, E5 to F3, B3 to F7), and not by narrative statements such as: "The Queen, worried about the safety of the King, made a daring sortie to chase the knights of the opposing army back into their camp." As we have seen in chapter 4, sports games are much more amenable to narration than chess, even though they are not built around stories, but this is mostly because sports broadcasters constantly inject the action on the playfield with information concerning real-world and human interests. It is only when the development of the game starts resembling the deep structure of a dramatic plot, with sudden reversals of fortune or heroic deeds by the underdog, that the broadcast can concentrate exclusively on the action on the field. But the main source of the tellability of sports games lies in the fact that the spectators/hearers develop emotional relations to the players as persons and care passionately about the outcome, as if the fate of their city depended on the performance of its team. The strength of this link to the real world, as well as their attractiveness as spectacle, make sports unique among abstract games.

For the vast majority of games, (re)tellability is a function of the particular nature of the generated events. It is easy to narrate the adventures of your Sims family—how Bob got depressed about not finding a job, how the house caught fire, how Betty saved everybody by calling the fire department—but it is hard, if not impossible, to tell stories about fitting blocks of various shapes falling from the top of the screen into a neat row. Murray's allegorical reading of *Tetris* is not a narration of a particular playing session but a subjective interpretation of the game, as defined by its timeless rules. Other players may interpret the game very differently, but most likely they will not interpret it at all. For a game to inspire *specific* retellings, to be *narratively designed,* it must involve actions whose purpose is not just winning or losing but fulfilling a concrete goal. It cannot, therefore, be about aligning three tokens on a line on a game board, nor about kicking a ball into a net. But it can be about stealing cars or using cars to chase bank robbers. Above all, it must take place in a fictional world, and not merely on a playfield. While retellings should not be confused with the live game experience—players, like fishermen, are prone to aggrandizing their exploits—they suggests that a mental act with narrative content takes place during the playing of the game. Players learn from past mistakes and plan strategies for future actions by mentally constructing the developing story of the game. The greater our urge to tell stories about games, the stronger the suggestion that we *experienced the game narratively.*

Figure 14 represents the contrast between abstract and narrative games by tracing it back to a distinction between two types of human action: practical and ludic. The ultimate purpose of practical actions is to ensure our survival (for instance, by acquiring material goods), while the purpose of ludic actions (playing games) is to provide entertainment. According to Huizinga, ludic actions take place in their own time and space, and they are not connected with material interests (1955, 13). But they are supported by gestures that take place in the real world, just as the actions of drama characters in the fictional world are supported by the gestures of actors on the stage. Ludic actions must therefore be analyzed into a physical and a symbolic, game-specific component. This game-specific component can either mimic other actions or constitute a species without equivalent outside the game of which the actions are a part. A mimetic ludic action can in turn simulate either a practical or a ludic action: the first case is represented by children's games of make-believe and by the type of computer games that I call narrative, the second case by games that simulate other games, such as computer versions of chess, Go, football, or golf. Most of these simulations concern abstract games, but it is not out

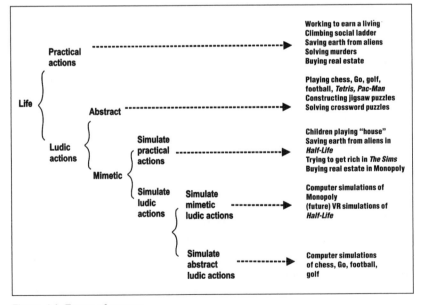

Figure 14. Types of games

of the question that an advanced computer technology may one day simulate older, narrative computer games. An example of this situation would be a full-body version of a first-person shooter taking place in either virtual reality or augmented reality. For a game to convey a story, then, it must either simulate practical actions or simulate other games that themselves simulate this type of action.

The Aesthetic and Functional Question

When the antinarrativist school runs out of suitable theoretical materials in its efforts to build a protective wall around game territory, it switches to aesthetic arguments: "Adventure games seldom, if ever, contain good stories," writes Espen Aarseth (2004a, 51), in an apparent concession to narrativism: for a bad story is still a story, unless one works aesthetics and tellability into the definition of narrative. "Much of the vast journey that it takes to complete Half-life would be excruciatingly dull if retold in any detail," writes Jesper Juul (2001, 5), mindless of the fact that people don't particularly care for detailed retelling of novels and movies either.

In 2001 the hypertext promoter and theorist Mark Bernstein issued a challenge to the game community: find me a game that speaks of serious human interests, such as sexuality (as does literature, and by extension literary hypertext).[7] Whether or not some games have met this challenge is a matter of opinion, but the question betrays a dubious desire to find the same kind of gratification in both games and literary narrative and to submit them to similar evaluation criteria. A game does not need to tell stories that would provide suitable literary material to immerse the player in the fate of its fictional world, because the thrill of being in a world, of acting in it and of controlling its history, makes up for the intellectual challenge, the subtlety of plot, and the complexity of characterization that the best of literature has to offer. The pursuit of large audiences by the game industry and its reluctance to take risks explains in part why it has been sticking so far to stereotyped narrative themes and formulae, such as medieval fantasy, science fiction, thrillers, horror, and the mystery story. But through their emphasis on action, setting, and imaginary creatures of fantastic appearance, these narrative genres are much more adaptable to the interactive and fundamentally visual nature of games than "high" literature focused on existential concerns, psychological issues, and moral dilemmas. Literature seeks the gray area of the ambiguous, while games and popular genres thrive in the Manichean world of "the good guys" versus "the bad guys" (Krzywinska 2002): if players had to debate the morality of their actions, the pace of the game, not to mention its strategic appeal, would seriously suffer.

Many commentators attribute the difficulty of creating truly good game stories—not necessarily the equivalent of *Hamlet*, but, more modestly, stories as engrossing as the novels and films of popular culture—to the inherent incompatibility of interactivity and narrativity. According to the game designer Greg Costikyan, "Creating a 'storytelling game' (or a story with game elements) is attempting to square the circle, trying to invent a synthesis between the antitheses of game and story" (online, 9). As I have observed in chapter 5, the root of the conflict between narrative design and interactivity (or gameplay) lies in the difficulty of integrating the bottom-up input of the player within the top-down structure of a narrative script: if the player's choices are too broad, there will be no guarantee of narrative coherence; if the choices are too narrow, the game will be boring. But a conflict can be seen as a challenge, and its resolution as an artistic feat. This is how Costikyan envisions the situation:

> Precisely because the two things—game and story—stand in opposition, the space that lies between them has produced a ferment of interesting game-story hybrids. And yet the fact remains: game and story are in opposition, and any compromise between the two must struggle to be successful . . . So should designers eschew attempts to inject story into the games they design? By no means; past efforts to do so have been fruitful, and have led to interesting and successful games. What designers must do, however, is understand that they are not involved in the creation of stories; gaming is not inherently a story-telling medium. (online, 9)

For Costikyan, a game is primarily a game, not a story, and an interesting gameplay represents the only valid criterion of success; otherwise game designers could just as well switch to the writing of novels or movie scripts. When conflict arises between story and gameplay, story should be subordinated to gameplay, rather than gameplay to story.

In many types of computer games, as I observe in chapter 5, the narrative design is not the focus of the player's attention but an "affective hook"[8] that lures players into the game. This is particularly true of first-person shooters (FPS). Once players are absorbed in the fire of the action, they usually forget whether they are terrorists or counterterrorists, humans defending the earth from invasion by evil aliens or aliens conquering the earth. Having fulfilled its role as a lure, the story disappears from the player's mind, displaced by the adrenaline rush of the competition.

This ancillary role of narrative offers a better justification for an opposition of games to the traditional narrative genres of novels and movies than the narratological considerations mentioned previously. Yet games are not the only texts that use stories as a means toward goal, rather than displaying them for their own sake: sermons, philosophical writings, political speeches, and advertisements frequently make their point through parables and narrative examples. In the opera, similarly, the plot of the libretto functions as a support for music, and while a good libretto enhances the work, the opera is evaluated on the basis of the music and not the plot. It is certainly not on the basis of the story that *The Magic Flute* is recognized as one of the greatest operas ever composed. If an opera or advertisement can tell stories without ceasing to be an opera or advertisement, why couldn't a game do the same thing? Narrative is not a genre that excludes other genres but a type of meaning that permeates a wide variety of cultural artifacts, and the ludologist claim that game and story form mutually exclusive categories betrays a lack of understanding of the nature of narrative. The fact that games may subordinate narrative to gameplay rather than making it a focus of interest can be easily accounted for by recognizing an instrumental mode of narrativity. Tweaking an expression coined by David Herman, we may call the games that use this mode "narratively organized systems for playing."[9]

Yet some game narratives are more memorable than others: it may not matter to serious chess players whether their pieces are called kings and queens or cats and dogs; and shooters will be mostly remembered for the sophistication of their weapons, not for the concrete mission given to the player; but as Stuart Moulthrop observes, you could not replace Lara Croft of *Tomb Raiders* with a "less salacious anatomy" (2004, 47) without a significant impact on the game experience. Or to take another example, the appeal of the Harry Potter video games resides as much, if not more, in finding oneself in a favorite fictional world with beloved characters and familiar activities, such as Quidditch matches, as in solving the particular problems presented by the game. Appealing in variable proportions to the strategic mind and to the imagination, computer games are an art of compromise between narrative and gameplay. If designers had truly fascinating stories to tell, they would write novels and film scripts rather than games. If the rules were as productive as those of chess and Go, we would not need the narrative. But a stereotyped story can be redeemed by interesting player action, while a game without originality on the level of rules can be improved by narrative packaging. In the design of games, gameplay and narrative remediate each other's deficiency.

The idea of an instrumental mode of narrativity explains why stereotyped game-stories can do their job without rivaling the aesthetic appeal of literature, yet it does not do justice to the diversity of computer games, nor to the diversity of interests found among their players. Following Plato, Roger Callois (1961) distinguished two types of games: *ludus* and *paidia*. *Ludus* corresponds to what Jesper Juul calls the "prototypical game situation," a situation he defines through the following conditions: (1) prototypical games are rule-based; (2) they have a variable, quantifiable outcome; (3) values are attached to the outcomes (winning or losing); (4) players invest efforts to influence the outcome; (5) players are attached to the outcome—they want to win and hate to lose (2005, 36).[10] *Paidia,* meanwhile, is a free play without computable outcome, characterized by "fun, turbulence, free improvisation, and fantasy" (Motte 1995, 7). While *ludus* dominates board games, sports, and many computer games, especially FPS, *paidia* is represented by all the games that are played for the sake of an imaginative experience: children's games of make-believe, playground activities, the use of toys, the transgression of social rules that takes place during the carnival, and within video games, by the so-called simulation games *(SimCity, Civilization, The Sims)* in which players manage a complex system and observe its behavior, rather than trying to pass levels or to beat opponents.[11] It is perhaps the major contribution of the computer to human entertainment to have allowed a combination of *ludus* and *paidia* within the same game environment—a combination that Caillois thought impossible: for him, games were either rule-based or invitations to make-believe (1961, 8–9).

In a classic paper, the MUD designer Richard Bartle has distinguished four types of players among the denizens of virtual worlds:

killers, achievers, socializers, and explorers.[12] Though the labels are self-explanatory, let me quote Bartle for a thumbnail characterization of the four types:

> Achievers regard points-gathering and rising in levels as their main goal, and all is ultimately subservient to this. . . . Killers get their kicks from imposing themselves on others. . . . [They] attack other players with a view to killing off their personae. . . . Socialisers are interested in people, and what they have to say. The game is merely a backdrop, a common ground where things happen to players. . . . Explorers delight in having the game expose its internal machinations to them. . . . The real fun comes only from discovery, and making the most complete set of maps in existence.

Killers and achievers are primarily *ludus* players, socializers and explorers *paidia* players. We can expect these four types of players to display significantly different attitudes toward narrative. Killers and achievers may regard the game-story as a quickly forgotten, disposable commodity, good only to provide clues for progressing in the game. Socializers will exchange stories about the game-world, perform small narrative scripts of their own invention, and generally enjoy the enactment through role-playing of the narrative design written into the game. As for explorers, they will view the game-world as a space full of stories awaiting discovery: the legends that explain landscape features, the gossips of nonplaying characters about people and places, the knowledge of the natives that will lead them into new territories. When explorers play games of emergence such as *The Sims*—games without a built-in script— they find their pleasure in coaxing new stories out of the system to find out how it works.

Far from being always subordinated to gameplay, narrative sometimes forms the purpose of playing. In both online and singleplayer virtual worlds, many players use "walkthroughs"—solutions posted on the Web—to perform the tasks given to them by the game. For these players, being taken step by step through the storyline of a quest, and getting to see more of the fictional world in the process, is more important than solving problems all by themselves. Interest in game-worlds as narrative environments has been boosted by the phenomenon of the game camera. *The Sims,* for example, features a camera that enables players to save screenshots from the game. Some players put these screenshots together into stories, adding text to the images, and post the results on a Web site specially dedicated to this type of project.[13] The stories do not necessarily retell the events generated by the player during the game session. But players have been known to manipulate the game in order to produce certain shots that will fit into the stories they want to tell. From a "narratively organized system for playing," *The Sims* database has been subverted into a "ludically organized system for storytelling." These formulae describe the two ends of a spectrum that accommodates a wide variety of games and player preferences.

The Methodological Question

Jesper Juul has recently made a conciliatory move toward narrativism by endorsing the concept of fictional world: "While all games have rules, most video games also project a fictional world" (2005, 121).[14] For a narratologist (or at least, for a narratologist of the cognitivist school), capturing a fictional world that evolves in time under the action of intelligent agents is all it takes for a semiotic artifact to fulfill the semantic conditions of narrativity—and no ludologist would deny that game worlds present these properties. It may turn out in the end that the quarrel between ludologists and narrativists (if I may speak for this elusive class) revolves more around the scope of the term "narrative" than around the nature of games, for I am not aware of any narrativist claiming that games are the same thing as novels and movies. But whether we speak of "narrative" or of "fictional world," these terms capture a dimension of video games that ludology cannot ignore any longer: the thrill of immersing oneself in an alternative reality.

The standard narrative approach to games has so far been comparative studies of games adapted from film or literary narratives, or vice versa, of the less common occurrence of movies adapted from games. But as the following list suggests, the concept of narrative has more "ludologic," more game-centered contributions to make to the new discipline:

1. Investigate the heuristic use of narrative. As Salen and Zimmerman have shown (2003, 396), creating a game-story, rather than listing a series of abstract rules, is an efficient way to facilitate the learning process. If an object on the screen is an abstract shape, we must learn from the user's manual how to manipulate it; but if it looks like a car, and if it is involved in a narrative scenario rele-

vant to cars, the user will know that it can be used to move around in the gameworld, for instance, to escape enemies.

2. Explore the various roles and manifestations of narrative in computer games:

- the narrative script that is designed into the game
- the narrative that players write though their actions, actualizing a particular sequence of events within the range of possibilities offered by the built-in script
- the narrative that lures players into the game (cut scenes and background information that introduce the game; text on the box)
- the narrative that rewards the player (cut scenes that follow the successful completion of a mission)
- the microstories told by nonplaying characters
- (for games with recording devices): the narratives that players make out of the materials provided by the game

3. Describe the various structural types of game narrative. For instance: *narratives of progression* (Juul 2005, 72–73), structured according to the flowchart, where players follow a fixed, predominantly linear narrative script that takes them through discrete levels; *narratives of emergence* (Salen and Zimmerman 2003), structured as a playground, where players choose their own goals and actions in a world teeming with narrative possibilities; and *narratives of discovery,* featuring two layers of story, "one relatively unstructured and controlled by the players as they explore the game space and unlock its secrets; the other pre-structured but embedded within the mise-en-scène awaiting discovery" (Jenkins 2004, 126).

4. Investigate how the game story is dynamically revealed to the player: how much of this story is told top-down, through noninteractive cut scenes, how much is discovered when the player takes the right action or finds the right information within the gameworld, and how much emerges bottom-up, through the choices of the player. Are the player's actions an integral part of the plot, or merely a way to gain access to spaces where more of the story will be revealed? How are the personality and past history of the avatar presented to the player? When the player gets to know his avatar only gradually, how can he take meaningful actions for this character when he is still incompletely acquainted with him? Which elements in the dialogue between the avatar and nonplaying

characters have ludological functions (that is, provide clues on how to solve problems), and which ones serve the narrative function of fleshing out the characters and the fictional world?

5. Map the fictional world and its objects against the rules of the game. We can distinguish several types of game objects, and several types of relations between objects and rules: (1) Objects internal to the fictional world attached to rules. The player can manipulate them, and they fulfill both a strategic and an imaginative function—what Kendall Walton calls "a prop in a game of make-believe." The rules, however, may or may not be consistent with the nature of the object, as we will see below. (2) Objects internal to the fictional world not attached to rules. The player cannot do anything with them, and their function is purely imaginative. They are the video game equivalent of Barthes's "reality effect." (3) Objects external to the fictional world attached to rules, such as the buttons of a menu. The function of these objects is purely strategic. Theoretically we could have objects external to the fictional world not attached to rules, but these objects would be useless.

6. Evaluate the connection between gameplay and narrative: could the same system of rules be narrativized in many different ways, or is there an organic, necessary connection between rules and narrative?[15] Do the problems presented to the player grow out of the narrative theme, or are they arbitrarily slapped upon it? (Critics of the game *Myst* argue, for instance, that there is little connection between the game-story and the problems that need to be solved in order to unfold it.) When the player solves a problem, does he understand the narrative logic of the actions that led to the solution, or do the problem-solving actions appear random to him?

7. Ask whether the rules and the events they create are consistent with the fictional world. Why is it, for instance, that in *The Sims* you must pay for commodities, but there is always food in the fridge, even when there is no money left in the bank? As Juul observes,

> in many cases, the fictional world gives the impression that many things are possible which are not implemented by the rules. The reverse case is when the rules allow for actions that the fictional world does not cue the player into expecting. Many first person shooters of the late 1990's featured wooden crates which turned out to contain medical kits and other items that the player could

pick up. For an inexperienced player this is nonsensical and not cued by the representation: only the trained player knowing the conventions of the game genre would understand it. (2005, 179)

The main reason for using narrative concepts in game studies is to come to terms with the imaginative dimension of computer games—a dimension that will be overlooked if we concentrate exclusively on rules, problem-solving, and competition. As I suggest above, the major innovation of computer games compared to standard board and sports games is to allow a combination of strategic action and make-believe within the same environment. The ludologists' approach, so far, has heavily favored the point of view of a specific type of player, namely, the "hard-core gamers" who devote most of their free time to games, play in a ruthlessly competitive spirit, know the system well enough to modify the rules or to program new levels, and are so familiar with the structures and conventions of games that they can jump right in, "ignoring game guides, opening cinematic, and in-game cut scenes" (Salen and Zimmerman 2003, 411). But as Bartle's player typology indicates, not all game players are killers and achievers, and even those players who prefer *ludus* to *paidia* are not necessarily insensitive to the particular embodiment of the game-world. I am not proposing a literary approach that isolates narrative scripts from the rules of the game and studies them for their intrinsic aesthetic merit (though such an approach would be justified if game narratives rose to an appropriate aesthetic level), but rather, a functional ludo-narrativism that studies how the fictional world, realm of make-believe, relates to the playfield, space of agency. By connecting the strategic dimension of gameplay to the imaginative experience of a fictional world, this approach should do justice to the dual nature of video games.

9. Metaleptic Machines

Metalepsis, a rhetorical and narrative figure described as early as the seventeenth century,[1] has become one of the favorite conceptual toys of postmodern culture and contemporary critical discourse. In this chapter I propose to explore its special affinities with computers, as well as its multiple manifestations in digital culture. Before I get to computers, however, let me survey other areas of metaleptic activity, starting with its literary homeland.

Narrative

To explain the concept of metalepsis, I will resort to the metaphor of the stack (Figure 15), a metaphor that should be familiar to every computer programmer.[2] A stack is a multileveled data structure whose components are processed in an order known as LIFO: last in, first out, as opposed to the queue, whose order of processing is first in, first out. The notion of diegetic levels introduced by Gérard Genette to describe the phenomenon of the proliferation of stories within stories offers a narratological equivalent of the computer stack. Every language-based fictional narrative involves at least two levels: a real-world level, on which an author communicates with a reader, and a primary fictional level, on which a narrator communicates with a narratee within an imaginary world. Whenever a narrative generates another narrative it adds another level to the narrative stack. This process is commonly known as *framing* or *embedding,* but here I will avoid these terms for fear of mixing my metaphors.

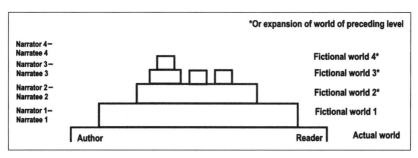

Figure 15. The narrative stack

The border between levels may be of two kinds: illocutionary or ontological. The first type occurs when a text-internal storyteller presents a story as true fact, as happens when a newly introduced character explains the circumstances that brought him on the scene. Here the boundary marks a change of speaker, but the represented world remains the same. The second type occurs when a story is told as fiction, creating not only a change of narrating voice but also a change of world. In this case the reader must recenter herself into a new fictional world and start building its mental image from scratch, rather than viewing this world as an expansion of the world of the preceding level. The pushing of a new story on the top of the stack interrupts the current story and divides the cognitive activity of the reader between the tale of the highest level, which always occupies the center of attention, and the unfinished stories of the lower levels, which remain present in the back of the mind. This division of attention explains why narrative stacks rarely reach more than three or four levels.

When a story is completed, it is popped from the stack, and the narration returns to the preceding level. The narrative stack, like the stacks maintained by the operating system of the computer, must be taken apart in the reverse order of its construction. It would be logically dangerous for a narrative to jump from the third to the first story level without revisiting and closing the story of the second level. Take, for instance, the case of *The Arabian Nights,* a work with an exceptionally tall stack: on the first fictional level, the text tells the story of Scheherazade and the Sultan. On the second fictional level, Scheherazade's storytelling creates the world of the "Three Ladies of Baghdad." Within this story, each of the three ladies tells her life story. Within Amina's story a young man does the same thing. When the young man concludes his narration, the reader expects the narrative to return to Amina's tale, then to the main tale of the "Three Ladies of Baghdad," and from there to the story of Scheherazade and the Sultan. A jump from the young man's tale to the story of Scheherazade, leaving the other stories hanging, would constitute a violation of narrative closure and a betrayal of the reader's expectations.

But literature thrives on transgressions, especially in the present age, and with its rigid boundaries and fixed order of processing, the stack offers a particularly tempting target for transgressive activities. Metalepsis is the operation by which narrative challenges the structure of the stack. Etymology tells us that the term is composed of two Greek roots: the prefix *meta*, "what is above or encompasses," and a suffix from the verb *lambanein*, "to grab." Metalepsis is a grabbing gesture that reaches across levels and ignores boundaries, bringing to the bottom what belongs to the top or vice versa. Though narratologists have not undertaken a systematic typology of metalepsis, the use of the term in the current literature falls into two main categories: (1) the rhetorical type, described by Gérard Genette,[3] and (2) the ontological type, described by Brian McHale in conjunction with postmodern narrative.

Nearly all the metalepses found in literature before the twentieth century belong to the first type. Rhetorical metalepsis interrupts the representation of the current level through a voice that originates in or addresses a lower level, but without popping the top level from the stack. This operation is represented in Figure 16. Genette illustrates the figure through the following quote from Diderot's *Jacques le fataliste*: "Qu'est-ce qui peut m'empêcher de marier le Maître et de le faire cocu" ("What prevents me from marrying the master and making him a cuckold?") (1972, 244).

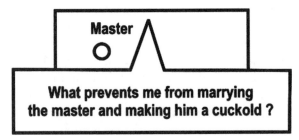

Figure 16. Rhetorical metalepsis

This sentence is not spoken by a prospective bride but by an authorial figure who wonders what he should do with his character.
Another example would be this sentence from John Fowles's *The
French Lieutenant's Woman,* where an authorial voice looks at his
characters from what could be the ground level of the stack: "These
characters I created never existed outside my own mind" (1969,
80). An aside to the audience in drama would constitute a rhetorical metalepsis looking in the other direction: from the fictional
world toward the real one. Rhetorical metalepsis opens a small
window that allows a quick glance across levels, but the window
closes after a few sentences, and the operation ends up reassert-
ing the existence of boundaries. This temporary breach of illusion
does not threaten the basic structure of the narrative universe. In
the rhetorical brand of metalepsis, the author may speak *about* her
characters, presenting them as creations of her imagination rather
than as autonomous human beings, but she doesn't speak *to* them,
because they belong to another level of reality. Communication
presupposes indeed that all participants belong to the same world;
this is why speaking to the spirit world is generally considered a
paranormal activity.

   Whereas rhetorical metalepsis maintains the levels of the stack
distinct from each other, ontological metalepsis opens a passage between levels that results in their interpenetration, or mutual contamination. These levels, needless to say, must be separated by the
type of boundary that I call ontological: a switch between two radi-
cally distinct worlds, such as "the real" versus "the imaginary," or
the world of "normal" (or lucid) mental activity versus the world of
dream or hallucination. Though McHale does not distinguish two
types of metalepsis, he clearly envisions an ontological operation
when he compares the figure to the "strange loops" and "tangled
hierarchies" described by Douglas Hofstadter in *Gödel, Escher,
Bach.* According to Hofstadter, "A Tangled Hierarchy occurs when
what you presume are clean hierarchical levels take you by surprise
and fold back into a hierarchy-violating way" (1980, 691). In a narrative work, ontological levels will become entangled when an existent belongs to two or more levels at the same time, or when an
existent migrates from one level to the next, causing two separate
environments to blend. The consequences of this operation for the
narrative stack are shown in Figure 17. We may compare rhetorical
metalepsis to a benign growth that leaves the neighboring tissues

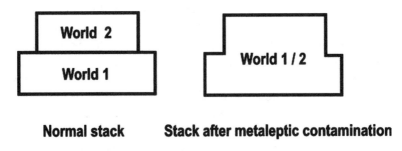

Normal stack   Stack after metaleptic contamination

Figure 17. Ontological metalepsis

unaffected, and ontological metalepsis to an invasive growth that destroys the structure of these tissues.

A classic example of ontological metalepsis is the short story by Woody Allen, "The Kugelmass Episode." In this story, the hero visits a psychoanalyst who offers to solve his problems by transporting him by means of a special machine into the world of the novel of his choice. Kugelmass selects Flaubert's *Madame Bovary,* and he begins a love affair with the heroine. This greatly upsets the literature professors of the Ivy League, for when they open the book to discuss it in class, they find Emma Bovary making love to a New York Jew instead of eloping with Rodolphe or Léon. Through the metaleptic operation, the imaginary Emma has migrated into the fictionally real world of Kugelmass, and the fictionally real Kugelmass has migrated into what is from his point of view the imaginary world of *Madame Bovary.* Should we say that Emma becomes real when she visits New York in the primary fictional world, or that Kugelmass becomes fictional when he visits Emma in the France of Flaubert's novel? The two levels are so hopelessly entangled that it becomes a moot question. Other examples of ontological metalepsis would be the meeting and interacting of author and characters in the same space, such as we find in Pirandello's *Six Characters in Search of an Author,* where characters beg the author to turn their lifestory into a drama, or in John Fowles's *The French Lieutenant's Woman,* where an author persona travels in the same train carriage as the hero of his novel.

Another way to represent ontological metalepsis is through the image of the snake that bites its own tail, a literal rendering of the concept of the strange loop. A strange loop phenomenon, according to Hofstadter, "occurs whenever, by moving upwards (or downwards) through the levels of some hierarchical system, we un-expectedly find ourselves right back where we started" (1980, 10). Though the strange loop is largely equivalent to the tangled hier-archy, some narrative situations are more easily described through the first image, and others through the second. An example that can be mapped equally well by both models is the very short story by Julio Cortázar, "Continuity of Parks." In this story, a reader character becomes absorbed in a novel about a plot by a woman and her lover to assassinate the woman's husband. The characters of the book within the story are first presented as two-dimensional literary creations, but the imagination of the reader-character gradu-ally fleshes them out into three-dimensional live individuals. At the height of the reader's immersion, the boundary between fiction and reality collapses, and the reader becomes the victim of the murder. The strange loop model explains the phenomenon by claiming that the stack curves back on itself, as its top level become the ground level, while the tangled hierarchy model would say that the world of the reader and the world of the book collapse into each other. Though the two models are formally equivalent, the image of the strange loop is more efficient when metalepsis involves overt self-reference—a phenomenon to which I will return below—while the tangled hierarchy is better at explaining those situations where characters travel between ontological domains. Though all meta-leptic phenomena arguably draw the reader's attention to the stack-ing of realities that defines the structure of the fictional text, only a subset of them offers *literal* cases of self-reference.

In all the examples I have discussed, the so-called reality that becomes affected by the events of a higher level is not the world in which the actual reader and author are located but the first level of the fictional tower. A story can represent the murder of a fictional reader by the protagonist of a fictional novel, but the only way for a real-world author to kill the actual reader would be by nonliterary means, for instance, by sprinkling anthrax between the pages of the book. In other words, the actual base of the narrative stack, the world of ground zero, remains protected from metaleptic phe-nomena. Though Hofstadter does not use the term "metalepsis," he comes to a similar conclusion when he claims that in the "strange loop" etchings of Escher, such as the one in which two hands draw each other, the paradox can be resolved by assuming that the artist and the spectator are located outside the system (1980, 716).

This protection of the real-world foundation of the stack means that ontological metalepsis, in contrast to the rhetorical version, is incompatible with a realistic framework. We all know that in everyday life we will never meet Emma Bovary, and that we have nothing to fear literally from fictional murderers. Since ontological transgressions cannot involve the ground level of reality, they cannot, by analogy, occur in a fictional world that claims to respect the logical and physical laws of the real world, unless they are confined to the private sphere of an insane individual who confuses the real and the imaginary, such as Don Quixote. Rather than challenging our mental models of the world we live in, metalepsis represents an attempt to expand the empire of fiction toward the most remote worlds within the universe of the imaginatively possible. The current thriving of the fantastic demonstrates that literature encounters no difficulties in revoking the physical laws of the real world and in introducing new species in a fictional world, such as orcs or hobbits; but transgressing the laws of logic is an infinitely more delicate operation, because, as Umberto Eco (1979) has argued, if contradiction makes its way into a fictional world, every descriptive statement will be true and false at the same time, and it will become impossible for the reader to imagine a concrete universe with stable properties. Though metalepsis denies some fundamental logical distinctions, it limits its destabilization to certain types of oppositions, and it does not throw the fictional world into complete chaos. The characters of a metaleptic fiction may transgress the principle of noncontradiction on the level of what Terence Parsons (1980) calls extranuclear properties—being real or imaginary—but they remain consistent on the level of their concrete, nuclear properties: the reader-character of "Continuity of Parks" may belong to two incompatible worlds at the same time, but in each of these worlds he is either dead or alive.

This containment of contradiction, and the fact that the ground level of reality remains protected in fiction by a make-believe reality, turn the literary manifestations of metalepsis into a relatively harmless game, at least if we read them literally rather than allegorically. Jean-Marie Schaeffer and John Pier (2002) have indeed observed that metalepsis lends itself far better to "comic and ironic" than to "tragic and lyric" effects.[4] But metalepsis is far more than a trick of the trade of the postmodern novelist, and the boundaries that it threatens involve other territories than the (fictionally) real and the imaginary. Any hierarchical system can be trumped, whether the levels are rhetorical or ontological, visual or musical, social or technological, spatial or temporal, semantic or cognitive. As Hofstadter's discussion of the strange loop phenomenon brilliantly demonstrates, metalepsis occurs not only in the arts but also in logic, mathematics, language, and science. When it affects these disciplines, metalepsis carries far more disturbing epistemological consequences than the playful subversion of narrative logic. For even if the metaleptic processes described in the next section do not necessarily invalidate logic, mathematics, and the scientific method, they certainly raise troubling questions about the limits of these modes of thinking.

Mathematics, Logic, and Experimental Science

The most famous example of the epistemological implications of metalepsis is the theorem proposed by the Viennese mathematician Kurt Gödel in his 1931 paper "On Formally Undecidable Propositions." The purpose of the theorem is to demonstrate that every formal mathematical system satisfying certain conditions— such as being capable of higher-level reasoning, that is, of reasoning about itself—is either incomplete or contradictory. A system is incomplete when it contains true propositions that cannot be proved, while a system is contradictory when some of its propositions are true and false at the same time, in violation of the principle of noncontradiction. In his presentation of Gödel's method, Hofstadter demonstrates that the proof is based on an idea similar to the paradox of Epimenides, the famous Cretan philosopher who pronounced the immortal judgment: all Cretans are liars. Since Epimenides was a Cretan, he was a born liar; consequently he lied; but if he lied, Cretans are truthful people; consequently he spoke the truth; and so on in an infinite series or reversals that represent the logical equivalent of a Möbius strip. The metaleptic dimension of the paradox resides in the fact that the utterance is self-referential, a feature more evident in its condensed version, "This sentence is false." In a normal situation, this type of sentence refers to another sentence, for instance: "This sentence is false: 'the earth is flat.'" The case of external reference can be represented by a snake ("This sentence is false") that bites another snake ("The earth is flat"). The first sentence is actively used by an imaginary speaker to express a proposition, while the second is merely mentioned as the subject matter of the propositional act. In a self-referential situation, by contrast, the snake bites its own tail, since the same words are both used and mentioned. Self-reference thus collapses the philosophical distinction between use and mention.

The implicit target of Gödel's theorem is the monumental project of Bertrand Russell and Alfred North Whitehead, *Principia Mathematica*, as well as any equivalent formal system. As Hofstadter explains, "*Principia Mathematica* was a mammoth exercise in exorcising Strange Loops from logic, set theory, and number theory" (1980, 21). To keep logical levels strictly separate, self-reference should be forbidden in formal systems, and these systems should only be allowed to speak about a language in a metalanguage. If such restrictions applied to natural languages, such as French or German, it would be necessary to invent an entirely new semiotic system to define the words of the lexicon. This operation would make it possible to avoid the notorious circularities of the dictionary, but at the exorbitant price of infinite recursion, since the semantics of this metalanguage could only be specified in a meta-meta-language, which itself would necessitate its own metalanguage. A paradoxical discipline, semantics must choose between the Charybdis of endlessly accumulating levels, and the Scylla of their confusion. But in formal mathematical systems, the strange loop of metalepsis appears inevitable. Gödel's proof consists of demonstrating that through perfectly legal manipulations, a system such as *Principia Mathematica* can be made to produce Cretan propositions that are true when they are false, and false when they are true. To reach this conclusion, Gödel introduces a system of numerical coding that makes it possible for a formula of the system to offer simultaneously a theorem of number theory and a statement concerning its own status as theorem of the system. This formula, which is rigorously derived and should therefore be regarded as a truth in the system, can be paraphrased by the sentence "I am not a theorem." Since the truth-status of the formula is unassailable, its existence offers two choices: if it is not accepted as a valid theorem, it constitutes a truth that cannot be proved, and the system is incomplete; but if the formula is accepted as theorem, the system allows contradiction. Metalepsis is the cancer that destroys from within the ambitions of totalitarian mathematical systems. But this cancer is not particularly aggressive, and while it cannot be cured, it will not kill the patient. Mathematical logic has not discarded its foundational concepts, and there are still truths waiting to be discovered and proved, still theorems waiting to be added to formal mathematical systems.

It is also through metaleptic arguments that some twentieth-century physicists have suggested the limits of science. What do these arguments tell us? That scientific objectivity, which presupposes a rigid separation between the observer and the observed phenomenon, is a partially utopian ideal, because in some circumstances the experimental process modifies its object.

This point is made by the famous thought experiment of Schrödinger's cat. Schrödinger took his inspiration for the story from the well-established fact that the behavior of subatomic particles—the subject matter of quantum mechanics—cannot be predicted with absolute certainty. As Brian Greene explains, "If a particular experiment involving an electron is repeated over and over again in an absolutely identical manner, the same answer for, say, the measured position of an electron will *not* be found over and over again" (1999, 107; italics original). We can determine the probability that a subatomic particle will be found in a specific location, but we cannot predict which one of these possibilities will be actualized. The sum of all the probabilities is known as the *wave function* of the particle, and it is captured, for the electron, by the famous Schrödinger equation. According to an interpretation widely associated with the Copenhagen school of quantum mechanics (Niels Bohr, Werner Heisenberg, Max Born),[5] the wave function collapses when an observation is made, so that elementary particles will be found in one specific location, rather than in all the possible states predicted by the wave function. But before the observation is made, the electron exists in a superposition of all possible states. Schrödinger exposed the paradox through the following story: a cat is sealed in a box together with an atom of uranium that has a 50 percent chance of decaying in a certain time span. Being a quantum phenomenon, the decay cannot be predicted. Now imagine that if the decay takes place, a poison gas will be released that kills the cat. Before you open the box, the atom will have both decayed and not decayed, and the cat will be in a superposition of states, dead and alive at the same time. It is the action of opening the door that sends the cat either to Hades or back to her favorite pillow.

According to the physicist Werner Heisenberg, famous for his formulation of the uncertainty principle,[6] "the transition from the 'possible' to the 'actual' state takes place during the act of observation" (quoted in Woolley 1992, 221). Schrödinger's imaginary experiment suggests the contamination of the world by the attempt to study its laws: it is no longer the referent that determines the content of the image but rather the construction of the image that determines the behavior of the referent.[7] The objectivist ideal represented in Figure 18a gives way to the subjectivist stance of Figure 18b.

In Figure 18a the complementary character of the relations of causality and mimesis confers stability to the image: here the world determines the content of the image, and the image represents the world. In 18b, by contrast, the world and the image are linked by the same relation, and they determine each other in a vicious circle that undermines the possibility of their absolute distinction. But the case of Schrödinger's cat, as well as Heisenberg's uncertainty principle, concerns quantum physics phenomena situated on the smallest scale of reality. As Brian Greene (1999, 3) has argued, the main problem that faces theoretical physics is that elementary particles seem to obey different laws than large-scale phenomena. According to Hofstadter, the principle of uncertainty should be kept in its proper context, and nothing authorizes its generalization into "The observer always interferes with the phenomenon under observation" (1984, 456), a formula that has become something of an article of faith in critical science studies. Objectivity may be elusive, but it remains a valid ideal, and the inevitability of some degree or some areas of metaleptic contamination does not necessarily threaten the entire scientific project.

Computer Science

When Alan Turing invented the machine that bears his name and laid down the foundations of informatics, he proposed a theorem

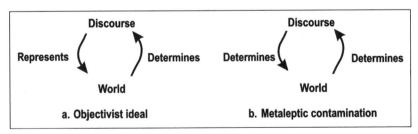

Figure 18. (a) Scientific realism; (b) scientific relativism

whose proof comes very close, in its spirit and method, to the proof of Gödel. This theorem demonstrates that the so-called halting problem cannot be solved.[8] The resolution of the halting problem consists of constructing an algorithm capable of determining, for all programs P and all inputs I, whether P operating on I will terminate properly or will lead to an infinite loop. This algorithm would itself be a program PP, which would take P and I as its inputs and would output the verdict "proper termination" or "infinite loop." The existence of such a metaprogram would make it superfluous to actually run the programs in order to know whether or not they terminate cleanly on a given input. Since a program could, at least in principle, run for a thousand years before terminating clearly, or alternatively, run forever, this could be a useful tool. We would know whether or not the program is worth running without waiting a thousand years (provided the metaprogram runs faster!). But the importance of Turing's theorem is mainly theoretical. The unsolvability of the halting problem means that there exist perfectly well-defined functions that cannot be computed by a Turing machine, and consequently by the most powerful computer. In other words, it does to computer science what Gödel's theorem does to mathematics. I will not go into the details of Turing's proof, but I will briefly sketch the metaleptic mechanism that makes it similar to Gödel's: a program is translated into a numeric coding that enables it to operate on itself, and this leads to a contradiction: if the program was going to terminate with itself as input, it goes into an infinite loop, and if it was going to go into an infinite loop, it terminates cleanly. The algorithm PP will consequently fail in at least one situation.

It is particularly easy for computers to create or fall by accident into strange loops and tangled hierarchies, because their binary language does not distinguish program instructions from input data, nor does it overtly mark the difference between numbers and alphanumeric characters. Take, for instance, the case of the binary sequence 01100001. The string may be interpreted by the machine as an instruction (such as rotate left or shift right the content of the processor), as a number (the decimal number 97), or as a letter (lowercase a). It is consequently not impossible for a computer to execute numerical or alphanumerical data as if they were program instructions, or conversely, for a program to be treated as input data. A program could even be made to store its results within the memory segment where it resides, thus overwriting its own code and replacing it with garbage. This self-modifying program would produce rather strange results on its second iteration. Disasters of this sort are usually prevented by the operating system and by the compiler or interpreter of the program. While the operating system partitions memory into sections devoted to data, and others reserved for instructions, so that programmers cannot make their programs overwrite themselves (unless they use instructions such as the infamous "peek" and "poke" of the BASIC language), the compiler or interpreter checks the compatibility of data and will not let the user add two variables declared as alphanumeric data. But every hacker familiar with the internal organization of the system knows how to get around these security features. Viruses, for instance, are instructions hidden in data files. Once they are inadvertently activated by the user, these metaleptic creatures ignore the levels of the machine's architecture, reproduce themselves uncontrollably, infect other files, and create chaos within the system. They are potentially far more invasive than the strange loops of mathematics and quantum physics, though it is only in science fiction (namely, in Neal Stephenson's *Snow Crash*) that they can cross the screen and infect the user.

In a more positive domain, it is to the metaleptic process of the feedback loop that Artificial Intelligence owes the power to create emergent systems, this is to say, systems capable of modifying themselves unpredictably, or of creating objects that adapt themselves dynamically to changing environments. In a feedback loop, the result of a function is recycled as input value, enabling this function to generate a system in constant evolution. If we place the function $f(x) = y$ in a feedback loop, for instance, the value of y obtained on the first evaluation yields the value of x for the second pass. It is this double role of the same value as input and output of the *same* function that suggests metalepsis, though the levels of the evaluation process remain clearly distinct.[9]

Another aspect of the computer that renders it hospitable, but also vulnerable, to metalepsis is the hierarchical character of its architecture. A computer is like a series of machines piled up on each other, the bottom ones so complicated that they are only understood by professionals, the top ones simple enough to be operated by the general public. (See Figure 19.)

On the ground level is the "real" machine, made of physical hard-

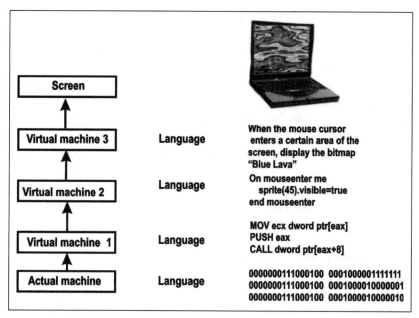

Figure 19. Computer architecture

ware. This machine, which cannot be changed, except by replacing electronic chips, and understands only machine language formulated in binary code, forms the support of a number of machines known in the jargon as "virtual," because they lack any material existence. These virtual machines accept instructions written in languages far easier to understand for human users than binary code, such as standard programming languages (BASIC, LISP, Java, C); high-level languages (PROLOG, Lingo) that look more and more like natural languages; click and drag actions that do not require coding from the user (as used in Flash, Director, or Dreamweaver), or, at the limit, spoken language itself. In order to be executed, the instructions given to these virtual machines must be translated by a compiler or interpreter into the binary language of the real machine. Virtual machines may lack physical existence, but to the user, they are as good as the real one, because they enable her to perform the tasks she has in mind without any detailed knowledge of the organization and mode of operation of the actual computer.

The stratified architecture of the computer is not in itself metaleptic, no more than the narrative stack of *The Arabian Nights,* but it creates opportunities for metaleptic operations of technological nature (viruses, programs that operate on themselves), as well as for manipulations that lead to ludic and artistic effects. The rest of this chapter will be devoted to metaleptic and quasimetaleptic features in digital texts. By metaleptic feature I understand a transgression of levels that involves contradiction, such as what I call above "ontological metalepsis," and by quasimetaleptic a form of playing with levels that remains compatible with a rational explanation, such as rhetorical metalepsis or effects of *trompe l'œil* that fool the user for a short period of time. To put it differently: in a genuine metalepsis one level actually and definitively invades another; in a pseudometalepsis, it only *seems* to invade or it does so only temporarily.

Code Poetry ("Codework")

As the architecture sketched in Figure 18 demonstrates, the behavior of all digital texts is regulated by the invisible code of a program. The presence of this code opens the possibility of moving down one level and playing with what we may call the "digital underwear" of the text. This gesture is the defining feature of a movement within new media literature known as "codework" poetry. The interplay of code and text can take many forms, offering various degrees of metaleptic contamination.

Dig out the code from under the screen. In an operation similar to "pressing the reveal code key" of the word processor, a digital text can offer a glimpse at the code that produces it, then return to a normal display. An example of this practice is found in a multimedia CD-ROM that I have coauthored, *Symbol Rock*,[10] made with the program Director. At one point in this text, the user explores an abandoned ranch by clicking on the rooms of the floor plan. But if she mouses over a hidden hot spot, the screen will display the Director code with which this particular screen was generated, as well as a pseudo assembly language translation of the Director code. This glimpse behind the stage shows how the text is made, but it does not present the code as an artwork, and it does not question the distinction between instrumental code and artistic text. It is therefore equivalent to what I describe above as rhetorical metalepsis.

Produce text that imitates code. Another way to play with the hierarchical organization of the computer is to create a blend of human and computer language. N. Katherine Hayles (2002, 50) calls this blend a "creolization" and illustrates it with the following excerpt from Talan Memmott's *Lexia to Perplexia*:

> From out of NO.where, Echo appears in the private space of Narcissus.tmp to form a solipstatic community (of 1, ON) with N.tmp, at the surface. The two machines—the originating and the simulative—collapse and collate to form the terminal-I. a Cell.f, or cell . . . (f) that processes the self as outside of itself—in realtime.

Neither operative code, nor traditional fiction or poetry, *Lexia to Perplexia* creates a predominantly graphic combination of alphabetical symbols—used to represent so-called natural languages—with graphemes borrowed from computer code and formal notation systems. If this text speaks to us, it is more on the metalevel, as symbolic gesture, than through the lexical meaning of its individual components. We may view this new idiom, allegorically, as the language of the cyborg or the posthuman, Donna Haraway's (1991) and Hayles's (1999) respective terms for the augmentation of human intelligence through the computer's unique capabilities. Alternatively, we could interpret this allusion to computer code as a new twist on McLuhan's self-reference–emphasizing, and therefore metalepsis-promoting, slogan, "the message is the medium."

A much closer imitation of computer language is found in Marjorie Luesebrink's adaptation of *Lexia to Perplexia*. Luesebrink took the real code of *Lexia to Perplexia*—the HTML and Java script code necessary to display the text properly on the screen, did some minor rewriting of the code to enhance visual appearance, tinkered with the fonts and the alignments, added an interesting graphic background, and posted the result as a poem in its own right (Figure 20).[11] More than a graphic blend, this text represents the metaleptic surfacing of a normally hidden layer of text and the accession of this layer to artistic status. But the operations performed by Luesebrink on the coded version of *Lexia to Perplexia* are purely cosmetic: by her own admission, she was not concerned with the integrity of the code. When I tried to execute the text, it worked for a while, displaying Memmott's text with certain fonts and colors and creating windows on the screen, but it eventually lead to a script error.

Combine the operative function of code and the aesthetic function of poetry. According to the digital poet John Cayley (2002, 7), a nonexecutable code poem is not a creole but a pidgin: a simplified

```
            <FONT class=whtT>Part of me is all used up, not enough,

  <A HREF="javascript:hide('TAB04');hide('TAB05');hide('TAB03');">[-1]</A> -

      the world has accelerated, raised stakes and frequency - pitched - at the edge,

           leaning out/into open [spaceless] space - the actualized delusion,

       dysillusion of the <A HREF="#" onmouseover="show('noteartaud');"

onmouseout="hide('noteartaud');">corpus artaud</A>, this sign and that are laid end to end,

      overlapped to extend the <A HREF="#" onmouseover="show('notepremise');"

   onmouseout="hide('notepremise');">premise</A>, the I that I am there.

       I am not who I want to be there - I am not enough - I am antiquated so

        <A HREF="javascript:closeOff();">pull the plug why don't you</A>
```

Figure 20. The code of Talan Memmott's *Leia to Perplexia*, displayed as poetry by Marjorie Luesebrink. Reprinted with permission.

language, a remix, a purely decorative collage. Trying to take the idea of code poetry beyond the stage of pseudocode, an active school of poet-programmers uses the language Perl to produce texts with a dual purpose. For a Perl text to be successful, it should not only address human concerns when read as a poem, but it should also generate a meaningful output when executed as code; otherwise we could just as well read regular code as poetry or feed the binary version of famous poems into the computer and watch them produce garbage.[12] For instance, Eric Andreychek's poem "Perl Port of Jabberwocky" is not only a humorous parody of Lewis Carroll's almost eponymous nonsense poem, it also outputs two lines of text when executed as code, and it launches three "dysfunctional" processes—processes that neither harm the system, nor do anything useful—corresponding to the three main characters of the poem: the speaker, his son, and the Jabberwock.[13] Here is an extract:

```
#!/usr/bin/perl

$brillig and $toves{slithy};
for $gyre ( @wabe ) {} for $gimble ( @wabe ) {}
map { s/^.*$/mimsy/g } @borogoves
and $mome{raths} = outgrabe;
```

tell $son, "And hast thou slain the Jabberwock?".
    "Come to my arms, my beamish boy!".
    "O frabjous day! Callooh! Callay!",
$_{joy} = chortle if $son;

$brillig and $toves{slithy};
for $gyre (@wabe) {} for $gimble (@wabe) {}
map { s/^.*$/mimsy/g } @borogoves
and $mome{raths} = outgrabe;[14]

Here is the output of the Perl code:

Beware the Jabberwock! at jabberwocky.pl line 8.,
Beware the Jujub bird at jabberwocky.pl line 10.

Another project of Perl poets is to write code that generates poetry automatically. In his essay "Pressing the Reveal Code Key," John Cayley describes an automaton of his invention that combines the ideas of the executable poem and of the poetry-generating code. This automaton produces text-code in the following steps:

1. Cayley writes an essay on the aesthetics of digital poetry.
2. He writes a program (in the high-level language HyperTalk) that produces a new text out of the old one by randomly selecting certain expressions and combining them acording to semi-aleatory processes.
3. He take the code of this program, and replaces the variables with fragments culled from the text produced in step 2.

Here is a truncated sample of the end product of this process (the original is far too long to quote):

on violation
set cursor to none
put false into subversive
put true into intimate
go to card reader
put empty into card field agents
hide card field agents
if performed then
put zero into poetic
hide message
put accuracy into change

```
put false into performed
end if
repeat until ideals are developed
if poetic is greater than change then exit repeat
if reader is not "code" then add one to ideals
if compromised then
put operations into card field agents
end if
if compromised then
lock screen
hide card field agents
do "unlock screen with dissolve " & fantasies
end if
end repeat
end violation
```

Of another of his code poems, similar in syntax to this one, Cayley writes:

> The text has genuinely ambiguous address—to a HyperTalk interpreter and to human readers. It could (and does, in some versions of the software) alter the behavior of a system, when included as one routine in a text generator. Its address to human concerns is clearly ludic and, perhaps, pretends more than it delivers in terms of significance and effect, but at least we can say, with little qualification, that this code is the text. (2002, 13)

Cayley's claim that the texts generated through the algorithm described above produce meaningful output when executed as code is fully believable. All that he has done is take operative code and change the names of the variables, which does not affect the syntax. If the replacement of variable names is consistent, the manipulated version should therefore work just as well as the original code. The products of Cayley's efforts are certainly more executable than run-of-the-mill poems, and thanks to the words that were chosen to fill the variables—*subversive, intimate, poetic, violation*—they are more poetic than run-of-the-mill code, but they cannot compete with human-generated poetry in the area of aesthetic appeal and human interest. The skeptics will say that code poetry constitutes a pointless hybridization. But if art is defined as the overcoming of self-imposed constraints and of "needless obstacles," as it is for OULIPO (Ouvoir de Littérature Potentielle) school of literature, then this text is indeed an impressive achievement. It all depends on whether it is judged on the basis of the originality of the process through which it was created, or on the basis of the output. Rejecting the WYSIWYG (what you see is what you get) approach that dominates interface design, code poetry tells us that in order to appreciate the text we have to dig below its surface and understand how it was made.

This philosophy is pervasive in digital arts, whether visual, textual, or mixed. As Christiane Paul observes: "A notable characteristic of digital images that focus on aspects of encoding and visualization is that the process and meaning of an image do not always reveal themselves on the visual level but often rely on external contextual information to help 'explain' the work" (2003, 51). For Lev Manovich, today's Web artist is no longer the modernist / romanticist who creates from scratch, nor the postmodernist who denatures and recycles artworks to draw attention to the representation of reality by media, but the "software artist" who leaves "his/her mark on the world by writing original code" (on-line, 6). When applied to the appreciation of computer-generated poems and stories, this philosophy can turn dull texts into exciting programming feats. Most attempts to write programs that produce literary texts have been disappointing, especially in the narrative domain: hardly anybody would read a computer-generated story for entertainment, unless some bug in the program introduced inadvertent comic effects.[15] But the reader familiar with Artificial Intelligence may admire a story-generating system, such as Talespin (Meehan), Minstrel (Turner), or Brutus (Bringsjord) for the sophistication of its algorithm rather than for the aesthetic quality of its output. Performing "reverse engineering," this reader derives pleasure from imagining the hidden code of the system, from assessing the extent of its internal representation of the narrative world—what we may call its narrative intelligence—and from guessing the heuristics that underlie the program's decisions. The same approach can be taken to the work of poets such as John Cayley or Loss Pequeño Glazier, who instead of writing poetry directly focus their artistic activity on the production of poetry-generating algorithms. The appreciation of the underlying code pushes traditional literary aesthetics, which is linked to the surface text, below the aesthetics of programming on the stack of the reader's priorities, in an inversion of levels that may not be strictly metaleptic but still challenges the structure of a hierarchical system.

Computer Games

Computer games offer a particularly favorable environment for metalepsis: as programs that produce fictional worlds, they can play with the levels of world and code; as worlds that invite the player to play the role of a character, they can exploit the contrast between the player's real and fictional identities; and as fictional worlds, they can resort to many of the metaleptic tricks of standard literary fiction.

Jesper Juul observes that if the fictional world of a video game is a world in a traditional sense, "it would make sense to assume that the characters in that world are generally unaware of their being fictional characters or of being part of a game at all" (2005, 183). But Juul mentions a game that contradicts this assumption. In *Super Mario Sunshine,* a Nintendo game played on the GameCube, an object that is part of the gameworld talks about the layout of the GameCube controller. When the player meets this object, it introduces itself as "The FLUDD," and offers to provide instructions, such as telling the player which button to press on the GameCube controller in order to operate a nozzle. In so doing, it communicates with the player on the real-world level, though the nozzle is part of the game world. As Juul concludes: "It is a mixing of fictional levels when an object in the fictional world knows about things in the real world and knows that it is a part of a GameCube game" (183). This metaleptic effect is much more user-friendly than what we find in postmodern literature. The function of the FLUDD is not to break the game of make-believe that makes the player regard the fictional world as real but, on the contrary, to enable the player to learn how to play the game without having to leave the fictional world. The FLUDD is therefore an immersion-preserving device that integrates real-world discourse—the instructions of the game—into the fictional world. At first sight this process may seem to contradict what I write above about the immunity of the real world from metaleptic processes, but all that happens in this case is a transfer of information between levels that combines the features of rhetorical and ontological metalepsis. The operation is ontological, because the Flubb is aware of the operation of the computer in the real world, but it is also rhetorical, because once the Flubb disappears, the fictional world regains its autonomy with respect to reality.

The computer game *Metal Gear Solid 2* offers a case of metalepsis that operates in the other direction: a phenomenon native to the fictional world invading, or rather pretending to invade, the real world.[16] In *Metal Gear Solid 2*, the player impersonates the agent Raiden, who is on a mission for the U.S. army. Toward the end of the game Raiden infects a computer within the game world with a virus. His superior, Colonel Campbell, shouts: "Raiden, turn off the console, now! . . . Don't worry, it is just a game. It is a game just like the usual. You ruin your eyes sitting this close to your TV." The speech act of Colonel Campbell is first addressed to the character Raiden, who is of course unaware that he is a fictional character manipulated by a player. But the discourse gradually crosses the ontological boundary that separates the player's avatar from the player himself, and it ends up describing the actual situation of the player: wasting his time with a game, rather than accomplishing heroic missions. This is the video-game equivalent of Pirandello's characters addressing their author.

In another metaleptic move, *Metal Gear Solid 2* simulates the transmission of the virus from the computer within the game-world to the machine that runs the game. After Colonel Campbell's warning, the screen flashes the message "Fission Mailed" (instead of "Mission Failed"), and it seems for a while that the game is actually over. When the game resumes, it does not fill the whole screen but plays in a small window, as if the virus had actually damaged the player's system, though without fully destroying it. In *Metal Gear Solid 2*, metalepsis is pure bluff: the game pretends to infect the real-world computer but doesn't really dare to affect the system.

Recent games have devised much more invasive ways to affect the real world than the make-believe metalepsis of *Metal Gear Solid 2*. In the somewhat mislabeled genre of "alternative reality gaming," the gameworld spills into the real world by making its gamemasters contact the user in person at any time of the day or night by phone, e-mail, or even by ringing his doorbell.[17] As a result of this intrusion, the playing field and playing time are no longer separated from the space and time of ordinary life, as they are in standard games. The appearance (rather than the actual occurrence) of a fusion of fiction and reality may someday be made possible by the much-talked-about technology of Augmented Reality.

In Augmented Reality, games will project the images of characters on a real landscape, rather than on a computer screen, and the fictional world will blend for the senses with the real world.

What would it take for metalepsis to *really* spill into the real world and affect it *physically*? It would be fairly easy to write a computer game that destroys the user's system. Such a feature would of course be self-defeating from a commercial point of view, since once the word got out, nobody would buy the product. But this reasoning does not apply to free gifts, as the damages caused by a type of digital creature known as a "Trojan Horse" demonstrate. According to the 2002 user's guide for Norton's antivirus software, "Trojan Horses are programs that appear to serve a useful purpose or provide entertainment, which encourage you to run them. But the programs also serve a covert purpose, which may be to damage files or place a virus on your computer."

In the artistic domain, the only form of representation that could conceivably create a metaleptic bleeding of the textual world into reality is dramatic acting. Jean Genet demonstrates how this could be done in his play *Les Bonnes (The Maids)*. Solange and Claire are two maids who stage a play in which they represent the murder of their hated mistress, Madame. Solange, who plays Claire, offers a poisoned drink to Claire, who plays Madame. This results in the death of Claire, and in the criminal conviction of Solange. A real-world actor, similarly, could stab another actor to death rather than faking a murder. It is from this metaleptic possibility that "snuff" movies derive their perverse appeal.

Virtual Reality

We all know that the experience of Kugelmass, who penetrates into the world of *Madame Bovary*, is only possible in a novel or film. But if the technology of Virtual Reality ever reaches the level of sophistication promised by its early prophets, it will someday be possible to simulate imaginary worlds through three-dimensional displays. The immersive-interactive experience of VR will not only open these worlds to our bodies for a multisensory apprehension of the environment; it will also enable us to manipulate the objects that furnish virtual worlds and to converse with their inhabitants. In a VR system shaped after the Holodeck, the visitor experiences the narrative in a variety of ways: as a character in the plot, she lives her destiny; as coauthor of the script, she writes the lifestory of her character; as an actor, she impersonates her character; and as a spectator, or at least as the beneficiary of the show, she is supposed to be entertained by her own performance. This accumulation of roles realizes a metaleptic blending of the various modes of participation in a dramatic action. Whether or not interactive drama in a virtual environment represents the artistic future of VR technology, it takes little effort to read its basic concept as the metaleptic dream of a corporeal, and therefore literal, passage into an imaginary world. As Brenda Laurel puts it, the goal of VR is to make it possible to "take your body with you into worlds of the imagination" (1993, 124). But the body that participates in a computer simulation remains anchored in the real, just as the body of an actor inhabits the space of the stage and not the world of the play. If the body that reaches imaginary worlds is a virtual or make-believe body, then the technology itself can accomplish nothing more than a virtual or make-believe metalepsis.

VR technology is still in infancy, and not many of us have personally experienced a three-dimensional, multisensory electronic simulation. But the fascination exercised by the idea of virtual reality on the popular imagination is so strong that the term tends to be associated with the totality of the realm of information that we access through the Internet, in other words, with the mythical cyberspace itself, without distinguishing the elaborate make-believe worlds of multiplayer games such as *EverQuest* or *Ultima Online* from the Web sites where we conduct the business of the real world, such as eBay or Amazon. In the language of the media, all these domains are equally virtual. Since the Internet plays an increasing role in our daily life, it is not surprising that the philosopher Jean Baudrillard, prophet of doom of the culture of mass media, has appropriated the concept—or is it only the phrase?—of virtual reality and turned it, at least for a while, into the culprit of the ultimate metaleptic nightmare: the advent of the hyperreal, which means the replacement of the real by a simulation. In an essay that precedes by over a decade the popularization of the idea of VR, Baudrillard distinguishes four stages in the development of the image:

1. It is the reflection of a basic reality
2. It masks and perverts a basic reality
3. It masks the absence of a basic reality
4. It bears no relation to any reality whatsoever: it is its own pure simulacrum. (1994, 6)

This evolution can be read as a critical interrogation of the phenomenon of representation. If the image can be truthful (1), it can also lie (2); if it lies, it hides the fact that it does not correspond to an external state of affairs (3); if it does not depict an external referent, it takes the place of this missing referent (4). In this last stage, the levels of the representational stack collapse into each other, and we inhabit simulacra. In a more recent text Baudrillard finds a name for the perpetrator of this "perfect crime" against reality:

> With the Virtual, we enter not only upon the era of the liquidation of the Real and Referential, but that of the extermination of the Other.
> It is the equivalent of an ethnic cleansing which would not just affect particular populations but unrelentingly pursue all forms of otherness.
> The otherness [. . .]
> Of the world—dispelled by Virtual Reality. (1996, 109)

If we take Baudrillard to the letter, metalepsis has finally managed to penetrate the ground level of reality. But this philosophy is a vast hyperbole; and most of us read it metaphorically as a meditation on the obsession of contemporary culture with the mediated reality of the image rather than literally as stating the fait accompli of the disappearance of any reality other than the products of our own simulative activity.

It is only in fiction—for instance, in *The Matrix,* a movie that makes explicit reference to Baudrillard's philosophy—that we become truly prisoners of a computer-generated virtual reality. In *The Matrix* and its sequels, *The Matrix Reloaded* and *The Matrix Revolution,* the world has been conquered by intelligent machines, but these machines are dependent on the electric signals produced by the human brain. In order to maintain this source of energy, they imprison humanity in a VR simulation, an image so perfect that the prisoners have no idea of their own enslavement. Only a small community, living in a spaceship that represents one of the last pockets of the free world, remains aware of the truth. The movie represents the efforts of these people to liberate the world from the illusion of the Matrix, but the "real world" that underlies the simulation is a world of doom and destruction, and the movie raises the philosophical question of what is preferable: the pleasant simulation of the Matrix, or what the leader of the free world, Morpheus, describes as "the desert of the real"—an expression quoted from Baudrillard. At least, this was the question that was raised after the first part of the trilogy. If I had been the scriptwriter of the two sequels, this is how the trilogy would end: Neo and Morpheus free the world from the Matrix, and it returns to its real state, the state of desolation shown in the first movie. Because this world is much less pleasant than the virtual reality created by the machines, there is a revolt of the freed humanity, and to retain their power, Morpheus and Neo are forced to create a simulation that makes the world look exactly the way it did under the Matrix. In other words, Neo and Morpheus become the new masters of the image. Unfortunately, the scriptwriters seem to have entirely forgotten the theme of the "desert of the real," and when the Matrix is defeated, reality is shown as an idyllic landscape where nature and technology, trees and skyscrapers, humans and creatures generated by AI live in harmony. The need for a happy ending and the obsession of popular culture with the religious archetype of the victory of good over evil have squelched whatever interesting philosophical themes the movie presented in the first installment.

Some philosophers (for instance, David Weberman and Philip Zhai) would argue that Baudrillard's vision of a metaleptic takeover of the real by a simulation is only impossible in the present state of technology. If VR were perfect (and it could become so someday), if a computer could create images of objects and feed into our brains sensory stimuli similar to those occasioned by the real object, there would be no way to distinguish the two versions, and the simulated would become the real. But the day when technology becomes sophisticated enough to make us perceive images as the real thing, its "victims" will have no knowledge of the metaleptic takeover. Metalepsis could thus affect the real world, but we would be unaware of it. Let me therefore rephrase the issue from the perspective of human experience and consciousness, and from the perspective of the current state of technology.

Metalepsis impacts our world through the strange loops of logic and experimental science, which place limits on knowledge, through the viruses that occasionally threaten our software, through the confusion of real-world self and fictional persona that reportedly affects some of the visitors of online virtual worlds (Turkle 1995), and through some medical or military VR applications in which users operate on real objects by manipulating their digital image.

But in its artistic manifestations, the phenomenon remains a pure thought experiment, a fantasy game played on a field securely fenced off from the lifeworld. Metaleptic texts make us *play* with the idea that we are fictional, the product of a mind that inhabits a world closer to the ground level than we do, but they cannot turn themselves into the command language that scripts our lives, into the matrix of irreality that envelopes our existence, and in the end, they cannot shake our conviction that we inhabit the only world that exists "for real," because this world is the one that we inhabit corporeally. We can visit other worlds in imagination, but our bodies tie us to the base of the stack.

Notes

Introduction

1. The Web sites for these conferences: Darmstadt conference, http://www.virtualstorytelling.com/ICVS2003/; Toulouse conference, http://www.virtualstorytelling.com/ICVS2003/; UCLA conference, http://dc-mrg.english.ucsb.edu/gradconf.html; and Sedona Festival, http://www.dstory.com/dsfsedona_04/. All sites accessed September 2004.

2. Quoted from the conference Web page.

3. See also the Web site InteractiveStory.Net, maintained by Mateas and Stern, at http://www.quvu.net/interactivestory.net/.

4. Lev Manovich, for instance, in his book *The Language of New Media,* titles one of the sections "What New Media Is," and another "What New Media Is Not."

1. Narrative, Media, and Modes

1. Quoted from Seymour Chatman, *Story and Discourse,* 20 (original in Bremond 1973, 12).

2. As Werner Wolf has argued (2003, 181–82), an example of a definition of narrative that seems too broad for transmedial narratology is Monika Fludernik's suggestion that narrative is in essence an expression of human experience, and that plot is not a necessary dimension. I am certainly not questioning the importance given by this definition to human (or anthropomorphic) experience. But if "experientiality" makes plot dispensable, any piece of music that arouses emotions (and don't they all?), any abstract painting titled *War, Anguish,* or *Serenity,* and any lyrical poem would be every bit as narrative as a classical novel, and more narrative than a historical chronicle that focuses on external events. While

a plot presupposes human experience, the converse does not hold true. According to my definition, a text with human-like characters engaged in physical actions will be perceived as more narrative than a text that consists exclusively of a representation of mental life and cogitations, such as *The Unnameable* by Samuel Beckett.

3. As Hayden White (1981) has convincingly argued.

4. Degree of narrativity can be understood in two ways, one pertaining to story and the other to discourse. In the story sense, the one I am using here, it means the extent to which the mental representation conveyed by a text fulfills the definition of story. In the discourse sense (developed in Prince 1982), it means the importance of the story within the global economy of the text and the ease of retrieving it. The same text can present full narrativity in sense 1, but low narrativity in sense 2, when it tells a well-formed story but the progress of the action is slowed down by descriptions, general comments, and digressions. See also the concept of "diluted narrativity" in Ryan 1992, 375.

5. For this statement to describe science fiction accurately, the concept of the fictional world must include not just its geographic configuration, but also its social organization.

6. This view is most forcefully defended in Schank and Abelson 1995.

7. Comparison may admittedly operate between temporally ordered items and thus participate in the building of narrative meaning, for instance, when we compare an initial and final situation and decide that a change of state has occurred. But since comparison does not in itself imply chronology, it does not necessarily produce narrative meaning.

8. I borrow this comparison from Fotis Jannidis (2003, 40).

9. My interpretation of the contrast representative / simulative clearly differs from that of Katherine Hayles, who, relying on Baudrillard's notion of simulation, writes: "Broadly speaking, representation assumes a referent in the real world, however mediated; there is an actor playing the role of Neo [in the movie *The Matrix*] . . . In simulation, the referent has no counterpart in the real world; there is no actor playing the Princess [in *Shrek*, an animation film], only ones and zeros in a machine" (2002, 5). This interpretation is widespread among theorists of digital media, especially among those who focus on film. (See also Paul 2003, 86–87.)

10. Meyerowitz suggests a third metaphor, media as environments, but it does not seem to me to stand on the same level as the other two: while the language and conduit metaphors capture not only an approach to media but also their *function,* and consequently their nature, medium as environment leads one to ask "What are the characteristics of each medium (or of each type of media) that makes it physically, psychologically, and socially different from other media and from live interaction" (61). But media are not environments all by themselves; they are rather

members of an environment. The third metaphor suggests therefore to me an approach to media, rather than a definition. Meyerowitz also suggests that "any use of media involves all three [metaphors] simultaneously" (65). But if the metaphors stand for function, not approach, then, as I have suggested, media can be conduits without being languages.

11. The cognitive researcher Mark Turner (1996) has even argued that language is a product, not a cause, of the human need to tell stories. This need, as Dautenhahn (2003) argues, can be attributed to the complex social organization of humans, compared to that of apes.

12. Some artists, however, have used the Xerox machine in a creative way, by placing three-dimensional objects on the glass plate.

13. This list should also make room for the kinds of objects that support these various modes of inscription: papyrus scrolls, codex books, the computer screen, and space itself for VR technology.

14. Against Ong's claim that the dramatic plot is a product of writing, one could argue that it has its sources in spontaneous oral storytelling. As William Labov has observed, conversational narratives of personal experience follow a pattern of exposition, complication, resolution, and coda which bears striking resemblance to the Aristotelian plot. Rather than creating this structure ex nihilo, writing allowed its expansion from the small stories of conversation to the relatively large frame of dramatic performance.

15. Some scholars disagree with this. Margaret Anne Doody regards, for instance, the romances of Greek and Roman literature (such as *The Golden Ass,* by Apuleius) as the earliest form of the novel.

16. I am thinking in particular of the indebtedness of early hypertext fiction to the aesthetics of the postmodern novel. The generally accepted explanation for this phenomenon is that the forms of the postmodern novel anticipate the new medium; but one could just as well argue that what Richard Lanham calls the "extraordinary convergence" of digital writing and postmodern theory is in fact a print tradition that continues in a new medium because of cultural habits.

17. Media such as oral storytelling may seem at first sight to illustrate the purely temporal category, but insofar as they use visual information— gestures and facial expressions—they belong to the spatio-temporal category. This leaves only media of long-distance communication (radio and telephone) as purely temporal manifestations of oral language. A case could also be made for placing print texts in the spatial category, because of the two-dimensionality of the page, but as the phenomenon of books on tape demonstrates, the vast majority of print narratives can easily be transposed into a purely temporal format and consequently do not take advantage of this spatiality. When a print text relies on graphic effects— illustrated children's books, artists' books, or calligrammes—it should be categorized as spatiotemporal.

18. I use "touch" as an umbrella term for (1) tactile sensations, such as smoothness, wetness, and warmth; (2) kinesthetics, the sense of one's body moving; (3) proprioception, "the perception of relative motion between one's body and the external world"; and (4) haptics, or "force feedback," "a combination of skin sensation, pressure sensing, and kinaesthetics" (all quotes, and the list, from Back 2003, 174).

19. As the title of her book suggests: *"A Voyage on the North Sea": Art in the Age of the Post-Medium Condition.*

20. This may be what leads Kittler to correct himself: "But right now there are still media; there is still entertainment" (32).

21. The exploitation of the spatiality of print for artistic purpose is not exclusive to twentieth-century literature. The Baroque age presents several examples of figurative texts shaped according to a certain figure, such as a cross or a labyrinth. For reproductions of some of these texts, see Simanowski 2004.

22. As in books on tape.

2. Drawing and Transgressing Fictional Boundaries

1. An example of a fiction that describes a particular world, without creating individuated characters, or subjecting this world to changes of state, is Jorge Luis Borges's piece of pseudo-anthropology, "Tlön, Uqbar, Orbis, Tertius."

2. A seeming exception to this statement is fictional narratives representing the utilitarian mode described in chapter 1: parables, *romans à thèse,* and didactic novels. But these fictions will not be very efficient if their world is unable to attract the reader's interest.

3. An exception must be made for Félix Martínez-Bonati, who addressed the logical problem of fiction in Spanish-language publications as early as 1960. This work wasn't, however, translated into English until 1981.

4. Among the many proposals that have been made to reconcile the phenomenon of unreliable narration with the truth-as-say-so of fiction, the most persuasive in my view is that of Félix Martínez-Bonati. He suggests that what holds true in a fictional world is assessed by the reader on the basis of two factors: the textual statements, but also the general world-model suggested by the text. When the statements of an individuated narrator clash with the world-model, and when an explanation consistent with the character's personality can be provided (such as hallucination), then it is justified to regard these statements as not yielding facts for the fictional world.

5. This is a simplified rewording of Currie's definition (1990, 31–33); the technical differences should not matter for the purpose of this discussion. Here is Currie's exact formulation:

U's [utterer] of S is fictive if and only if U utters A intending that the audience will (1) recognize that S means P; (2) recognize that S is intended by U to mean P; (3) recognize that U intends them (the audience) to make-believe that P; (4) make-believe that P; and further intending that (5) 2 will be a reason for 3; (6) 3 will be a reason for 4.

Currie adds two rewordings to take into consideration two special cases: fictional utterances conveyed through gesture rather than speech, and the situation of an author who is not addressing a particular audience (i.e., an author of written texts, in contrast to an oral storyteller).

6. Peter Rabinowitz argues that music can occasionally involve the pretense of another performance; in Rimsky-Korsakov's *Mozart and Salieri*, for instance, the soloist is made by the score to pretend that he is "an old blind violinist scratching out Mozart" (2004, 317). In the musical *Showboat*, when the heroine performs an audition song for a fictional audience, the actual audience in the theater and the fictional audience in the story do not hear the same song: for the actual audience the song is a "good parody of 'bad' music"; but for the fictional audience, the song is "an aesthetic sellout" (319). In these moments of musical duplicity, the actual listener believes that he is witnessing a certain performance and make-believes that he is hearing another; but examples of such situations are few and far between, and this type of "fictionality," in contrast to the fictionality of other media, affects only certain passages within a work. Whether or not we accept Rabinowitz's proposal, most music, like most paintings, remains immune to the dichotomy fiction/nonfiction. As for architecture, it could be argued that it does serve as a "prop in a game of make-believe" in amusement parks.

7. The hospitability of autobiography to representations of mental life make it the hardest genre of nonfiction to distinguish from fiction on the basis of formal features. This claim is supported by an experiment conducted by Malcolm Hayward. He presented subjects with unlabeled passages from historical and fictional texts and asked them to identify the genre. The proportion of errors (15 percent) was minimal. Most cases of misidentification came from confusion between autobiography and first-person fictional narratives.

8. Quoted by Cohn (1999, 10).

9. The Library of Congress cataloging data, reproduced in the book, lists *Austerlitz* and *The Emigrants* as "fiction," but these descriptions are made by librarians, and authors are not consulted. Coetzee's *Boyhood*, mentioned above, is cataloged as "biography." I am indebted to Emma Kafalenos for drawing my attention to this information.

10. Jonathan Long reports that in an interview with *The Guardian*, Sebald confessed that "he had always collected 'stray photographs' because 'there is a lot of memory in them'" (2003, 117).

11. Let's note, in passing, the opposition between Walton and Barthes: for Barthes all language is fictional, but images (photos) can make truth claims; for Walton, all images are fictional, but language can make truth claims.

12. Title of the second chapter of Foucault's *Les Mots et les choses* (English: *The Order of Things*).

13. For arguments different from mine in favor of the binary model, see Barbara Foley in "The Documentary Novel."

14. This remark does not apply to fictional activities in a larger sense, a sense that includes children's games of make-believe. As Jean-Marie Schaeffer observes (1999, 16), such games are probably found in all human communities (as well as among some animal species), and these communities are presumably able to tell the difference between ludic and practical activities.

15. These remarks concern the role of myth in oral societies, not in literate societies like ancient Greece. In *Did the Greeks Believe in Their Myths?*, Paul Veyne suggests that late Greek historians saw a historical basis in myth, but this truth had to be recovered by stripping myth of its fantastic elements (1988, 60). Stoic philosophers, on the other hand, ascribed a figurative truth to myth that was compatible with the fantastic (62). There is no documentation on the mode of beliefs inspired by myths in archaic Greece, when the myths were still in their oral stage.

16. In today's society, myth (or what remains of it) is interpreted in four different ways: (1) as authoritative, inspired, community-defining literal truths (the fundamentalist mode); (2) as authoritative, inspired, community-defining but potentially figural truths (the mainstream religion mode); (3) as literary truths, offering one source of inspiration among many others; (4) as fictional truths, forming entertaining narratives about imaginary worlds. Of these four modes of reading, the first two retain the conception of truth that I propose here as constitutive of myth, while the last two effectively kill myth but keep its memory alive by recycling its narrative material into another genre.

17. For instance, this comment in the *New York Times* by Michiko Kakutani: "[The] narrator appears in the foot-notes to the book alongside real-life sources, and he makes the reader think: if Morris won't tell the truth about himself, why should we believe what he has to say about the President or anyone else?" If the approach was generalized, according to another critic, it would be the end of scholarship, the triumph of entertainment over the pursuit of truth, and the vindication of "the professors who deny that objectivity is possible" (Dowd 1999).

3. Narrative in Fake and Real Reality TV

1. In this chapter, *The Truman Show* refers to the actual movie, and the Truman show to the fictional show within the movie.

2. European audiences, whose RTV programs were more of the Big Brother type—less script, more surveillance—display more tolerance for raw spectacles. Europeans seem also much more fascinated than Americans by webcams. According to Sella, France contributes a disproportionate amount of hits to the webcam show Nerdman, "the real life Truman" (found at http://www.nerdman.com).

3. In the final weeks of the show, in part because the voters were the audience at large, not the participants themselves, all the villains had been voted out, and the remaining participants got along so well that there wasn't any conflict in the house. No conflict, no drama. The producers tried to boost the ratings by luring out some of the remaining participants with cash prizes, in the hope of replacing them with more colorful players. But no participant took the bribes, and the show had to stick to the bitter end with the happy family that it had inadvertently created.

4. Narrative in Real Time

1. Examples of contemporary novels using the present as primary narrative tense include Margaret Atwood, *The Handmaid's Tale* (1985), J. M. Coetzee, *Waiting for the Barbarians* and *In the Heart of the Country* (both 1982), Michel Butor, *La Modification* (1957), and sections of Marguerite Duras, *L'Amant* (1984). The present seems indeed on its way to becoming the dominant tense of contemporary "literary" novels. See Cohn (1999) on the question of present-tense fiction, especially in the first person (as are all of the above examples except Butor).

2. This story by an eleven-year-old girl illustrates what I mean by "present of vividness": "There were these teenagers hanging around in the park, and I walked past them, and there is this girl, and she goes: 'What kind of battery did it take to light up your shirt?'" (the narrator was wearing a neon-bright orange shirt on that day).

3. Another such context is a radio conversation between a pilot and an air controller, or a cell phone report of live events. "Live now, tell later," the formula coined by Dorrit Cohn (1999, 96), has lost much of its validity in the age of the mobile phone. The convergence of life and narrative produced drama of unbearable intensity in the calls of the passengers on the doomed flights of September 11.

4. In the transcriptions from the broadcast I employ two conventions: italics indicate speaker emphasis; square brackets mark editorial comments.

5. Toward an Interactive Narratology

1. Advocates of this model include Genette, Prince, and Chatman.

2. Several scholars have proposed lists of fundamental properties of digital media. But these lists tend to mix properties of the system with design strategies and specific uses of system properties. Below are the lists proposed by Janet Murray and Lev Manovich. In parentheses are

occasional short explanations of what the items mean; in square brackets, comments on what technological category the item represents, or references to properties of my own list. Murray's list:

1. Digital environments are procedural. [Other term for programmability]
2. Digital environments are participatory. [Attributable to interactivity and networking]
3. Digital environments are spatial. [The sense that users can move around a digital environment is attributable to interactivity, volatility, and multimedia]
4. Digital environments are encyclopedic. [Specific use of a property not on my list: large amounts of storage] (Murray 1997, 71–90)

Manovich's list:

1. Numerical representation. [Type of encoding of data used by computers]
2. Modularity. [Design strategy that exploits the ease of reproduction offered by computers]
3. Automation. (= the computer now takes over tasks that had to be performed by humans, for instance, searching databases or transforming images in Photoshop). [Application of programmability]
4. Variability. (= new media objects easily undergo transformations). [Attributable to volatility and automation]
5. Transcoding. (= distinction between a "cultural layer" of New Media objects and a "computer layer" on which objects are represented in computer code). [A direct consequence of "numerical representation" rather than a separate property] (Manovich 2001, 27–49)

3. An exception to this statement is Noah Wardrip-Fruin's and Brion Moss's *The Impermanence Agent,* a noninteractive digital text that crucially depends on the programmability of the computer. A "stalker text" that operates by exploring the user's hard disk, *The Impermanence Agent* consists of two windows on the screen. One of them contains a textual narrative, the story of the life and death of the narrator's grandmother, Nana, illustrated with family photos. The other window contains texts from various authors and memorial imagery from multiple cultures. The content of both windows scrolls down slowly by itself, then returns to the top, in an infinite loop. Running continuously over a week, *The Impermanence Agent* modifies the content of each window by gradually replacing the original data with materials culled from the user's "scrapbook"—the file in which the Internet browser of the user's system stores text and images from the Web sites most recently visited. At the

end of the run, the original story has completely disappeared, replaced by a grammatically correct but semantically incoherent collage of words and phrases randomly selected from the scrapbook.

4. For instance, a cat toy at my local supermarket is labeled "interactive."

5. In *Cybertexts,* for instance, Espen Aarseth writes: "The word interactive operates textually rather than analytically, as it connotes various vague ideas of computer screens, user freedom, and personalized media, while denoting nothing" (1997, 48). He proposes to replace the notion of interactivity with that of ergodism: "In ergodic literature, nontrivial effort is required to allow the reader to traverse the text" (1997, 1). By Aarseth's standards, nontriviality has to do with choice: turning a page in a book is a trivial effort, but skipping a number of pages in a multiple-choice print text or shuffling a deck of cards to produce various combinations of words is nontrivial. I believe, however, that "ergodic" captures a different set of texts than "interactive," and that, properly defined, both terms have a place in the semiotics of textuality (Ryan 2001, 206–10). For me, a genuinely interactive text involves not only choice but also a two-sided effort operating in real time that creates a feedback loop. The two sides can be either two human minds, as in conversation or oral storytelling, or a human and a programmable system that simulates a communicative partner, as in digital texts. This conception of interactivity excludes branching or free-order print texts such as Julio Cortázar's *Hopscotch* and Milorad Pavíc's *Dictionary of the Khazars,* because a printed text does not perform any action, nor does it modify itself. In a digital text, by contrast, the system processes the user's input by executing certain operations, which lead to the display of certain signs. My inclination is to call the branching print texts ergodic (with Aarseth), and the digital ones both ergodic and interactive. But even though ergodic print texts are not literally interactive, they present at least some of the same types of architecture as digital texts because they rely on choice. This is why some of the models outlined in this chapter apply to both print and digital texts. But genuinely interactive digital texts offer a much wider range of narrative possibilities and user experiences than ergodic print texts.

6. I have already discussed some of these architectures in Ryan 2001, but here I do so with a different emphasis: their capability to generate variety on the levels of discourse and story. My discussion is indebted to the typology and examples of Katherine Phelps, though I am not incorporating all her categories. I am also adopting some of Phelps' structure diagrams under a different name: my "vector with side branches" corresponds to her "enhanced path," and my "flowchart" to her "sequential set."

7. For graph theory, the sea-anemone is technically a tree. This can be shown by lifting the anemone by its central node and letting its arms drop.

8. My dichotomy internal-external corresponds roughly to Aarseth's distinction between personal and impersonal perspective, and my category exploratory to Aarseth's user function by the same name. The closest to my ontological category in Aarseth's taxonomy is a user function he calls "configurative," in which "scriptons [Aarseth's term for recombinable chunks of text] are in part chosen or created by the user" (1997, 64). But my ontological category does not require from the user the creation of elements that will become a permanent part of the system. Nor is the selection of elements—Aarseth's second form of configuration—sufficient to ontological participation: it is the principal way of fulfilling the exploratory function.

9. In the third-person perspective, the user sees both the virtual world and the body of the avatar, while in the first-person, his apprehension of the virtual world corresponds to what the avatar can see (including some body parts of the avatar such as hands holding a gun). This distinction resembles only superficially the narratological categories of first-person and third-person narration; it would be more appropriate to describe third-person perspective as external focalization, and first-person as internal, or character focalization.

10. The on-line, multiplayer version of *The Sims* belongs to the internal-ontological group, because the player identifies with a specific character. In the CD-ROM, single-player version, by contrast, the user manipulates several characters.

11. In a brilliant analysis of the apparently crude shooter *Duke Nukem,* Eva Liestøl has argued, for instance, that the game invites adolescent boys to assert their masculinity in a world increasingly dominated by women by playing a supermacho hero who conquers a labyrinth symbolic of the inside of a female body and slays a female monster whose countless offspring are invading the city of Los Angeles.

12. Another type of action that is easily simulated by operating a control device, and that leads to instant, spectacular metamorphosis, is casting a spell. In medieval fantasy games, spells have become as prominent as weapons as a mean to defeat or escape enemies.

13. A case in point is Raymond Queneau's *Cent mille milliards de poèmes,* a work that combines the 14 lines of 12 sonnets into 1,214 different poems.

6. Interactive Fiction and Storyspace Hypertext

1. In some versions the art gallery becomes a technological exhibit.

2. IF survives in small Internet niches, practiced without commercial and theoretical pressures by enthusiastic writers and programmers who freely share their work with a devoted community. *Galatea* and *Spider and Web* are products of this noncommercial afterlife.

3. Other proponents of the convergence of hypertext writing and post-modern theory are Lanham (1993) and Landow (1997).

4. Nelson's concept of hypertext was broader than what is generally understood today by the term: he regarded hypertext as a subset of hypermedia, which he defined as "branching or performing presentations which respond to user actions." Hypertext was the language-based form of hypermedia: "Hypertext means forms of writing which branch or perform on request; they best are presented on computer display screens. . . . Discrete, or chunk style hypertexts consist of separate pieces of text connected by links." Today most people associate hypertext with the chunk-style, linked-based version, which is found both in the structure of the Web and in Storyspace products, but for Nelson it was only one of two variants. The other was what he called the stretch text: a nonbranching text whose "performance on request" consists of a changed appearance. For instance, the user can zoom in and out, make the display of the text longer or shorter, or, through a clicking action, cause the insertion of additional words in the middle of the text. On the contemporary hypermedia scene, stretch texts are represented by animated Flash movies whose objects alter their shape in response to the user's actions, and by the interactive maps (which Nelson would call "hypermaps") of the Web site Topozone.com. The user can change scale by zooming in and out of the maps or can get maps of adjacent quadrants. It should be noted that the three components of Nelson's definition, "branching," "performing," and "on request" are separable features. Performing is applicable to texts that are driven by computer code, but not to print texts: when the reader of digital texts clicks on a link, the system performs an action in order to display more text, but with a print text, it is the reader who turns the pages, even when the text offers a choice of continuation. The code of a digital text is like a musical score meant to be performed on an instrument called a computer. Branching occurs in both performing digital texts and nonperforming print texts, such as the *Choose Your Own Adventures* children's books. And finally, performing digital texts may branch, but not on the user's request. The branching may, for instance, be made conditional on the status of a variable internal to the system, such as the computer clock. What then is hypertext? If we adhere to Nelson's definition, it is restricted to digital texts but includes both linked-based branching texts and nonbranching stretch texts. Alternatively, we can limit hypertext to digital texts based on a link-node structure. This is my inclination. Some people finally regard branching as the necessary and sufficient condition of hypertextuality and will include nonlinear print text, as well as IF and computer games based on the structure of the labyrinth, in the category. (All Nelson quotes from Noah Wardrip-Fruin's "What Is Hypertext?" Wardrip-Fruin's source is Ted Nelson's article "No More Teachers' Dirty Looks.")

5. Storyspace allows the reader to write notes in special areas, the digital equivalent of scribbling in the margins of a text, but these notes are external to the text, and they do not move the plot forward.

6. Guard fields can work on other conditions as well. As Stuart Moulthrop explains: "'Guard fields' list criteria that must be met before a link can operate: the reader must have already visited certain places, or some places and not others, or must nominate certain words either by clicking them on-screen or typing them from the keyboard." (CD-ROM accompanying Wardrip-Fruin and Montfort 2003).

7. One author who openly chose "The Garden of Forking Paths" as a model is Stuart Moulthrop. In 1987, when Storyspace was still in the Beta stage, he wrote with the software an unpublished hypertext version of Borges's story that involved quoted fragments of the original text. It was an attempt to impart the structure of Ts'ui Pên's novel to Borges's linear story. To do this Moulthrop quoted passages of Borges's text but added alternate branches of his own invention. The 1987 version of "The Garden of Forking Paths" is reproduced (in a documentary, noninteractive version) in the CD-ROM that accompanies *The New Media Reader*. By the author's own admission, *Victory Garden* was also an attempt to implement the idea of the Garden of Forking Paths.

8. Standard manifestations of this process include metaphors such as "life is a journey," the future is "ahead of us," the past is "behind"; and when you face a decision in life, you stand "at a crossroad."

9. In the many-worlds interpretation of quantum mechanics, this splitting occurs incessantly. See note 6 in chapter 9.

10. Philosophers (such as A. N. Prior) generally agree that time splits toward the future, because the future is open to all possibilities, but it cannot split toward the past, because the past is already written and unchangeable. If time allowed backward branching, this would mean that a given individual would have several different personal histories, and mutually incompatible propositions would be true: for instance, "x was an enemy of y" and "x was a friend of y." Time can only branch backward from an epistemological perspective: for instance, a detective may consider several possible courses of past events that led to a murder; but this is a matter of not knowing which one is actual, not an ontological matter of multiple actualities. Once the case is solved, all but one of the branches are discarded.

11. Some authors take advantage of this feature by turning Storyspace maps into illustrations of the entities represented in the text; for instance, the nodes of the map shown in figure 5 are arranged to look like a patchwork quilt. Similarly, Stephanie Strickland shapes one of the maps of *True North* as a breast to represent "the pressure that language puts on women's bodies," another as an irregular blue sphere to represent "the pressure

scientific language puts on the earth," and another as a feather to symbol-ize "a different sort of navigation, a recaptured time/space that connects prehistory with the present" (1997a, 4).

12. Not all these texts are Storyspace products: *Califia* and *Marble Springs* (mentioned in the next paragraph) were made with Macintosh utilities, SuperCard and HyperCard.

13. "The medium is the message."

14. I borrow this concept of archive from Raine Koskimaa, who was the first to mention the structural shift of more recent hypertexts.

7. Web-Based Narrative, Multimedia, and Interactive Drama

1. These adaptations include: (1) A text-only version, in Russian and English, readable by scrolling down, that reproduces the dialogue. (2) An interactive version with realistic color pictures instead of the binary black and white of the original. This version operates like its model through successive divisions of the screen, though not as systematically: sometimes it reverts to larger frames or to a full-screen picture. In an intertextual tribute, one of the screens is directly borrowed from the original. Though relying much more extensively on pictures than Lialina's text, this version uses some Russian text toward the end. (3) A noninteractive Flash movie, in which the individual images of the original move down the screen, while the dialogue is spoken by two frequently overlapping voices against a background of music. The movie repeats itself in an infinite loop. (4) A static gouache rendering of one of the screens of the original. (5) A Flash movie that simulates the dynamics of the reading process: the windows open by themselves, rather than being operated by the user. (6) A movie with a navigable display that alters itself dynamically in response to cur-sor movements, as we find in computer games. Elements from the original text are projected on the architecture of *Castle Wolfenstein,* the game that pioneered the genre of the first-person shooters. (7) A blog Web site, on which the various lines of the text are presented as "posts" by Olia Lialina, to which readers can reply with comments. (Other versions are still listed but no longer accessible.)

2. Storyspace tries to alleviate this problem by allowing several text windows (corresponding to different lexia, or pages) to be displayed on the screen, either in a so-called cascading (i.e., stacking) pattern, where the newest window hides all but the edges of the earlier ones, so that only the titles of the earlier windows appear, or in a tiling pattern, where the screen is divided into horizontal strips that show the title and part of the text of each window. This feature enables the reader to move back and forth between several windows by clicking on their visible titles, an action that brings the window to the foreground. But few readers take advantage of this possibility, because it is rather clumsy. The complexity

of typical Storyspace networks quickly leads to an unmanageable prolif-eration of windows, and the text of the various windows can only be seen partially (in the tiling pattern), or not at all (in the cascading pattern).

3. Storyspace also offers the possibility of dividing the screen into distinct areas—text and picture, for instance—but this feature has been rarely exploited in hypertext fiction. One Storyspace text that makes use of distinct frames is Michael Joyce's *Twelve Blue*: one for the text, the other for the (non-system-generated) map.

4. Some Storyspace texts present a modest use of temporal resources: in *its name was Penelope,* by Judy Malloy, certain screens are displayed for a limited time and replaced by another lexia without user intervention. But the limited graphic capabilities of Storyspace do not make it possible to animate pictures.

5. An example of noninteractive Flash poem is the charming poem-cum-photograph "Young Couple at Ohio State Fair" by Felix Jung and Dipti Vadya. The text performs a reading of the picture by drawing attention to particular visual elements. As the poem writes itself dynamically on the screen, line by line, at a comfortable reading pace, the segment of the image described by the current line appears briefly, inviting the reader to focus on the visual referent. When the entire poem has been played, the fragments reappear on the screen and arrange themselves into a complete image.

6. For instance, Talan Memmott, *Lexia to Perplexia.*

7. My description of the features of Director is based on version 7. The current version (9) has many new features, which make the program more suitable for the creation of computer games.

8. On the respective importance of experientiality and plot for a defi-nition of narrative, see note 2 of chapter 1.

9. See chapter 8 for a more extensive discussion of these concepts, which were borrowed by Roger Caillois from Plato.

10. This means from standard programming languages such as Java, Jess, and C++ using standard OpenGL and Windows libraries. (Author's communication.)

11. Present-day CD-ROM–based games average forty to sixty hours, and online games take for some users over twenty hours a week for sev-eral months.

8. Computer Games as Narrative

1. By this criterion, computer versions of board games (chess, Mo-nopoly) or TV games *(Wheel of Fortune)* are not genuine video games, while computerized sports games (baseball, football, car racing) are, be-cause of the significant difference between the "real thing" and its com-puter version: the participation of the whole body.

2. Or, at least, the computer has greatly facilitated this integration.

As Greg Costykian observes in "A Farewell to Hexes," there existed, between 1958 and 1996, a rich tradition of paper and pencil war games that combined strategy and narrative themes. The board game Monopoly can also be considered an example of this combination, though its narrativity is rudimentary, compared to that of recent computer games.

3. See Margolin 1999 on nonretrospective narratives.

4. The computer is also a state-transition machine, and this explains the particular affinity of computers for games, but the states of the computer are much more finely grained than the strategic states of a game. For instance, some games allow players to get two different views of the same situation: vertical projection (map view) and horizontal (point of view of the avatar). Switching from one view to the other does not alter the game state, but the two views correspond to different computer states, triggered by different inputs. Similarly, when a player makes a Sim character walk from the fridge to the mailbox, the action mediates between two relevant game states where different actions are possible, but the animation that shows the character walking requires a very large number of different computer states—at least one for every frame.

5. Frasca recognizes that the output of a simulation does indeed look like a cinematic narrative: "To an external observer, the sequence of signs produced by both the film and the simulation could look exactly the same. This is what many supporters of the narrative paradigm fail to understand: their semiotic sequences might be identical, but simulation cannot be understood by just its output" (2003, 224). This observation amounts to equating narrative to a process of production, not to the product itself.

6. We customarily speak of winning and losing wars, but in human conflicts these outcomes are not nearly as clear-cut as in games: the winner always loses something, and the loser may profit. Wars, moreover, are fought for practical interests, not just to see who has the better army.

7. A discussion of this challenge can be found on Grand Text Auto, October 2003, at http://steel.lcc.gatech.edu/cgi-bin/mt/mt-comments .cgi?entry_id=99 (accessed March 2004).

8. Term proposed by J. Yellowlees Douglas (2004, 36).

9. The original is "narratively organized systems for thinking" (Herman 2003, 308) and it is meant to explain the importance of narrative as a cognitive tool.

10. Juul suggests a sixth rule: the same game can be played with or without real-life consequences. I find the constitutive status of this rule problematic: isn't the ludic status of the game diminished when we play it for money or for life? Playing professional sports is no longer a game; it is a job. On the other hand, there are some games, such as roulette or extreme sports, which wouldn't be thrilling if they did not put something real at stake.

11. The relation of simulation games to *paidia* has been noted by Gonzalo Frasca in "Ludology Meets Narratology." (Note that Frasca's own concept of simulation applies to all games, not just to the game type represented by *The Sims* family).

12. MUD stands for Multi Users Dungeon—a label inspired by the paper-and-pencil games Dungeons and Dragons. Bartle's typology was meant for text-based MUDs, but it applies equally well to MMORPGS (Massively Multi-Player Online Role-Playing Games), such as *EverQuest*. In addition, different individual games will attract different types of players.

13. http://thesims.ea.com/us/exchange/index.html.

14. Gonzalo Frasca has taken a similar turn. In a review of *Grand Theft Auto,* he writes: "Both *GTA3* and *Shenmue* tell a story. Yes, here you have a ludologist publicly say that games do tell stories. Spread the news!" (2003b, 5–6). In another article ("Ludologists Love Stories Too") he claims that the debate between narrativists and ludologists never happened. It may have been a one-sided affair, rather than a dialogue, but if the articles by Aarseth, Juul, Eskelinen, and Frasca quoted in the present chapter don't take a stance against the idea of games telling stories, what will it take to start a polemic? See also the quotes in Jenkins 2004, 118, as evidence that the debate did indeed happen.

15. Salen and Zimmerman (2003, 127–38) propose several examples of isomorphic games that dress up the same set of rules in different garb, some narrative and some not. For instance, the thematically concrete and therefore mildly narrative board game Chutes and Ladders could be transposed into a totally abstract game in which players would pick numbers, rather than falling through chutes and climbing ladders.

9. Metaleptic Machines

1. The concept of metalepsis was introduced in contemporary narratology by Gérard Genette. His source was the seventeenth-century French rhetorician Fontanier, who describes metalepsis as "pretending that the poet creates himself the effects that he is singing" ("feindre que le poète opère lui-même les effets qu'il chante"), such as saying that "Virgil kills Dido" (Genette, 1972, 244). The process I am trying to capture is not coextensive with all the uses of metalepsis in rhetorical literature. As Klaus Meyer-Minnemann has shown, early rhetoricians (Donatus, fourth century; Melanchton, sixteenth century) conceived metalepsis as a type of metonymy—a definition that will not be taken into consideration in this chapter. On the other hand, contemporary theorists have described the phenomenon I have in mind under other names. This is notably the case with Douglas Hofstadter's concepts of Strange Loops and Tangled Hierarchies. The present study will expand Hofstadter's treatment of these

phenomena to areas not covered in *Gödel, Escher, Bach*. Finally, some critics have proposed other terms that partially overlap with my interpretation of metalepsis. William Egginton's concept of "reality bleeding" is a forceful description of what happens in the narrative texts that I propose as examples of metalepsis, "Continuity of Parks" and "The Kugelmass Episode," but in contrast to my use of metalepsis, Egginton expands "bleeding" to any text that thematizes an interplay of multiple realities, whether or not these realities interpenetrate each other, and whether or not the text involves a paradox.

2. See Ryan 1991 for a more detailed discussion.

3. In *Figures III* (1972), Genette describes some cases of metalepsis that I would describe as ontological, though he does not regard them as a distinct species. But in his 2004 book *Métalepse,* he draws a distinction between "figural" and "fictional" metalepsis that corresponds roughly to my categories "rhetorical" and "ontological."

4. A critic who disagrees with this view is Debra Malina. She regards metalepsis as a violent, destructive operation that challenges the rational identity of the Cartesian subject and reconstructs postmodern subjectivity as unstable multiplicity. But it could be argued that even when postmodern literature uses metalepsis to express serious concerns, it does so in a light mood.

5. There is actually no such thing as a unified Copenhagen interpretation of quantum mechanics. What is known under this name is rather a myth invented retrospectively by the enemies of Bohr's school of thought. (Bruce 2004, 64.)

6. The uncertainty principle says that we cannot know simultaneously the position of an electron and its speed, because "there is always a minimal disruption that we cause to the electron's velocity through our measurement of its position" (Greene 1999, 113).

7. The Copenhagen interpretation has been more recently contested by a model related to Possible Worlds Theory. As Max Tegmark explains: "Many legitimate wave functions correspond to counterintuitive situations, such as a cat being dead and alive at the same time, in a so-called superposition. In the 1920s physicists explained away the weirdness by postulating that the wave function 'collapsed' into some definite classical outcome whenever someone made an observation. This add-on had the virtue of explaining observations, but it turned an elegant theory into a kludgy, non-unitary one . . . Over the years many physicists have abandoned this view in favor of one developed in 1957 by Princeton graduate student Hugh Everett III. He showed that the collapse postulate is unnecessary. Unadulterated quantum theory does not in fact, pose any contradiction" (2003, 46). What Everett suggested is that random quantum processes cause the universe to split into multiple copies, one for every

possible outcome. The cat, consequently, is dead in one parallel universe, and alive in another. Besides Tegmark, another physicist who defends the Parallel Universes model is David Deutsch.

Another interpretation of the cat situation involves no paradox at all. In quantum mechanics, the exact path of particles can only be described in terms of probabilities. If the release of the poison gas is triggered by a quantum phenomenon that has a 50-50 percent chance of happening, then the cat has a 50-50 percent chance of being dead or alive in the box, and the opening of the door leads only to the discovery of the cat's state, not to its triggering. This particular interpretation of the cat's story does not, however, invalidate Heisenberg's uncertainty principle, which is widely accepted in physics.

8. On the halting problem and the proof of its insolvability, see Savitch, 1982, 128–37.

9. Turning output into input is not uncommon in computer programming. For instance, the output of a subroutine becomes the input of the program that activated the subroutine. But this process is not metaleptic because the subroutine and the calling program are distinct pieces of code. In recursive functions, by contrast, outputs are fed back as input to the very same code that produced them.

10. Noncommercial CD, available on demand from the author.

11. I am indepted to Marjorie Luesebrink for these details (private e-mail). The text is to be found in her on-line essay "The Personalization of Complexity."

12. Since only a small subset of the binary digit combinations that can fit into a computer "word" (= memory unit) correspond to recognizable and executable instructions, feeding the binary coding of a poem to a machine as a program to be executed would quickly result in an "unknown instruction" error.

13. I am indebted to the author for this information.

14. Poem found at http://c2.com/cgi/wiki?PerlPoetry.

For comparison, here is the the first strophe of Carroll's poem:

> 'Twas brillig, and the slithy toves
> Did gyre and gimble in the wabe:
> All mimsy were the borogoves,
> And the mome raths outgrabe.
> (Carroll 1995, 130)

15. As does Espen Aarseth (1997, 130–31).

16. I take this example from Christian Andersen (2002).

17. On the phenomenon of alternate reality gaming, see http://www.unfiction.com.

Bibliography

Aarseth, Espen. 1997. *Cybertext: Perspectives on Ergodic Literature.*
Baltimore: Johns Hopkins University Press.

———. 1999. "Aporia and Epiphany in *Doom and the Speaking Clock*:
The Temporality of Ergodic Art." In Ryan 1999, 31–41.

———. 2003a. "Playing Research: Methodological Approaches to Game
Analysis." Papers of the 2003 DAC conference, Melbourne. hypertext
.rmit.edu.au/dac/papers/Aarseth.pdf (accessed March 2004).

———. 2003b. "We All Want to Change the World: The Ideology of
Innovation in Digital Media." In Liestøl, Morrison, and Rasmussen
2003, 416–39.

———. 2004a. "Genre Trouble: Narrativism and the Art of Simulation."
In Wardrip-Fruin and Harrigan 2004, 45–55.

———. 2004b. "Quest Games as Post-Narrative Discourse." In Ryan
2004, 61–90.

Abbott, H. Porter. 2002. *The Cambridge Introduction to Narrative.*
Cambridge: Cambridge University Press.

Allen, Woody. 1981. "The Kugelmass Episode." In *The Treasury of
American Short Stories,* ed. Nancy Sullivan, 680–90. New York:
Doubleday.

Amerika, Mark. 2004. "Expanding the Concept of Writing: Notes on
Net Art, Digital Narrative, and Viral Ethics." *Leonardo* 37, no. 1:
9–13.

———. FILMTEXT. http://www.markamerika.com/filmtext/ (accessed
September 2004).

Amerika, Mark, and Talan Memmott. "Active/onBlur: An interview
with Talan Memmott conducted by Mark Amerika." http://trace.ntu
.ac.uk/newmedia/interview.cfm (accessed January 13, 2003).

Andersen, Christian. 2002. "Morphology of the Action/Adventure Game." Manuscript, Aarhus University.

Andreychek, Eric. "Perl Port of Jabberwocky." http://c2.com/cgi/ wiki?PerlPoetry (accessed September 2004).

Ankerson, Ingrid, and Megan Sapnar. "Cruising." http://www .poemsthatgo.com/gallery/spring2001/crusing-launch.html (accessed June 2004).

Aristotle. 1996. *Poetics*. Trans. and with an introduction by Malcolm Heath. London: Penguin Books.

Arloz the Little Rhinoceros. http://turbulence.org/works/nature/objects/ rhino/index.html (accessed November 30, 2002). No longer available.

Auletta, Ken. 1999. "What I Did at Summer Camp." *New Yorker* 7, no. 26: 46–51.

Austin, J. L. 1962. *How to Do Things with Words*. Oxford: Oxford University Press.

———. 1970. "Truth." In *Philosophical Papers*, ed. J. O. Urmson and G. J. Warnock, 117–33. Oxford: Oxford University Press.

Back, Maribeth. 2003. "The Reading Senses: Designing Texts for Multisensory Systems." In Liestøl, Morrison, and Rasmussen 2003, 157–82.

Banfield, Ann. 1982. *Unspeakable Sentences: Narration and Representation in the Language of Fiction*. London: Routledge.

Barthes, Roland. 1977. "Introduction to the Structural Analysis of Narrative." In *Image, Music, Text*, trans. Stephen Heath, 79–124. New York: Hill and Wang.

———. 1981a. *Camera Lucida: Reflections on Photography*. Trans. Richard Howard. New York: Hill and Wang.

———. 1981b. "The Discourse of History." In *Comparative Criticism: A Yearbook*, vol. 3, ed. E. S. Shaffer, trans. Stephen Bann, 7–20. Cambridge: Cambridge University Press.

———. 1982. "The Reality Effect." In *French Literary Theory Today*, ed. Tzvetan Todorov, 11–17. Cambridge: Cambridge University Press.

Bartle, Richard. 1996. "Hearts, Clubs, Diamonds, Spades: Players Who Suit Muds." http://www.mud.co.uk/richard/hcds.htm (accessed March 2004).

Baudrillard, Jean. 1988. "On Seduction." In *Selected Writings*, ed. Mark Poster, 149–65. Stanford, Calif.: Stanford University Press.

———. 1994. "The Precession of Simulacra." In *Simulacra and Simulations*, trans. Sheila Faria Glaser, 1–42. Ann Arbor: University of Michigan Press.

———. 1996. *The Perfect Crime*. Trans. Chris Turner. London: Verso.

Ben-Amos, Dan. 1969. "Analytical Categories and Ethnic Genres" *Genre* 2: 275–301.

Benveniste, Emile. 1971. *Problems in General Linguistics*. Trans. Mary Elizabeth Meek. Coral Gables, Fla.: University of Miami Press.

Bernstein, Mark. 1998. "Patterns of Hypertext." http://www.eastgate .com/patterns/Patterns.html (accessed August 2004).

————. 2000. "More Than Legible: On Links That Readers Don't Want to Follow." http://portal.acm.org/citation.cfm?doid=336296.336370 (accessed August 2004).

————."Hypertext Gardens: Delightful Vistas." http://www.eastgate .com/garden/ (accessed February 2001).

Blank, Marc. 1982. *Deadline*. Interactive fiction software. Cambridge, Mass.: Infocom.

Bolter, Jay David. 1991. *Writing Space: The Computer, Hypertext, and the History of Writing*. Hillsdale, N.J.: Lawrence Erlbaum.

————. 1992. "Literature in the Electronic Writing Space." In *Literacy Online: The Promises (and Perils) of Reading and Writing with Computers*, ed. Myron C. Tuman, 19–42. Pittsburgh: University of Pittsburgh Press.

Bolter, Jay David, and Richard Grusin. 1999. *Remediation: Understanding New Media*. Cambridge, Mass.: MIT Press.

Booth, Wayne. 1996. "Where Is the Autorial Audience in Biblical Narrative—and in Other 'Authoritative' Texts?" *Narrative* 4, no. 3: 218–53.

Bordwell, David. 1985. *Narration in the Fiction Film*. Madison: University of Wisconsin Press.

Bordwell, David, and Kristin Thompson. 1990. *Film Art*. 3rd ed. New York: McGraw Hill.

Borges, Jorge Luis. 1983 [1962]. *Labyrinths. Selected Stories and Other Writings*. Ed. Donald A. Yates and James E. Irby. New York: Modern Library.

————. 1970. *The Aleph and Other Stories*. Ed. and trans. Norman Thomas di Giovanni. New York: E. P. Dutton.

Bremond, Claude. 1973. *Logique du récit*. Paris: Seuil.

Brewer, William F. 1995. "To Assert That Esentially All Human Knowledge and Memory Is Represented in Terms of Stories Is Certainly Wrong." In *Knowledge and Memory: The Real Story: Advances in Social Cognitions VII*, ed. Robert S. Wyer, 109–19. Hillsdale, N.J.: Lawrence Erlbaum.

Bringsjord, Selmer, and David Ferrucci. 1999. *Artificial Intelligence and Literary Creativity: Inside the Mind of Brutus, a Storytelling Machine*. Hillsdale, N.J.: Lawrence Erlbaum.

Bruce, Colin. 2004. *Schrödinger's Rabbits: The Many Worlds of Quantum*. Washington, D.C.: Joseph Henry Press.

Bruner, Jerome. 1991. "The Narrative Construction of Reality." *Critical Inquiry* 18, no. 1: 1–22.

Bukatman, Scott. 1993. *Terminal Identity: The Virtual Subject in Postmodern Science Fiction.* Durham, N.C.: Duke University Press.

Caillois, Roger. 1961. *Men, Play, and Games.* Trans. Meyer Burach. New York: Free Press.

Campbell, Joseph. 1968. *The Hero with a Thousand Faces.* 2nd ed. Princeton, N.J.: Princeton University Press.

Campbell, P. Michael. 1987. "Interactive Fiction and Narrative Theory: Towards an Anti-Theory." *New England Review and Bread Loaf Quarterly* 10, no. 1: 76–84.

Carroll, Lewis. 1995. *Alice's Adventures in Wonderland and Through the Looking-Glass.* New York: Rand McNally.

Carroll, Noël. 1996. "Nonfiction Film and Postmodern Skepticism." In *Post-Theory: Reconstructing Film Studies,* ed. David Bordwell and Noël Carroll, 283–306. Madison: University of Wisconsin Press.

Cassell, Justine, and Henry Jenkins, eds. 1998. *From Barbie to Mortal Kombat.* Cambridge, Mass.: MIT Press.

Cayley, John. 1996. "Pressing the Reveal Code Key." *EJournal.* http://www.hanover.edu/philos/ejournal/archive/ej-6-1.txt (accessed September 2004).

———. 2002. "The Code Is Not the Text (Unless It Is the Text)." http://www.electronicbookreview.com/thread/electropoetics/literal (accessed January 2005).

Center for Digital Storytelling. Online. http://www.storycenter.org/.

Chatman, Seymour. 1978. *Story and Discourse: Narrative Structure in Fiction and Film.* Ithaca, N.Y.: Cornell University Press.

———. 1990. *Coming to Terms: The Rhetoric of Narrative in Fiction and Film.* Ithaca, N.Y.: Cornell University Press.

Coetzee, J. M. 1997. *Boyhood: Scenes from Provincial Life.* New York: Viking.

Cohn, Dorrit. 1999. *The Distinction of Fiction.* Baltimore: Johns Hopkins University Press.

Cortázar, Julio. 1967. "Continuity of Parks." In *Blow-up and Other Stories,* trans. Paul Blackburn, 63–65. New York: Pantheon.

Costikyan, Greg. Online. "Where Stories End and Games Begin." http://www.costik.com/gamstry.html (accessed March 2004).

———. Online. "A Farewell to Hexes." http://www.costik.com/spisins.html (accessed September 2004).

Coverley, M. D. 2001. *Califia.* Hypertext software. Cambridge, Mass.: Eastgate Systems.

Crawford, Chris. 2002. "Assumptions Underlying the Erasmatron Storytelling System." In Mateas and Sengers 2003, 189–97.

———. 2003. "Interactive Storytelling." In Wolf and Perron 2003, 259–73.

———. 2004. *Chris Crawford on Interactive Storytelling.* Berkeley, Calif.: New Riders.

Currie, Gregory. 1990. *The Nature of Fiction.* Cambridge: Cambridge University Press.

Darley, Andrew. 2000. *Visual Digital Culture: Surface Play and Spectacle in New Media Genres.* London: Routledge.

Dautenhahn, Kerstin. 2003. "Stories of Lemurs and Robots: The Social Origin of Story-Telling." In Mateas and Sengers 2003, 63–90.

Dawkins, Richard. 1976. *The Selfish Gene.* New York: Oxford University Press.

Deutsch, David. 1997. *The Fabric of Reality.* Penguin Books.

Discovering Lewis and Clark. Online. http://www.lewis-clark.org/.

Ditlea, Steve. 1998. "False Starts Aside, Virtual Reality Finds New Roles." *New York Times,* March 23, C3.

Doležel, Lubomír. 1999. "Fictional and Historical Narrative: Meeting the Postmodernist Challenge." In Herman 1999, 247–73.

Don, Abbe. 1990. "Narrative and the Interface." In *The Art of Computer Interface,* ed. Brenda Laurel, 383–91. Reading, Mass.: Addison-Wesley.

———. Online. Bubbe's Back Porch. http://www.bubbe.com/dsb/index.html.

Doody, Margaret Anne. 1996. *The True Story of the Novel.* New Brunswick, N.J.: Rutgers University Press.

Douglas, J. Yellowlees. 2000. *The End of Books, or Books without End? Reading Interactive Narratives.* Ann Arbor: University of Michigan Press.

———. 2004. "Response to Markku Eskelinen." In Wardrip-Fruin and Harrigan 2004, 36–37.

Douglas, J. Yellowlees, and Andrew Hargadon. "The Pleasures of Immersion and Interaction: Schemas, Scripts, and the Fifth Business." In Wardrip-Fruin and Harrigan 2004, 192–206.

Dowd, Maureen. 1999. "Forrest Gump Biography." *New York Times,* September 22.

Eco, Umberto. 1979. *The Role of the Reader.* Bloomington: Indiana University Press.

———. 1989. *The Open Work.* Cambridge, Mass.: Harvard University Press.

Egginton, William. 2001. "Reality Is Bleeding: A Brief History of Film from the Sixteenth Century." *Configurations* 9, no. 2: 207–30.

Eliade, Mircea. 1975. *Myths, Rites, and Symbols: A Mircea Eliade Reader.* Ed. Wendell C. Beane and William G. Doty. Vol. 1. New York: Harper and Row.

Elliott, Kamilla. 2004. "Literary Film Adaptation and the Form/Content Dilemma." In Ryan 2004, 220–43.

Eskelinen, Markku. 2001. "The Gaming Situation." Game Studies 1, no. 1. http:///www.gamestudies.org/0101/eskelinen/ (accessed March 2004).

———. 2004. "Towards Computer Game Studies." In Wardrip-Fruin and Harrigan 2004, 36–44.

EverQuest Atlas: The Maps of Myrist. Published by Sony On-line Entertainment, Inc.

Ferguson, Niall, ed. 1997. *Virtual History: Alternatives and Counterfactuals.* London: Macmillan.

Fleischman, Suzanne. 1990. *Tense and Narrativity: From Medieval Performance to Modern Fiction.* Austin: University of Texas Press.

Fludernik, Monika. 1996. *Towards a "Natural" Narratology.* London: Routledge.

Foley, Barbara. 2005. "Documentary Novel and the Problems of Borders." In *Essentials of the Theory of Fiction,* ed. Michael J. Hoffman and Patrick Murphy, 239–54. Durham, N.C.: Duke University Press.

Foucault, Michel. 1971. *The Order of Things: An Archeaology of the Human Sciences.* New York: Pantheon Books.

Fowles, John. 1969. *The French Lieutenant's Woman.* Chicago: New American Library, Signet Books.

Frank, Joseph. 1991. *The Idea of Spatial Form.* New Brunswick, N.J.: Rutgers University Press.

Frasca, Gonzalo. Online a. "Ludology Meets Narratology: Similitude and Difference between (Video)games and Narrative." http://www.jacaranda.org/frasca/ludology.htm (accessed March 2004).

———. Online b. "Ludologists Love Stories, Too: Note from a Debate That Never Took Place." http://www.ludology.org (accessed March 2004).

———. 2003a. "Simulation versus Narrative: Introduction to Ludology." In Wolf and Perron 2003, 221–35.

———. 2003b. "Sim Sin City: Some Thoughts about *Grand Theft Auto 3.*" *Game Studies* 3, no. 2. http://www.gamestudies.org/0302/frasca/ (accessed March 2004).

Freeland, Cynthia. 2004. "Ordinary Horror in Reality TV." In Ryan 2004, 244–66.

Gaudreault, André, and François Jost. 1990. *Le récit cinématographique.* Paris: Nathan.

Genet, Jean. 1984 [1947]. *Les Bonnes.* Paris: Gallimard.

Genette, Gérard. 1972. *Figure III.* Paris: Seuil.

———. 1988. *Narrative Discourse Revisited.* Trans. Jane E. Lewin. Ithaca, N.Y: Cornell University Press.

———. 1991. *Fiction et diction*. Paris: Seuil.

———. 2004. *Métalepse: De la figure à la fiction*. Paris: Seuil.

Glaser, Michelle, Andrew Hutchison, and Marie-Louise Xavier. 2001. *Juvenate: An Interactive Narrative*. CD-ROM. Produced in association with the Australian Film Commission. http://multimedia.design. curtin.edu.au/juvenate/ (accessed June 2004).

Glassner, Andrew. 2004. *Interactive Storytelling: Techniques for 21st Century Fiction*. Natick, Mass.: A. K. Peters.

Glazier, Loss Pequeño. 2002. *Digital Poetics: The Making of E-Poetries*. Tuscaloosa: University of Alabama Press.

Greene, Brian. *The Elegant Universe: Superstrings, Hidden Dimensions, and the Quest for the Ultimate Theory*. New York: Random House, 1999.

Grice, H. Paul. 1975. "Logic and Conversation." In *Syntax and Semantics 3: Speech Acts*, ed. Peter Cole and Jerry Morgan, 41–58. New York: Academic Press.

Grodal, Torben. 2003. "Stories for Eye, Ear, and Muscle: Video Games, Media, and Embodied Experience." In Wolf and Perron 2003, 129–55.

Gulland, Sandra. 1999. *The Many Lives of Josephine B*. New York: Touchstone.

Gunder, Anna. 2004. *Hyperworks: On Digital Literature and Computer Games*. Uppsala, Sweden: Publications from the Section for Sociology of Literature and the Department of Literature, Uppsala University.

Haraway, Donna. 1991. *Simians, Cyborgs, and Woman: The Reinvention of Nature*. London: Routledge.

Harpold, Terry. 2005. "Digital Narrative." In Herman, Jahn, and Ryan 2005, 108–12.

Hayles, N. Katherine. 1999a. "Artificial Life and Literary Culture." In *Cyberspace Textuality: Computer Technology and Literary Theory*, ed. Marie-Laure Ryan, 205–23. Bloomington: Indiana University Press.

———. 1999b. *How We Became Posthuman: Virtual Bodies in Cybernetics, Literature, and Informatics*. Chicago: University of Chicago Press.

———. 2002. *Writing Machines*. Cambridge, Mass.: MIT Press.

———. 2003. "Translating Media: Why We Should Rethink Textuality." *Yale Journal of Criticism* 16, no. 2: 263–90.

———. 2004. "Print Is Flat, Code Is Deep: The Importance of Media-Specific Analysis." *Poetics Today* 25, no. 1: 67–90.

Hayward, Malcolm. 1994. "Genre Recognition of History and Fiction." *Poetics* 22: 409–21.

Heise, Ursula K. 2002. "Unnatural Ecologies: The Metaphor of the Environment in Media Theory." *Configurations* 10, no. 1: 149–68.

Herman, David, ed. 1999. *Narratologies: New Perspecives on Narrative Analysis*. Columbus: Ohio State University Press.

————. 2003. "Regrounding Narratology: The Study of Narratively Organized Systems for Thinking." In *What Is Narratology?*, ed. Tom Kindt and Hans Harald Müller, 303–32. Berlin: Walter de Gruyter.

Herman, David, Manfred Jahn, and Marie-Laure Ryan, eds. 2005. *The Routledge Encyclopedia of Narrative Theory*. London: Routledge.

Hildesheimer, Wolfgang. 1983. *Marbot: A Biography*. Trans. Patricia Crampton. New York: Braziller.

Hofstadter, Douglas. 1980. *Gödel, Escher, Bach: An Eternal Golden Braid*. New York: Vintage Books.

————. 1984. *Metamagical Themas: Questing for the Essence of Mind and Pattern*. New York: Vintage Books.

Huizinga, Johan. 1955. *Homo Ludens: A Study of the Play Element in Culture*. Boston: Beacon Press.

I'm Your Man. 1998. Interactive movie. Dir. Bob Bejean. Performed by Mark Metcalf, Colleen Quinn, and Kevin M. Seal. A Choice Point Film. Presented by Planet Theory in association with DVD international. DVD edition produced by Bill Franzblau.

Inform Web site. Online. http://www.inform-fiction.org/introduction/index.html.

InteractiveStory Net. Online. http://www.quvu.net/interactivestory.net/.

Iser, Wolfgang. 1980. "The Reading Process." In *Reader-Response Criticism: From Formalism to Poststructuralism*, ed. Jane Tompkins, 50–69. Baltimore: Johns Hopkins University Press.

Jackson, Shelley. 1995. *Patchwork Girl*. Hypertext software. Cambridge, Mass.: Eastgate Systems.

Jahn, Manfred. 2003. "'Awake! Open Your Eyes!' The Cognitive Logic of External and Internal Stories." In *Narrative Theory and the Cognitive Sciences*, ed. David Herman, 195–213. Stanford, Calif.: CLSI Publications.

Jakobson, Roman. 1960. "Linguistics and Poetics." In *Style and Language*, ed. Thomas Sebeok, 350–77. Cambridge: MIT Press.

Jannidis, Fotis. 2003. "Narratology and the Narrative." In *What Is Narratology?*, ed. Tom Kindt and Hans-Harald Müller, 35–54. Berlin: Walter de Gruyter.

Jenkins, Henry. 2004. "Game Design as Narrative Architecture." In Wardrip-Fruin and Harrigan 2004, 118–30.

Jennings, Pamela. 1996. "Narrative Structures for New Media: Towards a New Definition." *Leonardo* 29, no. 5: 345–50.

Johnson, Steven. 1997. *Interface Culture: How New Technology Transforms the Way We Create and Communicate*. San Francisco: HarperEdge.

Joyce, Michael. 1987. *afternoon, a story.* Hypertext software. Cambridge, Mass.: Eastgate Systems.

———. 1995. *Of Two Minds: Hypertext, Pedagogy, and Poetics.* Ann Arbor: University of Michigan Press.

———. 1996 and 1997. *Twelve Blue: Story in Eight Bars.* World Wide Web hyperfiction. Postmodern Culture and Eastgate Systems. http://www.eastgate.com/TwelveBlue (accessed February 2004).

Jung, Felix, and Dipti Vadya. "Young Couple, Ohio State Fair." http://webdelsol.com/Synesthesia/# (accessed May 28, 2004).

Juul, Jesper. 2001. "Games Telling Stories: A Brief Note on Games and Narratives." *Game Studies* 1, no. 1. http:///www.gamestudies.org/0101/juul-gts/ (accessed March 2004).

———. 2004. "Introduction to Game Time." In Wardrip-Fruin and Harrigan 2004, 131–42.

———. 2005. *Half-Real: Video Games between Real Rules and Fictional Worlds.* Cambridge, Mass.: MIT Press.

Kakutani, Michiko. 1999. "Biography as Mirror Reflecting Biographer." *New York Times,* October 2.

Kittler, Friedrich. 1997. *Literature, Media, Information Systems.* Ed. John Johnston. Amsterdam: G + B Arts International.

Klastrup, Lisbeth. 2003. "A Poetics of Virtual Worlds." Digital Arts and Culture Conference, Melbourne, 100–109. http://hypertext.rmit.edu.au/dac/papers/ (accessed September 2004).

Koskimaa, Raine. 2000. "Digital Literature: From Text to Hypertext and Beyond." Ph.D. diss., University of Jyväskylä, Finland http://www.cc.jyu.fi/~koskimaa/thesis/.

Kozloff, Sarah. 1992. "Narrative Theory and Television." In *Channels of Discourse, Reassembled,* ed. Robert Allen, 43–71. Chapel Hill: University of North Carolina Press.

Krauss, Rosalind. 1999. *"A Voyage on the North Sea": Art in the Age of the Post-Medium Condition.* London: Thames and Hudson.

Krzywinska, Tanya. 2002. "Hands-On Horror." In *Screenplay,* ed. Geoff King and Tanya Krzywinska, 206–23. London: Wallflower Press.

Labov, William, and Joshua Waletzky. 1967. "Narrative Analysis: Oral Versions of Personal Experience." In *Essays on the Verbal and Visual Arts,* ed. June Helm, 12–44. Seattle: University of Washington Press.

Landow, George Press. 1997. *Hypertext 2.0: The Convergence of Contemporary Critical Theory and Technology.* Baltimore: Johns Hopkins University Press.

Lanham, Richard. 1993. *The Electronic Word: Democracy, Technology, and the Arts.* Chicago: University of Chicago Press.

Larsen, Deena. 1993. *Marble Springs.* Hypertext software. Cambridge, Mass.: Eastgate Systems.

Laurel, Brenda. 1991. *Computers as Theatre*. Menlo Park, Calif.: Addison-Wesley.

———. 1993. "Art and Activism in VR." *Wide Angle* 15, no. 4: 13–21.

———. 2001. *Utopian Entrepreneur*. Cambridge, Mass.: MIT Press.

Lejeune, Philippe. 1980. *Je est un autre: L'autobiographie, de la littérature aux médias*. Paris: Seuil.

Lessing, Gotthold Ephraim. 1984. *Laocoön: An Essay on the Limits of Painting and Poetry*. Trans. Edward Allen McCormick. Baltimore: Johns Hopkins University Press.

Lewis, David. 1978. "Truth in Fiction." *American Philosophical Quarterly* 15: 37–46.

Lewis, Jason. "Nine." http://www.poemsthatgo.com/gallery/fall2003/nine/nine.htm (accessed June 2003).

Lialina, Olia. 1996. *My Boyfriend Came Back from the War*. http://www.teleportacia.org/war/ (accessed June 2003).

Liestøl, Eva. 2003. "Computer Games and the Ludic Structure of Interpretation." In Liestøl, Morrison, and Rasmussen 2003, 327–57.

Liestøl, Gunnar, Andrew Morrison, and Terje Rasmussen, eds. 2003. *Digital Media Revisited*. Cambridge: MIT Press.

Liu, Alan. 2004. *The Laws of Cool: Knowledge Work and the Culture of Information*. Chicago: University of Chicago Press.

Long, Jonathan. 2003. "History, Narrative, and Photography in W. G. Sebald's *Die Ausgewanderten*." *Modern Language Review* 98, no. 1: 117–37.

Luesebrink, Marjorie. "The Personalization of Complexity." http://califia.hispeed.com/Complexity/ (accessed January 2003).

Lunenfeld, Peter. 2004. "The Myth of Interactive Cinema." In Ryan 2004, 377–90.

Lyotard, Jean-François. 1984. *The Postmodern Condition: A Report on Knowledge*. Trans. Geoff Bennington and Brian Massumi. Minneapolis: University of Minnesota Press.

Malina, Debra. 2002. *Breaking the Frame: Metalepsis and the Construction of the Subject*. Columbus: Ohio State University Press.

Malloy, Judy. 1993. *Its Name Was Penelope*. Hypertext software. Cambridge, Mass.: Eastgate Systems.

Manovich, Lev. 2001. *The Language of New Media*. Cambridge, Mass.: MIT Press.

———. "Generation Flash." http://www.fdcw.unimaas.nl/is/generationflash.htm (accessed October 2003).

Margolin, Uri. 1999. "Of What Is Past, Is Passing, or to Come: Temporality, Aspectuality, Modality, and the Nature of Literary Narrative."' In *Narratologies: New Perspectives on Narrative Analysis,* ed. David Herman, 142–66. Columbus: Ohio State University Press.

Martínez-Bonati, Félix. 1981. *Fictive Discourse and the Structures of Literature*. Ithaca, N.Y.: Cornell University Press.

Mateas, Michael. "A Preliminary Poetics for Interactive Drama and Games." In Wardrip-Fruin and Harrigan 2004, 19–33.

Mateas, Michael, and Phoebe Sengers, eds. 2003. *Narrative Intelligence*. Amsterdam: John Benjamins.

Mateas, Michael, and Andrew Stern. 2002. "Façade: An Experiment in Building a Fully-Realized Interactive Drama." http://www.quvu.net/interactivestory.net/papers/MateasSternGDC03.pdf.

———. 2005. *Façade*. Interactive CD-ROM. Downloadable from http://interactivestory.net/download.

McHale, Brian. 1987. *Postmodernist Fiction*. New York: Methuen.

McLuhan, Marshall. 1996. *Essential McLuhan*. Ed. Eric McLuhan and Frank Zingrone. New York: Basic Books.

Meadows, Mark Stephen. 2003. *Pause and Effect: The Art of Interactive Narrative*. Indianapolis: New Riders.

Meehan, James. 1981. "Tale-Spin." In *Inside Computer Understanding*, ed. Roger Schank, 197–225. Hillsdale, N.J.: Lawrence Erlbaum.

Memmott, Talan. *Lexia to Perplexia*. http://www.altx.com/ebr/ebr11/11mem/ (accessed January 2004).

Metz, Christian. 1974. *Film Language: A Semiotics of the Cinema*. Trans. Michael Taylor. New York: Oxford University Press.

Meyer-Minnemann, Klaus. 2005. "Un procédé qui 'produit un effet de bizzarerie': La métalepse littéraire." In *Métalepses: Entorses au pacte de représentation*, ed. Jean-Marie Schaeffer and John Pier. Paris: Editions du Centre National de la Recherche Scientifique.

Meyerowitz, Joshua. 1993. "Images of Media: Hidden Ferment—and Harmony—in the Field." *Journal of Communications* 43, no. 3: 55–66.

Miller, Carolyn Handler. 2004. *Digital Storytelling: A Creator's Guide to Interactive Entertainment*. Amsterdam: Focal Press/Elsevier.

Montfort, Nick. 2002. "Toward a Theory of Interactive Fiction." Available at: http://nickm.com/if/toward.html (accessed February 2003).

———. 2003. *Twisty Little Passages: An Approach to Interactive Fiction*. Cambridge, Mass.: MIT Press.

———. 2004. "Interactive Fiction as 'Story,' 'Game,' 'Storygame,' 'Novel,' 'World,' 'Literature,' 'Puzzle,' 'Problem,' 'Riddle,' and 'Machine.'" In Wardrip-Fruin and Harrigan 2004, 310–17.

Morris, Edmund. 1999. *Dutch: A Memoir of Ronald Reagan*. New York: Random House.

Morrissey, Judd. 2000. *The Jew's Daughter*. http://www.thejewsdaughter.com/ (accessed February 2003).

Motte, Warren. 1995. *Playtexts: Ludics in Contemporary Literature*. Lincoln: University of Nebraska Press.

Moulthrop, Stuart. 1991. *Victory Garden*. Hypertext software. Watertown, Mass.: Eastgate Systems.

———. 2004. "Response to Espen Aarseth." In Wardrip-Fruin and Harrigan 2004, 47–48.

Murray, Janet. 1997. *Hamlet on the Holodeck: The Future of Narrative in Cyberspace*. New York: Free Press.

———. 2004. "From Game-Story to Cyberdrama." In Wardrip-Fruin and Harrigan 2004, 2–11.

Nattiez, Jean-Jacques. 1990. "Can One Speak of Narrativity in Music?" *Journal of the Royal Musical Association* 115, no. 2: 240–57. http://www.jstor.org/view/02690403/ap030008/03a00060/0 (accessed July 2004).

Nelson, Theodore. 1970. "No More Teachers' Dirty Looks." *Computer Decisions* 9, no. 8: 16–23.

Ong, Walter J. 1982. *Orality and Literacy: The Technologizing of the Word*. London: Methuen.

On-line Caroline. http://www.On-linecaroline.com (accessed October 2003).

Parker, Jeff. 2001. "A Poetics of the Link." *Electronic Book Review*. http://www.electronicbookreview.com/thread/electropoetics/linkletters (accessed January 2005).

———. *Long Wide Smile*. Hypertext fiction. http://www.hypertxt.com/parker/magnetic.

Parsons, Terence. 1980. *Nonexistent Objects*. New Haven, Conn.: Yale University Press.

Paul, Christiane. 2003. *Digital Art*. London: Thames and Hudson.

Pavel, Thomas. 1986. *Fictional Worlds*. Cambridge, Mass.: Harvard University Press.

Pearce, Celia. 2002a. "Game Noir: A Conversation with Thim Schafer." *Game Studies* 3, no. 2. http://www.gamestudies.org/0301/pearce/ (accessed March 2004).

———. 2002b. "Sims, BattleBots, Cellular Automata God and Go: A Conversation with Will Wright" *Game Studies* 1, no. 2. http://www.gamestudies.org/0102/pearce/ (accessed March 2004).

Perlstein, Steven. 2004. "Choice Is Overrated." *Washington Post,* September 10.

Phelps, Katherine. "Story Shapes for Digital Media." http://www.glasswings.com/Storytronics/Tronics/shapes/onshapes (accessed July 2004).

Pinsky, Robert. 1984. *Mindwheel: An Electronic Novel*. Steve Hale and William Mataga, programmers. Interactive fiction. San Rafael, Calif.: Brøderbund Software Corp.

Pirandello, Luigi. 1995. *"Six Characters in Search of an Author" and Other Plays*. Trans. Mark Musa. London: Penguin Books.

Plantinga, Carl. 1996. "Moving Pictures and the Rhetoric of Nonfiction Film: Two Approaches." In *Post-Theory: Reconstructing Film Studies*, ed. David Bordwell and Noël Carroll, 307–24. Madison: University of Wisconsin Press.

Plotkin, Andrew. *Spider and Web*. Interactive fiction. Downloadable from ftp://ftp.gmd.de/if-archive/games/infocom/Tangle.z5 or directly played from http://www.ifiction.org/games/play.phpz (accessed October 2004).

Ponech, Trevor. 1997. "What Is Non-Fictional Cinema?" In *Film Theory and Philosophy*, ed. Richard Allen and Murray Smith, 203–20. Oxford: Clarendon Press.

Powers, Richard. 1995. *Galatea 2.2*. New York: Farrar, Straus, and Giroux.

Pratt, Mary Louise. 1977. *Toward a Speech Act Theory of Literary Discourse*. Bloomington: Indiana University Press.

Prince, Gerald. 1982. *Narratology: The Forms and Functions of Narrative*. The Hague: Mouton.

———. 2003 [1987]. *Dictionary of Narratology*. Lincoln: University of Nebraska Press.

Prior, A. N. 2003. *Papers on Time and Tense*, ed. Per Hasle, Peter Øhrstrom, Torden Braüner, and Jack Copeland. Cambridge: Cambridge University Press.

Propp, Vladimir. 1968. *Morphology of the Folk Tale*. Trans. L. Scott, rev. by Louis A. Wagner. Austin: University of Texas Press.

Rabinowitz, Peter. 2004. "Music, Genre, and Narrative Theory." In Ryan 2004, 305–28.

Raley, Rita. 2002. "Interferences: [Net.Writing] and the Practice of Codework." Electronic Book Review. http://www.electronicbookreview.com/thread/electropoetics/net.writing (accessed January 2005).

Rettberg, Scott. 2002. "The Pleasure (and Pain) of Links Poetics. *Electronic Book Review*. http://www.electronicbookreview.com/thread/electropoetics/pragmatic (accessed January 2005).

Ricoeur, Paul. 1983, 1984, 1985. *Temps et récit*. 3 vols. Paris: Seuil.

Rothstein, Edward. 2000. "TV Shows in Which the Real Is Fake and the Fake Is Real." *New York Times*, August 5.

Ryan, Marie-Laure. 1991. *Possible Worlds, Artificial Intelligence, and Narrative Theory*. Bloomington: University of Indiana Press.

———. 1992. "The Modes of Narrativity and their Visual Metaphors." *Style* 26, no. 3: 368–87.

———. 1997. "Postmodernism and the Doctrine of Panfictionality." *Narrative* 5, no. 2: 165–87.

———, ed. 1999. *Cyberspace Textuality: Computer Technology and Literary Theory.* Bloomington: Indiana University Press.

———. 2001. *Narrative as Virtual Reality: Immersion and Interactivity in Literature and Electronic Media.* Baltimore: Johns Hopkins University Press.

———, ed. 2004. *Narrative across Media: The Languages of Storytelling.* Lincoln: University of Nebraska Press.

Ryan, Marie-Laure, and Jon Thiem. *Symbol Rock.* Interactive CD-ROM.

Salen, Katie, and Eric Zimmerman. 2003. *Rules of Play: Game Design Fundamentals.* Cambridge, Mass.: MIT Press.

Saussure, Ferdinand de. 1966. *Course in General Linguistics.* Trans. Wade Baskin. New York: McGraw Hill.

Savitch, Walter J. 1982. *Abstract Machines and Grammars.* Boston: Little, Brown.

Schaeffer, Jean-Marie. 1999. *Pourquoi la fiction?* Paris: Seuil.

Schaeffer, Jean-Marie, and John Pier. 2002. Introductory text to the international colloquium "La métalepse, aujoud'hui." Goethe Institut, Paris, November 29–30.

Schank, Roger. 1990. *Tell Me a Story: A New Look at Real and Artificial Memory.* New York: Scribner.

Schank, Roger, and Robert P. Abelson. 1995. "Knowledge and Memory: The Real Story." In *Advances in Social Cognition,* vol. 7, *Knowledge and Memory: The Real Story,* ed. Robert S. Wyer, 1–85. Hillsdale, N.J.: Lawrence Erlbaum.

Scholes, Robert. 1993. "Tlön and Truth: Reflections on Literary Theory and Philosophy." In *Realism and Representation: Essays on the Problem of Realism in Relation to Science, Literature, and Culture,* ed. George Levine, 179–81. Madison: University of Wisconsin Press.

Searle, John. 1975. "The Logical Status of Fictional Discourse." *New Literary History* 6: 319–32.

Sebald, W. G. 1996. *The Emigrants.* Trans. Michael Hulse. New York: New Directions.

———. 2001. *Austerlitz.* Trans. Anthea Bell. New York: Random House.

Sella, Marshall. 2000. "The Electronic Fishbowl." *New York Times Magazine* 2: 50–57.

Short, Emily. *Galatea.* Interactive fiction. Downloadable from http://www.wurb.com/if/game/1326.

Simanowski, Roberto. 2004. "Concrete Poetry in Digital Media: Its Predecessors, Its Presence, and Its Future." Dichtung-Digital. http://www.dichtung-digital.com/2004/3/simanowski/index.htm.

Steiner, Wendy. 2004. "Pictorial Narrativity." In Ryan 2004, 145–77.

Stephenson, Neal. 1993. *Snow Crash.* New York: Bantam Books.

Stern, Andrew. 2003. "Virtual Babyz: Believable Agents with Narrative Intelligence." In Mateas and Sengers 2003, 189–97.

Strickland, Stephanie. 1997a. "Poetry in the Digital Environment." *Electronic Book Review.* http://www.electronicbookreview.com/ thread/electropoetics/map-like (accessed January 2005).

———. 1997b. *True North.* Hypertext software. Cambridge, Mass.: Eastgate Systems.

Suits, Bernard. 1978. *The Grasshopper: Games, Life, and Utopia.* Toronto: University of Toronto Press.

Survivor. 2000–present. TV series. Created and produced by Mark Burnett.

Tegmark, Max. 2003. "Parallel Universes." *Scientific American,* May, 41–51.

The Truman Show. 1998. Film written by Andrew Niccol, directed by Peter Weir. With Jim Carey, Ed Harris, Laura Linney.

Thomas, Evan, and Jon Meacham. 1999. "The Book on Reagan." *Newsweek,* October 4, 23–25.

Tosca, Susana Pajares. 2000. "A Pragmatics of Links." *Journal of Digital Information* 1, no. 6. http://jodi.ecs.soton.ac.uk/Articles/v01/i06/ Pajares/ (accessed June 2002).

Turkle, Sherry. 1995. *Life on the Screen.* New York: Simon and Schuster.

Turner, Mark. 1996. *The Literary Mind.* Oxford: Oxford University Press.

Turner, Scott. 1994. *The Creative Process: A Computer Model for Storytelling and Creativity.* Hillsdale, N.J.: Lawrence Erlbaum.

Veyne, Paul. 1998. *Did the Greeks Believe in Their Myths? An Essay on the Conceptual Imagination.* Trans. Paula Wirrig. Chicago: University of Chicago Press.

Walker, Jill. 2004. "How I Was Played by On-line Caroline." In Wardrip-Fruin and Harrigan 2004, 302–9.

Walton, Kendall L. 1984. "Transparent Pictures." *Critical Inquiry* 11, no. 2: 246–77.

———. 1990. *Mimesis as Make-Believe: On the Foundations of the Representational Arts.* Cambridge, Mass.: Harvard University Press.

Wardrip-Fruin, Noah. "What Is Hypertext?" http://hyperfiction.org/ texts/whatHypertextIs.pdf (accessed January 2005).

Wardrip-Fruin, Noah, and Pat Harrigan, eds. 2004. *First Person: New Media as Story, Performance, and Game.* Cambridge, Mass.: MIT Press.

Wardrip-Fruin, Noah, and Nick Montfort, eds. 2003. *The New Media Reader.* Cambridge, Mass.: MIT Press.

———, and Brion Moss, with a. c. chapman and Duane Whitehurst. 2002. "The Impermanence Agent: Project and Context." In *CyberText*

Yearbook, ed. Markku Eskelinen and Raine Koskimaa, 13–58. Jyväskylä, Finland: University of Jyväskylä, Publications of the Research Centre for Contemporary Culture.

Weaver, Mike. 1984. *Julia Margaret Cameron, 1815–1879.* Boston: Little, Brown.

Weberman, David. 2002. "The Matrix: Simulation and the Postmodern Age." In *The Matrix and Philosophy,* ed. William Irwin, 225–39. Chicago: Open Court.

Weinstone, Ann. 2004. *Avatar Bodies: A Tantra for Posthumanism.* Minneapolis: University of Minnesota Press.

White, Hayden. 1978. *Tropics of Discourse: Essays in Cultural Criticism.* Baltimore: Johns Hopkins University Press.

———. 1981. "The Value of Narrativity in the Representation of History." In *On Narrative,* ed. W. J. T. Mitchell, 1–23. Chicago: University of Chicago Press.

———. 1987. *The Content of the Form: Narrative Discourse and Historical Representation.* Baltimore: Johns Hopkins University Press.

———. 1992. "Historical Emplotment and the Problem of Truth." In *Probing the Limits of Representation: Nazism and the Final Solution,* ed. Saul Friedlander, 37–53. Cambridge, Mass.: Harvard University Press.

Wolf, Mark J. P., and Bernard Perron, eds. 2003. *The Video Game Theory Reader.* New York: Routledge.

Wolf, Werner. 2002. "Das Problem de Narrativität in Literatur, Bildender Kunst und Musik: Ein Beitrag zu einer Intermedialen Erzähltheorie." In *Erzähltheorie transgenerisch, intermedial, interdisziplinär,* ed. Vera Nünning and Ansgar Nünning, 23–104. Trier: Wissenschaflicher Verlag Trier.

———. 2003. "Narrative and Narrativity: A Narratological Reconceptualization and its Applicability to the Visual Arts." *Word and Image* 19, no. 3: 180–97.

———. 2005. "Music and Narrative" and "Pictorial Narrativity." In Herman, Jahn, and Ryan 2005, 324–29 and 431–35.

Wolfe, Tom. 1973. "The New Journalism." In *The New Journalism,* ed. Tom Wolfe and E. W. Johnson, 1–52. New York: Harper and Row.

Woolley, Benjamin. 1992. *Virtual Worlds.* London: Blackwell.

Worth, Sol. 1981. "Pictures Can't Say Ain't." In *Studies in Visual Communication,* ed. and intro. Larry Gross. Philadelphia: University of Pennsylvania Press.

Zhai, Philip. 1999. *Get Real: A Philosophical Adventure in Virtual Reality.* New York: Rowman and Littlefield.

Zoesis Project. Online. http://www.zoesis.com/corporate/n-index.html.

Index

Aarseth, Espen, 97, 98, 107, 130, 131, 170, 179, 183, 189–90, 191, 192, 195, 239n.5, 240n.8, 246n.14, 248n.15
Abbott, H. Porter, 186, 192
Abelson, Robert P., 10, 232n.6
afternoon (Michael Joyce), 136, 138, 139, 145
A la recherche du temps perdu (Proust), 180
Allen, Woody, 208, 247n.1
alternate reality gaming, 225
Andersen, Christian, 248n.16
Andreychek, Eric, 220
animé film, 173
Ankerson, Ingrid, 159
Arabian Nights, The, 205
architecture, textual, xxii, 100–107; flowchart, 105; maze, 105; multistrand, 102, 104; network, 102–3; sea anemone, 104, 148; tree, 105; vector with side branches, 104
Aristotelian structure, xvii, xviii, 60, 63, 68, 172, 233n.14
Aristotle, xv, 49, 88, 172

Arloz the Little Rhinoceros (Flash text), 159
augmented reality, 195, 225–26
authoring systems, *see* Director, Flash, Inform, Storyspace
avatar, 190

Baroque architecture, 16
Barthes, Roland, 3, 38, 46, 47–48, 50, 56, 72, 202, 236n.11; kernels and satellites, 130
Bartle, Richard, 198–99
baseball broadcast. *See* sports broadcast
Bates, Joe, xvii
Bateson, Gregory, 39
Baudrillard, Jean, 59, 72, 227–29, 232n.9
Beckett, Samuel, 232n.2
believable characters, xviii
Ben-Amos, Dan, 55
Benveniste, Emile, 47
Bernstein, Mark, 109, 111, 136, 195
Big Brother, 61, 68, 69, 237n.2
biography, 44, 81

Marie-Laure Ryan is an independent scholar based in Colorado. She is the author of *Possible Worlds, Artificial Intelligence, and Narrative Theory* and *Narrative as Virtual Reality: Immersion and Interactivity in Literature and Electronic Media*; the editor of two collections of essays, *Cyberspace Textuality* and *Narrative across Media*; and the coeditor of *The Routledge Encyclopedia of Narrative Theory*.